MW01705903

SHOPPING THE WORLD

ANNE
GARBER

SHOPPING THE WORLD

OVER 300
MAIL ORDER
SOURCES
FOR
CANADIAN
CONSUMERS

KEY PORTER BOOKS

To my visionary friend, Bob Mercer, who was the catalyst for this book and who has suggested loudly on several occasions that he should have a large percentage of the royalties from it.

Bob, it is your destiny to be famous, not rich. As they say in the mail order business, "The cheque is in the mail."

Canadian Cataloguing in Publication Data

Garber, Anne
Shopping the world

ISBN 1-55013-259-8

1. Mail-order business – Canada – Directories.
2. Shopping – Canada – Directories. I. Title.

HF5466.G37 1990 381'.142'0294 C90–094369–6

Key Porter Books Limited
70 The Esplanade
Toronto, Ontario
Canada M5E 1R2

Typesetting: Southam Business Information and Communications Group Inc.

recycled paper

Printed and bound in Canada

90 91 92 93 94 6 5 4 3 2 1

CONTENTS

SUBJECT INDEX

AUTHOR'S WARNINGS, CAUTIONS AND MOTHERLY ADVICE

ALTHOUGH EVERY EFFORT has been made to ensure that all information in this book is factually accurate and completely up to date as we go to press, you may discover that some outlets have changed their mail order policies, after all. The author and publisher assume no responsibility for difficulties with mail order sources listed herein.

Keep in mind that great deals may be mixed in with not-so-great ones. Life's like that sometimes, so shop wisely.

Obviously, I have not ordered goods from every single source listed and have relied to some extent on referrals from friends and acquaintances to fill out some categories of goods. I also cannot personally guarantee the virtues of every product sold, though I must admit that "researching" (reading hundreds of captivating catalogues) enticed me into buying a great many of the items described. My personal experience, after years of mail ordering, is that I've rarely been disappointed. In fact, it's the most fun you can have for the price of a stamp.

Read the introductory chapters about consumer protection carefully. Choose the goods you order judiciously. Keep written records whenever possible. Caveat emptor. Now go outside, play nice with your little brother and don't get dirty!

ACKNOWLEDGEMENTS

IT WOULD BE thoughtless of me not to mention a few of the people who contributed to this book in ways more important than they imagine. My special thanks go to Deborah Ramsay, Michael Campbell, Bob Mercer, Joyce Woods, Allan MacDougall, Ian and Wendy Haysom, Peter Clough, Linda Olivier, Julie Glover, Murray McLauchlan and Kevin Barker (for encouragement and ideas), to David Oakes, Deborah Roitberg, Robert Mackwood, Sherry Killam, Priscilla Johnston, Lorraine Gannon, Kerry Moore, Lynne McNamara, June and Julian Ross, Jancis O'Mara and John Crawford (for support, relentless catalogue searching and brilliant discoveries), to Ronit Cohen, Astrid Gannon, Rebecca Johnson and Marilyn Rapanos (for thorough research and assistance) and to Richard Barazzuol (for computer programming, research, advice, support and consultation above and beyond the call of duty). And many thanks to Anna Porter and Phyllis Bruce for believing in this project and letting me do it "my way."

INTRODUCTION

SHOPPING BY MAIL is a concept that has been around for ages but is only now beginning to come into its own. In fact, Neiman-Marcus, which may very well have launched the Mail Order Age, introduced the idea as long ago as February 1908, with an ad that included the lines: "Will fill all mail orders with the utmost care. Garments will be fitted on models in sizes ordered before sending, assuring satisfactory garments."

Today, many firms still take the trouble to assure consumer satisfaction and uphold the motto that "the customer is always right."

On the other hand, there are risks inherent in mail order shopping. You might correctly guess that the larger the distance that the goods you've ordered have to travel, the greater the chance of loss, breakage or misrepresentation, and the better the chances that if something goes wrong, more effort will have to be put into sorting things out. Add to that possible misunderstandings due to different languages, methods of carrying on business and ethical standards, and the potential exists for real conflict.

So why do people persist in buying by mail? The answer is easy: with catalogues often only a postage stamp away, a whole, vast world of unique and wonderful products is opened up for you. It's almost like Christmas morning when you receive one of these packages in the mail and carefully unveil your long-awaited purchases from lands far away.

Sometimes there are substantial savings to be had. Often the goods are of superior quality, compared to local merchandise. And again, there's the lure of anticipation, looking forward to what the postman will bring tomorrow.

Personally, I've been a typical Canadian mail-orderer for more than three decades (Gulp! Now you know!) and I've bought items as diverse as an antique reproduction silver marrow spoon (from the Metropolitan Museum of Art in New York) or impossible-to-find baby items (from Mothercare in England). I've bought embroidered pillow shams from Hong Kong at a fraction of their cost in the Chinatowns of Vancouver or Toronto. I've even found great buys from Canadian mail order houses such as Jay Norris, Carole Martin or Regal Gifts, when I take the time to sort the wheat from the chaff.

As a nine-year-old, I sent away for stamp collections from ads found in the back of comic books, just as my daughter does today, even in the apparently more sophisticated milieu of the '90s.

These days, we're certainly not "too good" for this type of consumerism. Today, we're well-informed and discriminating, and we recognize a bargain for what it is. These days, shopping by mail makes good sense. In fact, in large urban centres, it has become downright trendy.

I hope you'll share with me my happy romp through some of the finest mail order sources in the world and capture a little of the sense of joy I felt in making these discoveries.

Please take the time to read through the introductory chapters carefully so you can avoid some of the pitfalls of mail order and reap the benefits of a hobby — or is it a way of life? — that is one of the favourite pastimes of Canadians from coast to coast.

1. HOW TO USE THIS BOOK

THIS IS THE easiest shopping guide you will ever use. It is divided into the following sections: introductory chapters (the part you're reading now), subject index, the listings, and a complete alphabetical index (including brand names).

Subject Index
Simply look for the TYPE of items you would like to find by browsing through the Subject Index, page 49. After the name of each mail order source in this index, you'll find a brief description of the goods they carry. Next, you can turn directly to the listings for the catalogues that caught your interest (starting on page 113), to read the complete description of that source. You'll find the entry you want by looking for its code number, not its page number. For example, J. Crew imports, code number 140, is found on page **186**.

You'll never have to read footnotes. You won't find notes in the text saying, "Please also see 'Housewares, Misc.'" And once you get to know your favourites, finding them again is easy.

The Alphabetical List of Sources
Instead of arranging the sources only in subject categories, this book also gives you a full listing for each entry in an alphabetized section in the middle of the book — kind of like a thesaurus. Every entry is written up completely in this section, so it appears in only one place in the book (to save you looking back and forth for little bits of information). Each listing has its own coding number.

Index
In addition, there is an extensive index in the back of this book, listing not only generic names for the types of goods you might be after, but many brand names, too. Again, numbers given next to entries are code numbers, not page numbers.

2. HOW TO SHOP BY MAIL

a. Using Canada Post
Most of your mail order goods will be shipped to you by the regular services of Canada Post.

Sometimes goods will be delivered directly to your door. Often, when the items originate in a foreign country (including the U.S.), you will have to go to a Canada Customs office to claim them, fill out forms or pay duty or Federal Sales Tax. Large packages normally go to your nearest Canada Post branch office and a card is sent to notify you where they are being held for you. You must bring personal identification with you to claim such parcels.

Here are limitations, restrictions and words of caution.

b. Canada Post Weight Limitations

Goods shipped to you by mail from most foreign countries must not exceed 20 kg. From the United States, the limit is 30 kg. For heavier parcels, you should deal with a courier service. In some cases, it is cheaper to send goods by courier than by mail anyway.

Exceptions to these rules may be found in the Postal Rate Guide at your local office of Canada Post (many Canadian towns and cities have advice-by-phone numbers in the telephone directory, too), or you can order the guide for $28 from:

Postal Rate Guide
PUBLISHING CENTRE
Supply & Services Canada
Ottawa, Ontario
K1A 0S9

c. Postal Rates

New postal rates came into effect at the beginning of 1991, and the new postal guide was published (and available) in April 1990. New rates are not anticipated "in the near future" at this writing.

"Oversize lettermail" rates are applicable for small packages not exceeding 38 cm x 27 cm x 2 cm in size and weighing 500 g or less. A 500 g package meeting these size requirements would cost $2.34 to mail anywhere in Canada.

"Small packets" (up to 1 kg) destined for most foreign countries cost $1.90 for 100 g and up to $13.60 for 1 kg, if sent by air. The same package at surface mail rates costs $1.20 (100 g) to $6.15 (1 kg). Remember: these rates are to foreign destinations FROM Canada.

Printed papers (including books) sent from Canada to foreign countries cost $22.50 for 2 kg by air, $8.60 by surface mail. Keep these figures in mind in case you have to return goods to their source — it can be very costly! Air parcels must carry an airmail sticker. Mailed items exceeding $300 Cdn. in value must be accompanied by a Customs Declaration form, available from the post office.

d. Insurance and Breakage

Insurance and breakage are covered by the country from which the goods are shipped. Each country has different rules. Insist that your goods are packed well at the source. Canada Post does not insure for breakage of fragile or perishable goods. Fragile means glass, plastics and electronics.

For goods that are lost or broken while in the care of Canada Post, you may claim a refund for value, IF they are not fragile, and IF they have been well-wrapped and protected.

"Registered Mail" does not insure your package, it only confirms delivery (i.e., the sender receives a notification that the parcel or letter arrived).

Insurance itself is referred to as "Security Registered" and costs $4.70 for the first $250 only for goods shipped WITHIN CANADA. For latest rates and extent of coverage, contact Canada Post. You will have to look up rates for outgoing international mail in the Rate Guide (e.g., if you are returning goods to their country of origin).

If you are returning goods to their source in the U.S. and wish to insure them, you can insure parcels only, at a cost of 45 cents per $100 of value, to a maximum of $4.50 on $1,000.

e. Types of Service

Lettermail rates are described above. Categories include regular letters and postcards, "non-standard" lettermail and oversize lettermail. There is also "special lettermail," "Priority Courier," "printed papers (including books)" rate and "Small Packets."

Two levels of service are available for parcels: first class (by air) or fourth class (by sea or surface transport).

Pamphlets describing these and other services are available from neighbourhood postal branches.

f. C.O.D. (Cash on Delivery)

Clearly a procedure on its way out. Ideally, this method should allow you to withhold payment until your goods arrive and you have examined them. What really happens, however, is that your postal worker is unlikely to stand on your icy doorstep while you open-and-inspect.

You may pay only in cash (no credit cards or cheques). C.O.D. works only within Canada. Only non-perishable goods may be sent this way. You cannot open and inspect your goods before paying. So C.O.D. is merely a payment-deferral plan these days, and no more than that.

g. What to Tell Sources About Mailing into Canada

Canada Post publishes a handy brochure in French and English to summarize how our postal system serves your mail order sources sending goods into Canada from abroad (or from the States). It is called "For Exporters Mailing Goods to Canada" and may be obtained from your branch post office. Highlights of the brochure are paragraphs about customs declarations, multiple shipments and the use of postal codes. For valuation of goods coming into this country, you may wish to write to:

The Director General
Assessment Programs Division
Revenue Canada, Customs and Excise
Ottawa, Canada
K1A 0L5.

More information on the subject is available in my description of customs regulations, further on.

h. Goods That May Not Be Imported by Mail

It is illegal to send anything by mail that has anything to do with:

Bookmaking
Pool setting (as in a hockey pool)
Unlawful lottery schemes
Betting
Wagering or
Lottery tickets of any kind.

It is legal to mail firearms, as long as the firing pin is mailed separately.

It is illegal to mail articles that are "obscene, indecent, immoral or scurrilous." It is also illegal to mail "any article relating to schemes to deceive or defraud the public" or "articles or special messages sent to any person with the intention to obtain money under false pretenses." These are Criminal Code offences.

The following dangerous articles are prohibited:

Celluloid, liquid celluloid, inflammable films
("safety" films may be mailed if packed in containers approved by Canada Post)
Compressed gases
Corrosive liquids
Explosive substances
Inflammable liquids or solids (e.g., matches)
Oxidizing substances
Radioactive substances

Live animals are not accepted for mailing. Exceptions are made for bees (but not from outside of Canada), day-old chicks and natural-enemy controllers of noxious insects, if they are packaged in a fashion acceptable to Canada Post.

Many pesticides, natural plants and plant matter and all fireworks are illegal to mail.

Tobacco and liquor are subject to Customs restrictions and alcohol is not permitted to be sent through the mail.

Chain letters are not permitted through the mails, but post office officials tell me that they are virtually powerless to stop them because the letters so rarely bear return addresses.

Pyramid sales schemes are completely illegal, and Canada Post will bring charges against any individuals who use the postal system for this purpose.

3. METHODS OF PAYMENT

a. Paying with Plastic

The only hesitation you need have about paying with your credit cards is that — occasionally — disreputable firms will attempt to charge you for items you did not order. Careful record-keeping (and a quick call to VISA or MasterCard or American Express) will handle any difficulties quickly and painlessly. Also, if the firm hopes to stay in business, it will not cross the credit-granting institution — or you.

One hidden advantage of paying by credit card is that some credit card companies are now applying automatic insurance on all purchases from the moment of purchase onward. That means that if you buy a Lalique vase from a source in the Virgin Islands on your American Express card — just as the advertisements show — your purchase will be insured as it's shipped, without additional cost to you. Amex's "Purchase Protection Plan" extends to 90 days after you buy the item; claims must be made within 45 days after the loss, theft or damage occurred. If you already have insurance, PPP will pay whatever the insurance company does not cover, up to a maximum of $60,000 in value, and it will pay your deductible in these cases. Exceptions are: jewellery not on your person (in order words, if it's stolen from your hotel room, you're out of luck); living plants or animals; tickets of any kind; travellers' cheques (they had better be American Express, anyway!); and cash. Claims in Canada are made to 1-800-668-9072. It takes about 35 days to be reimbursed for your loss.

A number of other credit-grantors are taking up this practice, such as Woodward's stores in British Columbia and Alberta. Royal Bank's VISA Gold card purchases are automatically protected against loss, theft or damage for up to 90 days from the date of purchase, on "almost anything you buy, anywhere in the world, at no additional charge." Inquire locally about benefits and limitations of your own cards. Royal Bank's Diners Club card credits you back a one percent cash rebate on all purchases, which helps to repay you for your annual users' fee for the card.

Most credit card companies will convert (at the bank's rate for the currency on the day your "chit" is deposited) the cost of your purchases into the currency of the country you are buying from, at no additional cost to you.

b. International Money Orders, Money Orders and Bank Drafts

Some firms will not accept payment in anything other than U.S. currency, so you have the sticky matter of buying an International Money Order (referred to in the text as an IMO) in U.S. dollars. Fortunately, most banks and post offices do this routinely and do not sniff and make awful faces when you ask for advice.

Within Canada, substitute "regular Canada Post money order" wherever I've mentioned IMO. Payments up to a maximum of $200 can be made with Canadian money orders, in Canadian or U.S. currency or British pounds sterling. Post offices will only accept cash for money orders. Canadian money orders may be enclosed with your correspondence.

When dealing with other countries, the post office can issue "advice," which is a form of payment that has to be cleared through Ottawa and converted to the foreign currency. Then, the payment is sent directly on to your correspondent. This takes about three weeks, costs $1.85 for most foreign countries and does not allow you to send the payment along with your order, so the potential for mistakes is increased.

On the other hand, most Canadian banks can issue IMOs or bank drafts immediately in forms that can be enclosed with your order and in the foreign currency you require.

Bank drafts cost more but are much more convenient. Banks can usually write IMOs in U.S. or Canadian funds or pounds sterling and will charge you anywhere from $2.50 to $3.50, depending on the currency required and the bank you select. Bank drafts cost $6 to $7.50 (again, depending on the bank) and can be written in any currency. (The cheapest rate for a bank draft I found, by the way, was at Central Guaranty Trust for only $5.) The currency conversion is written for you while you wait, and you'll naturally pay for the bank draft in cash, withdraw funds from your account or, in some cases, charge it to your VISA card. Bank rates vary considerably, so shop around for convenience and best rates.

c. Paying by Cheque

Cheques are sometimes acceptable to the mail order house, but I've generally found paying by cheque delays the order while the mail order source allows for time for the funds to clear their local bank. In Canada, I prefer not to pay by cheque because my home phone number appears on my personal cheques and I'd rather the domestic mail order houses not have a means of soliciting from me directly. I've discovered that ordering under a false name in Canada almost certainly means my fake name is sold to junk-mailers, because "Anne Garberini" certainly wins a lot of contests and "free" premiums!

Personal Data
It's wise not to divulge too much personal information by mail, for reasons of personal security and privacy. It's truly amazing what they know about us without much effort. If you must pay by personal cheque, cover your phone number with white-out or black marker.

Sending Cheques Abroad
My correspondents have begged me to tell you that when you send a cheque to their country (particularly to England and Scandinavia), the cost of depositing and clearing the item may cost more than the cheque itself is worth! When you are asked for one or two dollars for a catalogue, please don't send a cheque! In fact, I suppose I should go on record as saying "Use cheques only in North America, and only where you need a piece of paper confirming your payment." A money order will serve as well, often better.

Some cheques are deposited in the foreign country on a "Send on Collection" basis, which means the foreign bank sends the cheque back here to be cleared, then your bank sends the funds — the whole exercise may take months!

You may find a certified cheque works well to third world countries where banking is less efficient than in Canada. Having your cheque certified may cost about $3.50.

d. Cable Transfer (Wiring Money)
Movies of the '30s certainly glamorized this idea ("Oh! Now I'll have to get Daddy to wire me more money!"), and it's still in use today. It is a very quick method of moving money around, but it's very expensive and requires a trip to the bank. Wiring money is mostly used by businesses that must move large sums around quickly, so if you have an account with a gem house in India and need to wire money, this is for you. Costs run from about $7 per transaction between banks to more than $40, plus a "communication fee." Within Canada, this is the cost of the phone call the bank makes to the other bank to confirm the transfer of funds. You must get the merchant's account number, bank address and branch number to wire money. It takes one business day within Canada and about 48 hours outside of the country. Again, shop around between financial institutions for the best rates.

e. Currency Exchange
The best-known company dealing with foreign currencies in Canada is Deak International (formerly Deak-Perrera). They have offices around the globe and a company history dating back to 1928. For information about their services or their Thomas Cook travellers' cheques, there is a toll-free number in Canada: 1-800-268-8155. They also offer a free currency guide, which is updated periodically and gives tables of general foreign equivalents to U.S. and Canadian dollars.

4. HOW TO SHOP BY PHONE, FAX OR COMPUTER

a. Telephone Orders

Mail ordering by phone is usually easy. Complications arise when calling overseas; obviously a foreign language makes being understood more difficult.

Canada

When phoning places in Canada, it's simple: anything outside of your free-calling area is prefixed by the numeral "1" and the area code. In your own province, some long-distance calls will be prefixed only by "1." If in doubt, dial "0" for operator assistance. Information about long-distance dialling and toll charges is always free. Operator-assisted calls are more expensive than direct-dialling.

U. S. A.

When placing calls to the U.S., it's always wise to call directory assistance in that area to check the number first. To do that (and it's a free call), dial 1-area code-555-1212. The operator will ask you what city you are calling before he or she looks up the number for you.

Whoops!

Should you make a mistake in dialling, reach a wrong number or be given an incorrect number by long-distance information, always call your local operator ("0") and report the problem and you will receive a credit on your next phone bill, usually to a maximum of one minute's worth of toll charge.

Overseas

Ordering overseas by phone is more of a hassle, but it can be achieved. I try to order this way only with companies I've already had good experiences with via the postal service. Again, it's wise to check with the overseas operator before you begin dialling, to make sure you have the correct phone number, country code, area code and prefix. For many countries, the overseas prefix is 011.

Hong Kong

Hong Kong is a special case this year because, believe it or not, they changed virtually every number in Hong Kong, Kowloon and the New Territories on the last day of 1989! The old prefix number for calls to Hong Kong was "5," and the old Kowloon prefix was "3." Some numbers had seven digits in total (in which case the numbers should have remained the same), while others had the prefix, plus a seven-digit number, for a total of eight. In that case, the first number should have been dropped. So if a Kowloon number was 3-7654321, it is now 765-4321. If it was 3-

654321, it is now 365-4321. I know this is complicated, but I've called Hong Kong successfully in the past few months, so I know it can be done. The country code prefix for Hong Kong, by the way, is 852.

United Kingdom
To expand its range of available telephone numbers in response to what they refer to as a "phone number famine," British Telecom introduced code changes for the city of London, effective in May of 1990.

Prior to that time, Canadian callers reached London with the prefix "1". Under the new system, that code becomes either "71" or "81." For example, if you used to dial direct as 011-44-1-434-1000, that number would now be 011-44-71-434-1000.

Generally speaking, locations in the inner city core carry the "71" code and the outer areas the "81" code. All London numbers in the listings in this book have been updated, but remember when you receive catalogues from these sources, their own promotional material may not yet be updated. To make matters more complicated, some exchanges have both prefixes allocated to them. If you have trouble dialling or faxing to any of these numbers, please contact your local operator for assistance.

Credit Cards
Please also refer to the section on ordering via credit card (Methods of Payment: Paying with Plastic) for other details on credit card use. You will be expected to give your name, card number and expiry date when ordering by credit card over the phone. Unless you are prepared to wire money to a long-distance source (which 99 percent of them will *not* accept), you will pay by credit card. Again, deal only with reputable firms to avoid credit card fraud. If you have a problem when you have ordered by credit card, always call the local office of the credit institution (or their Canada 800 number, if they have one) to report the problem. VISA, MasterCard and American Express, which are the most commonly used cards, all have provisions to more or less "stop payment" to firms trying to scam you, so call quickly if you think there is a problem.

Lost cards (or problems) should be reported promptly, even though Canadian consumer protection legislation puts a $50 ceiling on the amount you are liable for with fraudulent use of your card. The problem number for American Express is (800) 268-9855; for Diners Club, it's (800) 387-2630; and for MasterCard, it's a toll-free line to Missouri (still free from Canada): (800) 826-2181. VISA cards have different toll-free numbers for each bank that issues them, and various parts of the country are served by special lines. Call 1-800-555-1212 for the one for your bank and region.

Remember, too, that some cards protect you against loss or breakage of the goods you have ordered and will pursue a claim for you if they can't refund or replace directly.

b. 800 Numbers

Canada 800 numbers
Wherever possible, I have included Canada 800 numbers in the text. Please read carefully, because many 800 numbers in the listings may only be used from within the continental United States. Each time I mention these numbers in the listings, they are prefaced with "U.S." or "Can." to avoid confusion.

For Canadian toll-free calls, you simply dial 1-800 and the number given. There is no long-distance charge payable by you.

Please remember that time differences may mean that the phones may not be open when you call, particularly if you are calling back East from the West Coast.

To check the accuracy of 800 numbers, you may call the 800 Service Directory Assistance Operator free at 1-800-555-1212.

A directory of Canadian 800 numbers costs $8.95 from Telecom Canada. To order a copy, dial 1-800-663-7862 (6:30 a.m. to 4:30 p.m. PACIFIC time). This directory includes both white and yellow page listings.

U.S. 800 numbers
U.S. 800 numbers are liberally sprinkled throughout the listings in this book. The only catch (but a big one) is that you can't use these numbers from Canada — unless (and that's a big unless) you subscribe to a telephone service that circumvents Canadian telecommunications systems by patching you through directly to the States (see below for details). So if you want to use U.S. 800 numbers, you must be in the States. By the same token, to FIND U.S. 800 numbers you don't have, you must be in the U.S. and dial 1-800-555-1212. If it's any comfort, Canadian 800 numbers don't work from the States, either.

How to...
Because I live in Vancouver, I find it easy to visit a friend's office just across the border in Blaine, Washington, to make my U.S. 800 calls, and of course, it costs my friend nothing because the calls are free. I also use his mailing address to receive my orders and he uses my address and phone in Canada, so everyone's happy. Similar friendships arise between Windsor and Detroit (it still costs only a dollar to take the bus from downtown to downtown between those two cities); Sault Ste. Marie and Soo Canals, Michigan; Toronto and Buffalo or Niagara Falls; Winnipeg and Pembina, North Dakota; Calgary and Kalispell,

Montana; Montreal and Plattsburg, New York; and New Brunswick and Maine. Feel guilty about your dollars flowing South? Did I mention the G.S.T.?

Alternative Ways of Calling U.S. 800 Numbers
Some entrepreneurial types spotted a service gap in Canadian telecommunications (perhaps a "cheapskate gap" would be more accurate) some years ago. These clever folks found out that toll charges for long-distance telephone calls within the continental United States were cheaper than similar distances within Canada. To circumvent the system, they bought lines to nearby points in the U.S. and sold time on their independent system to Canadian business subscribers who were big consumers of long-distance service. If you work in an office served by Cam-Net Telecommunications, chances are you would access the U.S. long-distance trunk lines by dialling "8" instead of "9" for an outside line. Smart cookies discovered they were then able to call U.S. 800 numbers directly! Not every area of Canada is served by these alternative systems, but if you suspect your office is, ask your boss. Remember, though, that although the 800 calls on these systems are free, the cost of connecting with the nearby bordertown (while nominal) does apply.

c. Fax Orders
It seems hard to believe that a scant five years ago no one (except perhaps the most devout gadget-freaks) had ever heard the term "facsimile machine."

Now, there's barely an office anywhere that doesn't have one and many folks have a personal fax machine at home, too.

A Facsimile Fable
Fax machines are a wonderful convenience to the mail order shopper. Not too long ago, I went to Hong Kong from Vancouver on business. Before I left, my mother (in Toronto) asked me to buy her a Diane Freis outfit while I was there. This is a designer line, and though they're not outrageously expensive, a $150 (Cdn) item is a big chunk out of one's $300 duty-free allowance, so I wanted to be sure I wasn't making a mistake. I went to the Pacific Place mall location of Diane Freis in Hong Kong Central and found two outfits I thought my mother would like. The salesgirl was able to give me magazine photos of the clothes, which I faxed to my dad's office in Toronto, and by that evening I had my reply and my dilemma was solved — for a grand total of $4 for the fax transmissions from my hotel and back.

This communications option is of obvious merit to the mail-orderer. Using faxes also allows you to keep hard copy proof of correspondence and shipping deadlines which you usually waive when ordering by phone.

Fax for Hire
If you don't have access to a business or personal fax, you will find that many stationery stores (and places where you can rent a postal box or office services) allow people to pay for use of their professional capacity facsimile machines. Even some drug stores have faxes for public use. These places often charge unfairly high rates, so shop around for the best prices.

Again, it's wise to check with the telephone company before running out hundreds of faxes at home, so you'll be sure not to get hit with an unexpected massive phone bill.

Many sources listed in this edition include facsimile numbers, and many others will acquire them soon.

Do not dial "01" for fax numbers, or you'll get the operator. Within your city, there is no prefix. In your own province (but outside of your free-calling area) dial "1" plus the fax number. Outside of your province (and also to the States), dial "1" plus the area code, plus the fax number. For overseas, dial "011," plus the country code, plus the city routing code, plus the fax number.

In the listings, any numbers in brackets before the phone or fax numbers are prefixes, country codes or city routing codes. When in doubt, call long-distance directory assistance or fax information before starting to make calls.

Facsimile Information
Directory assistance lists many fax numbers for businesses, but sometimes they can't find new numbers. In that case, there's an 800 number to call in Canada: 1-800-268-2770 for a free service called Dial-A-Dex. These people are directory publishers, and they operate this service to allow you access to not-yet-published fax numbers. In Toronto, call (416) 232-1791. In Vancouver, call (604) 683-5529. Before and after hours, numbers outside of Toronto are put on call-forward to Toronto (how did we ever manage without this technology?), so after you dial, your phone will go back to a dial tone, then you'll hear clicks and electronic noises, followed by some strange-sounding rings, and they will pick up in Toronto.

The company providing this free service is called Business Connections, and they publish a directory that goes by the same name and that covers all of Canada. Business Connections is also the sole agent for directories (one for fax and one for telex numbers) listing numbers for 131 countries, and published by Jaeger and Waldmann in Europe. If your own fax number is listed in one of these directories, you are entitled to receive one free. If you don't have your own fax line but wish to purchase one of these directories (which are published each August), you can do so via the 1-800-268-2770 number. They will invoice you directly for the Canadian edition or send you a form to order the worldwide one.

Business Connections (Canadian directory) costs $49.95 plus $4 postage if you aren't listed in it; the Jaeger and Waldmann directory costs $180, plus $20 postage.

The Toronto office is open weekdays from 8 to 8, Eastern time. For U.S. and off-shore fax numbers that you can't find through the usual long-distance directory assistance methods, Business Connections will research the numbers for you and call you back once they've found them; this service, again, is entirely free to Canadians. They make their money by selling advertising in the directories, in case you were wondering. Naturally, they can only give you fax numbers already on hand for listing in their directories, so sometimes you will still find those numbers elusive.

Keep all correspondence from mail order sources and make a note of any fax numbers that appear on their letterhead, for future use, even if you think you don't need those numbers today. Technology is very seductive, and even if you resist now, in a year you may suddenly realize you've become a convert. I know. I was a late convert to computerism and now I'm a fervent proponent, which brings us to our next topic:

d. Computer Services, Access Information and Fees (1990-1991)

Shopping by Computer

Electronic shopping using a personal computer is increasing in popularity. One advantage of electronic shopping is the ability to shop at any time of the night or day, from your home or office. Another advantage is a direct and instant contact with the source of the merchandise, although you still have to rely on the mail or parcel services for delivery.

You need three basic items to shop by computer: a modem, communications software and a computer. The modem is a device that connects your computer to the telephone line and allows you to send and receive information. Modems range in price from $75 to about $250, depending mainly on their speed of transmission. Communication software is often supplied with a modem. Shareware programs can be obtained free from local computer bulletin boards ("shareware" means that you can use the program for a while before sending in a nominal registration fee — a cost-effective alternative to regular marketing methods). Commercial programs cost in the range of $150 to $300. A basic computer that can also be used for word processing, accounting, etc., as well as communication can be purchased for less than $1000. So, for not much more than $1000, you can join the electronic age of shopping, banking, mail exchange, information retrieval and a multitude of other services and product sources available on-line.

CompuServe
Since its start in 1979, the CompuServe Information service has become the largest general computerized information service in the world. More than half a million members access CompuServe by using their computer, a modem and a local telephone call. The system offers more than 1400 databases, including electronic mail, personal computer support, financial and stock market information, news services, educational and reference services, entertainment, and much more, including, of course, computer shopping.

The Electronic Mall
CompuServe's Electronic Mall provides a convenient alternative to the long lines, crowded parking lots and restrictive business hours associated with traditional malls. The Electronic Mall is open 24 hours a day, seven days a week. More than 150 merchants, including such names as Brooks Brothers, Walden Books and Pepperidge Farms, offer merchandise ranging from flowers and fruit to BMWs, from computer equipment to kitchenware. Easy to follow menus guide you through the Mall, making shopping or browsing a breeze. There are menu selections that describe how to use the Mall, how to order products, how to check the status of an order; the menu also offers many useful tips. Products are ordered on-line and shipped directly to you.

Shopping the Mall is easy. You can shop by store, department or product. Shop by Department opens the doors (actually, menus on your computer screen) to all stores having a department you specify, such as men's apparel. To visit stores having a particular product that you specify, such as books or cameras, choose Shop by Merchant. Using the Product Category Index ushers you into the store you choose, where you can shop in any or all of the store's departments.

Free Shopping Weekends
Every weekend, the Electronic Mall offers free connect time when you can browse through participating merchants' on-line stores for those two days without paying standard CompuServe connect rates. In other words, you pay nothing while you explore a Mall store that's currently offering "free connect." Who says you can't get something for nothing?

Discounts with Shopper's Advantage
Shopper's Advantage is a discount shopping club that allows comparison shopping for more than 250,000 name-brand products at savings from 10 to 50 percent off the manufacturers' suggested retail price! You can browse for everything from air conditioners to computers to microwaves.

Like the Mall, Shopper's Advantage offers five choices from the main menus to guide you through its various offerings. For example, Best Buys highlights special bargains, The Department Store lets you shop by department, while Shop by Model Number provides the fastest way to shop. Enter the exact model number of a product and within moments, that product's price and description appears on your screen. Shop by Product Category takes you directly to product categories such as appliances, TV and video equipment, cars and auto accessories, and home furnishings, without going through a series of menus. Shop by Product Code offers a quick way to shop using convenient product and manufacturer codes.

Shopper's Advantage maintains no inventory. Instead, it arranges for shipping and delivery of products directly from participating manufacturers and distributors to its members. Members and nonmembers alike can browse, but to purchase products, you must be a member. Membership carries a low fee and requires a valid VISA or MasterCard.

The pricing and product information found in Shopper's Advantage Club is useful to comparison shop locally or to research many products before you buy. Members of Shopper's Advantage Club can purchase directly through the database and be assured of guaranteed savings on most products. If, within 30 days of placing an order with Shopper's Advantage Club, a member finds the exact item advertised elsewhere for less, including shipping, handling and applicable sales taxes, he need only send a copy of the ad and his Shopper's Advantage Club receipt, and a refund for the difference will be issued.

Shopper's Advantage Club offers only top quality brand-name products from manufacturers you know and trust. And all products are delivered with U.S. manufacturers' warranties in effect.

Every month Shopper's Advantage Club features helpful information on product lines such as stereo, camera, or TV and video. This valuable product information, available as a selection from the main menu during the feature month and then under the Glossary of Terms in the Info/Member Feedback Menu, can help members be smarter shoppers.

Check the What's New File often for current promotions and clearance sales.

Shopper's Advantage Club is provided to members at the standard annual membership fee of $30, unless otherwise stated. Once enrolled, members will be charged only for the standard CompuServe Information Service connect time rates while shopping.

Getting Started

To join CompuServe, you will need a membership kit, which is available for $39.95 (U.S.) at most computer stores or through CompuServe by calling toll-free in Canada to 1-800-848-8199. The kit provides everything you need to use CompuServe (except the computer and modem) including a User's Guide, a membership booklet containing a User ID number, a password and detailed instructions for accessing CompuServe. In addition, CompuServe offers a $25 on-line usage credit to allow new members time to explore the service. The fee for service varies depending on your modem speed and the time of day. The following table shows the current rates from Canada (assuming you are in a major centre with a local access number — otherwise there are additional carrier charges — see iNET 2000 later in this section for another access method):

CompuServe Connect Rates (per connect hour)

BAUD	Prime/ Daytime $/Hour	Standard/ Evening $/Hour
up to 300	$ 6.00	$ 6.00
450*	$ 6.00	$ 6.00
1200	$12.50	$12.50
2400*	$12.50	$12.50
4800**	$32.50	$29.00
9600**	$47.50	$44.00

* Not available from all locations
** Requires hard-wired network connection and is not available from all locations.

Connect time is billed in one-minute increments, with a minimum of one minute per session. Connect time rates do not include communication surcharges and product surcharges.

In addition to connect time charges, members are billed for network communication surcharges (e.g., CompuServe Network, Datapac, Telenet) for each session on the Information Service.

CompuServe (free) Help
The following menu from CompuServe is a list of areas for which there are no connect time charges levied by the service. However, the carrier surcharge is still in effect, so make sure you check Billing Information (7) to determine how much you are being charged for this "free" service.

1 Tour/Find a Topic
2 Command Summary/How to Use
3 Ask Customer Service
4 Membership Changes
5 What's New
6 Practice Forum
7 Billing Information
8 Telephone Access Numbers
9 Order from CompuServe
10 Rules of Operation/Copyright
11 Membership Directory
12 Specials/Contests

GEnie

GEnie, which stands for General Electric Network for Information Exchange, is a product of GE Information Services, a component of General Electric Company. GEnie offers hundreds of products and services and provides local access phone numbers to subscribers in the U.S.A., Canada and Japan. There are more than 150,000 subscribers using products ranging from RoundTable forums to travel services to business and financial services.

Shopping

GEnie has an electronic mall where you can shop at more than 35 stores ranging from Apparel Concepts for Men to Tiffany & Co. Shopping at the mall is similar to shopping at your local supermarket. First you enter one of the stores by either starting at the GEnie Main Mall menu and choosing the store, or by going directly to the store by typing the keyword for that store at the system prompt. After you enter the store, you can select items and they will be put into your "electronic shopping cart." If you decide you don't want an item in your basket, you can type REMOVE and you will be given the chance to remove it. If you want to know what is in your basket, just type DISPLAY. If you decide you no longer want anything in your basket, just type EMPTY. When you are done shopping, type CHECKOUT. You will be asked for all the information needed to complete your purchase. Payment can be made by VISA, MasterCard, the Discover Card, American Express, COD, personal cheque, or a mailed invoice, depending on the merchant.

The following policies are adhered to by all merchants:

1. All merchandise orders must be shipped within 12 days of order unless otherwise specified in the store's "ordering and shipping policy."

2. Your credit card will not be charged until the merchandise is shipped.

3. Your credit card number is not available to anyone except the store from which you ordered.

4. All stores have liberal return policies. (So your satisfaction on a purchase is guaranteed.)

5. If the product you order is not available, you will be notified within two business days after placing your order. If you have a problem with an order, you can take your complaint to the GEnie Mall Manager, whose electronic address is MALL.

6. All merchants will respond to any electronic mail inquiry within three business days.

Costs
The cost of using GEnie is a combination of a one-time subscription fee of $29.95 (U.S.) plus a basic rate based on the time you spend connected to the GEnie system and the speed of your modem. A remote access charge applies in some areas that do not have a local GEnie number. The basic rate in the U.S., effective May 1, 1989, is summarized below:

Modem Speed	Prime-time rate	Non-prime-time rate
300bps	$18/hr.	$5/hr.
1200bps	$18/hr.	$6/hr.
2400bps	$18/hr.	$10/hr.

The prime-time rate is in effect from 8:00 a.m. to 6:00 p.m. weekdays. The non-prime-time rate is in effect from 6:00 p.m. to 8:00 a.m. weekdays, and all day on the weekend and national (U.S.) holidays. The subscription fee includes a $10 usage credit, a subscription to GEnie's *Live Wire* newsletter and a GEnie User's Manual.

Accessing GEnie
To talk to a representative about signing up for GEnie, you can call GEnie Client Services toll-free at 1-800-638-9636 (in the U.S. and Canada). Their office hours are from 8:00 a.m. to midnight weekdays (EST) and noon to 8:00 p.m. on weekends and holidays.

Delphi
Delphi is one of the pioneers in the telecommunications field. It was founded in 1981 and was the first full-service system to offer 1200 bps access at no surcharge. It was the first to offer a surcharge-free 2400 bps access and the first to publish an on-line encyclopedia.

Delphi is known for its relaxed and friendly atmosphere, which gives the service a sense of community. Delphi offers all of the features of a leading information service: electronic mail, real-time conferencing, news wires, comprehensive business information, extensive travel information (with an instant reservation system) and on-line shopping.

Merchant's Row On-line Shopping
The following list is a sample of some of the many vendors available on Delphi's Merchant's Row:

- Chocolates by Godiva will ship chocolate anywhere.
- Long Distance Roses will send floral displays.
- Coffee Anyone??? offers a fine array of gourmet products.
- Mary Tac Industries offers many Tandy products.
- UNICEF Greeting Cards and Gifts for special occasions.

Delphi also offers access to a shopping service called Comp-u-Store Online (the same service is available from CompuServe where it is called Shopper's Advantage — see above). You will find more than 250,000 name-brand products to choose from, and most are available at guaranteed savings of 10 percent to 50 percent off manufacturers' list prices.

Accessing Delphi — The Delphi Advantage
Delphi Advantage members' rates are as low as eight cents per minute — that's only $4.80 per hour — for domestic U.S. access via TYMNET, Telenet or direct dial (and access from Canada via TYMNET) during the evenings and weekends. International access for Advantage members is 12 cents per minute 24 hours a day. To join the Delphi Advantage, there is a one-time membership fee of $19 (U.S.), with a commitment to use $24 worth of Delphi connect charges per month.

For more information, call Delphi Member Services at 1-800-544-4005. Delphi's mailing address is Delphi, Three Blackstone Street, Cambridge, MA 02139.

iNET 2000
iNet 2000 is a service offered by Telecom Canada to facilitate information management. It offers access to a wide range of information, both Canadian and American. Access to CompuServe is available through the iNET Gateway service. The surcharge is higher than direct connecting via the CompuServe Network (although the latter is not available in many Canadian cities, while iNET is available through Datapac in most Canadian cities).

Comp-U-Store
The shopping area on iNET is called Comp-U-Store. Unlike the other electronic shopping services mentioned so far, this one is Canadian, and so the prices are as listed, with no need to figure out exchange and duty.

Shopping and Ordering
Comp-U-Store contains discount price and product information for more than 50,000 brand-name products. All major brand names within categories of appliances, electronics and cameras are available.

To guide you to the product of your choice, Comp-U-Store will prompt you for the following information: product type, brand name, model number and product features. Once you have entered your product selection criteria, Comp-U-Store will display a complete description of the product including the Comp-U-Store discount price. If you choose to buy, Comp-U-Store will ask for a ship-to address and delivery instructions. The order will be processed and a detailed confirmation of the purchase will be mailed to you. Each product comes with the manufacturer's warranty in full effect.

Note: Unfortunately, Comp-U-Store is unable to ship products to the Northwest Territories.

USER NOTES
Members may print out any information obtained through Comp-U-Store. However, since prices are updated daily, Comp-U-Store will sell only at the price quoted at the time of order.

Cost:
$0.40 per minute at all times.

Offered by:
Comp-U-Card Canada Inc.
2000 Mansfield
Suite 600
Montreal, Quebec
H3A 2Z3

iNET 2000 Rates
One-time Service Charge
A one-time charge of $55 per individual user or organization is applied at the time of the initial order.

Consolidated Billing
Subscribers receive one monthly bill containing iNet 2000 charges and Information Service Provider charges for those Information Service Providers participating in Accounts Receivable Management.

iNet also offers on-line help, and tutorials are available on the system.

If you would like to learn more about the advantages of becoming an iNet 2000 user, call toll-free in Canada: 1-800-267-8480 or (613) 781-3842.

iNet 2000 Feature Usage Charges
A charge for iNet 2000 feature usage is applied on a per-user-connect hour basis as follows:

*Prime time $16.50/hr
Non-prime time $12.35/hr
* 8 a.m. - 6 p.m. local time on weekdays.

This feature rate applies only when the user is accessing iNet features including directories, filing, editing, messaging and data conferencing. This rate does not apply when the user is connected to a listed on-line service, at which time a service access charge is applied.

On-line Service Access Charges
When the user is connected to a listed on-line service, a communications charge is applied as follows:

Prime-time access to a Canadian service $6.60/hr
Non-prime-time access to a Canadian service $4.95/hr
Access to a U.S. service (i.e., CompuServe) $9.90/hr

Confused?
Shopping by computer is the wave of the future. Most of these companies know how nervous we are about new technology, and they are more than happy to assuage our fears with easy-to-decipher information (Hey, if I can learn this, you can learn this), so there's no reason to be shy about calling for free pamphlets or fact sheets.

5. CUSTOMS AND IMPORT DUTIES, RULES AND RESTRICTIONS

a. Free Trade and U.S. Imports

Due to changes in tariff agreements between the United States and Canada, dutiable goods will vary over the next few years and many restrictions will ease. Contact your local Revenue Canada Customs and Excise branch for updates on the information in this section.

The only effect the Free Trade Agreement will have over the phasing-out period (1990 through 1999) will be to remove Customs duty. All other charges, such as excise duty, federal sales tax and provincial liquor distribution fees, are still applicable.

b. Rules for Imports from the U.S. and Other Countries

Goods produced in countries other than the United States or Canada, but imported via the U.S. are subject to what is known as the "Most Favoured Nation Tariff Rate." If the goods are imported from the U.S. but have been produced in a developing nation, they are taxed under the "General Preferential Tariff." Goods imported directly from countries other than the U.S. are subject to "General Tariff." Agreements exist with some Commonwealth countries that lessen import tariffs. Among these are Great Britain, Australia, New Zealand and Caribbean countries. Items from Japan, England and Hong Kong come in at similar rates. Customs officials are often helpful (to a fault) in going through their reference books and trying to assign your goods to the cheapest category. For example, pretzels (which are subject to an additional 13.5 percent federal sales tax, calculated on the value declared to the purpose of paying duty) are imported at a rate of only 4 percent from the U.S. From other countries, the tariff is 5 percent, plus the F.S.T., of course.

The rate of tariff on some foodstuffs varies greatly. For instance, yeast imported from the States comes in free, although from other countries, you'll pay 12.5 percent (not subject to F.S.T.).

c. Common Tariffs

Here are some common goods you might order by mail and their varying tariffs, according to country of origin: puddings, sugar candy or cakes: 12.4 percent (from U.S.; 15.5 percent, other countries); chocolates: 10 percent, plus F.S.T. (12.5 percent plus F.S.T. from other countries); roasted coffee: 2.6 cents per kilogram from U.S. sources (4.41 cents per kilogram, other countries); tea or herbal teas are free from all sources (no F.S.T. either); jams and jellies: 8 percent (U.S.) (10 percent other countries), but strawberry jam has a higher tariff at 12 percent (15 percent). Raw nuts come in duty and tax free, but salted or candied nuts are dutiable at 8 percent and 12.4 percent respectively (higher for foreign countries) and those processed nuts are subject to F.S.T. also. There are thousands of other items, but I think you get the idea. The best bet is to request a free information circular from Customs and look up any goods you might consider importing, first, so you can factor in costs and determine in advance what your purchases will truly cost you. Alternatively, you can go down to Customs and look in their foot-wide book (which lists some 100,000 items and their rates) and look up your categories yourself.

d. Restrictions on Foods

Here's a surprise: among the goods you may not import are corn on the cob, fresh peaches, nectarines, apples, apricots, pears, plums, quince, hawthorn and potatoes. Your maximum on meat or meat products is 10 kg (22 lbs.) so if you're buying a ham from the States, remember your limit. A ham, by the way, would also require inspection by Agriculture Canada. We buy ours from Quebec and avoid the hassle.

e. Some Duty-free Goods from the U.S. and Some Other Countries

Here's an assortment of goods that are duty-free under U.S. tariff (though some require payment of F.S.T.): Corning Ware; disc drives; recorded magnetic tapes; contact lenses; dictionaries; dogs; Duraflame logs; hair dryers; eyeglasses; fertilizers; smoke detectors; domestic-made radios and receivers; battery-operated radios; compact disc players (when combined with automatic tuner or receiver); cellular phone for automotive installation; religious paraphernalia (calendars, pictures, scriptures); electric razors; football helmets; saxophones; underwater compasses; roofing shingles (except asphalt); snowmobiles; harmonicas; helmets (including football, but excluding all other sports); unstrung natural or cultured pearls; unmounted gems (emeralds, rubies, sapphires, diamonds); insulin; orthopedic shoes; pacemakers; hearing aids; Pyrex cookware; children's picture books; most other books; and printed music.

f. Goods You'd Rather Buy in the U.S.

A small difference exists in tariffs on certain goods, which, if manufactured overseas, are subject to the "Most Favoured Nation" tariff, but are non-dutiable if imported from the States. These include: computers, computer parts, modems, magnetic disc drives, video displays and monitors. Big differences in tariffs apply to roller skates or ice skates (tariff-free from U.S., 22.5 percent if manufactured elsewhere); downhill or cross-country skis (compare at 11.4 percent); fur gloves (compare at 25 percent!); and revolvers or pistols that are free if U.S.-made, tariffed at 5.5 percent if made abroad.

g. Goods Expensive to Bring in from the States

Some items are best bought from Canadian sources. Leather gloves, as an example, are tariffed at 20 percent (U.S. origin) or 25 percent (many other countries). Imitation jewellery, contact lens solution, toasters, water skis and felt hats are all relatively high in tariff rate, too. Most U.S. clothing comes in at 18 or 20 percent (22.5 or 25 percent under M.F.N. rate), including even garments for children.

h. Preferable Goods to Import from Abroad

It is a pleasant surprise to many that all forms of silk yard goods (that is, not made up into garments) may be imported into Canada duty-free. Unset gemstones, as mentioned above, are also non-dutiable, as are unstrung pearls. The latter can be strung on temporary strings, and this procedure is obvious to Customs officials who are used to seeing it.

i. Procedures

First, you'll want to arm yourself with Revenue Canada Customs and Excise's latest (free) edition of "Importing Goods into Canada? Documentation Simplified." Ah...yes and no. It is very helpful to have this booklet, but you will have to decide just how "easy" it actually makes things. It might also be useful, if you are going to become really serious about ordering goods from overseas, to obtain the pamphlet "Free Trade and the Commercial Sector," which helps to explain customs and tariff provisions affected by the Free Trade Agreement and what impact they have on goods from the U.S. or goods from other countries imported via the U.S.

You may want to consult that big, fat book at Customs, I mentioned earlier. This book (called *Customs Tariff*) is located in all Customs offices, but not in any other government offices, such as the post office. If there is no Customs office in your town, you can write to the "Tariffs and Values" office of Customs in your nearest Canadian city.

The purpose of looking up the tariff is to be prepared when you ultimately bring goods through Customs. You will know ahead of time what the cost will be and will be able to fill out the "Canada Customs Coding Form" in advance, thereby minimizing the hassle at the post office, airport or wherever your package arrives. However, all this advanced footwork is not really necessary. Personally, I've never done it. I just wait till the notice comes in the mailslot, then head down to Customs to pay the piper (I mean the taxman). Once in awhile, my package comes through to me directly, no tariff payable, no hassle, nice surprise. On the other hand, if you are planning to make some large purchases (a piece of furniture in a large crate is unlikely to slip through unnoticed), or if you will have many packages delivered to you at the same time, it might be wise to investigate the options before you make the commitment to spend your hard-earned money.

j. Where You Pay Duty

Duty can be paid at Customs offices at airports, post offices, marine offices or border crossings, which brings us to the next topic:

k. U.S. Drop-off Points

Here's a question I'm often asked regarding mail ordering from the United States: Is it worthwhile to keep a post office box or other type of mailing address in a nearby U.S. border town to simplify transactions?

In my own sphere, I enjoy several options, including friends and family in the continental United States who are willing to receive catalogues and goods for me at home and notify me of their arrival. This is a great convenience, especially when you're faced with wonderful sources, such as The Sharper Image, which steadfastly refuse to send their catalogue free to Canadian addresses, despite the fact that we do a great deal of business with them.

Canada Customs has no problem with the notion of Canadians keeping U.S. mailing addresses — provided, of course, that you are legitimately declaring, as you return to Canada, any goods you acquire that way.

Another advantage is that you may find you have some recourse (if you are dealing between U.S. addresses) to U.S. consumer protection legislation, which, at this writing at least, is considerably more stringent than our own. For example, the U.S. Federal Trade Commission has a mail order rule which states that if goods are not sent to you within 30 days, the vendor must give you the option of prompt refund. If no definite delivery date was given, one is estimated from the time you mailed your order. The vendor must also advise you of amended shipping dates along with the option to cancel (and receive a refund), and this choice must be placed before you in a method that costs you no further postage to reply.

A number of consumer protection provisos apply between U.S. addresses, too.

These regulations do not cover photo finishing, magazine subscriptions (except for the first issue), seeds or plants, or any orders that are placed by telephone (because you are not using the U.S. Postal Service).

There is also some protection in place about unsolicited goods between points in the U.S.

The Vancouver-Blaine friendship is one of the happier across-the-border relationships, but even so, there are some tensions. To ameliorate possible problems, the Americans held a congressional hearing in April 1990 in Blaine, noting that though officials had guessed border traffic would decline somewhat after Expo 86 in Vancouver, instead it has increased by some 60 percent. Washington Governor Booth Gardner called for an increase in customs and immigration manpower and testified that Canada is the largest importer of Washington State goods, the largest investor in Washington and the state's largest source of tourists, so "it is in our vital interest to let nothing stand in the way of this relationship."

Quintin Villanueva, U.S. Customs Pacific regional commissioner, said that options the U.S. Customs Service is considering include pre-approved identification cards for frequent, low-risk travellers, and an automatic licence-plate reader that would free inspectors from manually entering licence plates into their computers. These folks really want to be pals, don't you think?

The point is that Canadians usually save money by crossing the border. I'm not trying to anger all the "Buy Canadian" proponents, and heaven knows I try to honour that dictum whenever I can, but the fact is, dealing with the U.S. expands our world, and that's one aspect of what this book is all about.

l. Customs Brokers

Most consumers do not require the services of a broker, but if you are buying large items or shopping by mail overseas a great deal, it might be worth pursuing. The Yellow Pages lists many customs brokers. For individuals, it's unlikely the forms will be so complicated that you'll need one.

If you ship via a courier service, they will often clear your package of customs and settle with you upon delivery.

m. Gift Exemptions

Gifts sent from abroad to Canadian addresses come in duty-free if they are valued at under $40 (Cdn.) each. A written declaration from the sending party is all that is required.

On the other hand, you can't order in an item and say it's a gift to get the exemption — even if that is true. You must have the item shipped directly to your friend and marked clearly that it is a gift and what the value is. Many mail order sources, especially those dealing with you by credit card, will happily (and efficiently) send your gifts wherever you wish, enclosing a gift card with your greetings appropriate to each recipient. Many are sophisticated enough to send you a computer printout of all of these transactions, too. I know a growing number of individuals who handle their Christmas shopping regularly in this painless fashion.

The only caution I would offer here is to make sure that your source is one with which you have done business at least once or twice before you start firing gifts off worldwide, just to be on the safe side and know they can deliver the goods as promised.

n. "Duty-free" Shopping by Mail

Shopping from the duty-free shops situated near the American border, or at airports, can be done only in person, and you must be leaving Canada to shop there.

Some mail order sources advertise themselves as "duty-free" shops; what they mean by that is that the goods they bring into their shop come into their country sans duty, so there are some apparent savings. Perfume from France, for example, may have a very high import duty if brought directly into the country, but if it goes to a duty-free store in Nassau or the Virgin Islands, it may be much less expensive than shopping domestically — or not. Wise price comparisons are *de rigueur*, here.

Generally speaking, if the goods are discounted to the U.S. market, you will enjoy at least some saving by buying from that source by mail. However, call Customs before purchase, to be on the safe side.

o. Acceptable Tariff Payment Methods

Tariffs are usually payable only by cash or traveller's cheques, but certain locations will also take credit cards, such as major airport Customs, major border crossings from the United States and some Customs offices. It's wise to check before you head down to Customs so you won't wait in line, do the paperwork and then arrive at the counter to discover you don't have the cash in hand that you need.

6. COURIER SERVICES, FREIGHT AND SHIPPING

Courier services will sometimes be more efficient, safer, more reliable and even less costly than some postal services. Certainly, it will be worth your while to investigate costs and timing.

a. UPS

The most commonly used courier service in North America is United Parcel Service, or UPS. Within Canada, they serve every address accessible by road in Quebec and Ontario, and many addresses in Manitoba, Saskatchewan, Alberta and British Columbia. Since in most cases you would be the recipient of delivery, it is an easy matter to call your local UPS and find out if they will deliver to your home or business.

Internationally, UPS ships by air to and from more than 200 countries, including those often featured in this book, such as the United Kingdom, Hong Kong, Virgin Islands, Turkey, India.

UPS air rates are expensive. A one-kilogram parcel from the U.K., for example, would cost $42 (Cdn) to ship to you, compared to approximately $13.60 by airmail, or $6.15 by surface mail (boat). Rates quoted for post are for outgoing Canadian mail and are an approximation only, since costs will vary according to the country of origin. You may not ship more than 136 kg (300 lbs.) from one shipper to yourself on the same day. These would have to be divided into a number of packages, because the largest single parcel you can ship by UPS is 32 kg (70 lbs.), with total dimensions adding up to not more than 330 cm (130 inches).

UPS has a helpful booklet on packaging, labelling and shipping, called "Package With Care," which is free for the asking. Among the no-no's is using string to bind the parcel, a fact that was news to me.

Here are some serious restrictions: you must insure goods valued at over $100 for 25 cents for each additional $100, according to Warsaw Convention liability rules. You may not ship goods valued in excess of $25,000 by UPS. You may not ship articles of unusual value, nor ammunition, firearms, dangerous goods or hazardous materials.

UPS offers an automatic brokerage service between Canada and overseas, which is a great advantage. All packages must be prepaid.

Ground service rates are much cheaper than courier services.

b. Federal Express

This courier service is fast and efficient, and very good at making deliveries into Canada from the U.S. However, they are expensive to use and the cost of shipping FedEx is almost always borne by the consumer.

Within the U.S., an "economy" rate is offered, at about half the other "overnight" rate. Unfortunately, as soon as goods cross the border to Canada, they can only use the "overnight" rate.

If duty must be paid, someone has to meet your parcel at the FedEx office and pay it before it can be delivered.

Anything shipped by FedEx is considered "commercial," so no $40 duty-free gift exemptions apply.

c. Couriers

Purolator will not accept any perishables, even vaccuum-packed cookies, for instance. Unlike Federal Express, however, they will take goods through Customs; they are a "door-to-door" service.

In the U.S., Purolator uses "Airborne Express," both between U.S. points and into Canada from the States.

TNT Skypak is relatively expensive, quoting us $165 to deliver a 10-kg package to the Yukon from London, England.

Skypak International Express would have charged us $48 to bring a three-pound tin of cookies into Vancouver from L.A. You'd have to want those cookies BADLY.

The Yellow Pages are chock full of international and regional courier services. Again my advice is: shop around.

d. Trucking and Freight Companies

For large items, such as furniture, you may find it less costly to send goods by truck or rail. Most mail orderers dealing in large items can make these arrangements for you, forwarding lading or way-bills to you to check against deliveries. Again, you'll pay extra, usually equated according to how far you are from the shipping source (i.e., some places pay for the first 1,000 miles, then charge a substantial fee for additional distance).

Note that "F.O.B." a certain city means you pay for shipping once the order leaves those city limits.

e. Goods by Ship

Though the prospect of shipping by sea intimidates most of us, it is achievable. Again, if you're dealing with experienced mail order houses, they can advise you and usually make all the arrangements on your behalf. In Commonwealth countries, firms that perform moving, packing, crating and shipping services are usually called "removal" companies, a fact we Canadians find mildly disconcerting, but what's in a name, after all?

Most goods shipped by sea are either crated or sent in container shipments (or both) and it is a very slow but relatively safe mode of transport. And it's quite an experience to journey down to your own Port Authority Customs office to claim and "bail out" your goods.

Water damage is an occasional risk. Check liability limitations with the shipper before signing anything or paying for shipping.

7. PROVINCIAL AND FEDERAL SALES TAXES

a. Provincial Sales Taxes

Not every province has a P.S.T. Those that do charge a fixed percent on many purchased items and services. Hang onto your hats for some surprises: here's a list of provinces and their P.S. taxes:

British Columbia	6 %
Alberta	none
Saskatchewan	7 %
Manitoba	7 %
Ontario	8 %
Quebec	9 %

New Brunswick	11 %
Nova Scotia	10 %
Prince Edward Island	10 %
Newfoundland	12 % (wow!)

Most mail order purchases are taxed, and many of the mail order sources I've included leave room for applicable taxes on their order forms.

There are exemptions, which vary from province to province. Some exempt children's clothing, school supplies or books.

Consumer taxation authorities we talked to told us that mail order purchases are not of particular interest to them — they make up a small fraction of the total retail sales they tax. If you overlook a small P.S.T. charge, the taxman is not going to come after you with a truck in the night, but the general rule of thumb is that if you're buying goods in your home province, most of them will be subject to P.S.T. and it should be added into the purchase price and remitted with your order payment.

Goods shipped out of province (i.e., if you buy something from Quebec and live in B.C., and have the goods sent to your home) are P.S.T. exempt, even though both provinces have P.S.T.

If you are living in B.C. and you buy your friend (who lives in Quebec) a gift ham from a supplier in Quebec, you pay the P.S.T., because the goods are "being consumed" in the province of origin. If the ham is first sent to you and then you turn around and ship it back to your friend, however, no tax is paid.

b. Federal Sales Tax

Federal Sales Tax, or F.S.T., is levied on most items bought in Canada or imported into Canada. Usually, when you buy an item at a retail store, the F.S.T. has been added in at the manufacturing level.

When you import goods, however, you suddenly discover what F.S.T. is all about.

Exempt goods include foodstuffs (except for snack foods and chocolate bars), most clothing (but not sports helmets and things like hockey gloves or padded cycling tights). Generally speaking, clothing with protective elements is not exempt from F.S.T.

Foodstuffs include bakery goods and food and drink for human consumption (but not animal feed or beer). Fruit juice is exempt if it has at least 25 percent natural juice. Lollipops and ice cream are exempt.

With the G.S.T. (effective January 1991), all imported clothing is taxable. The G.S.T. replaces the F.S.T., so the new rate for all goods is 7 percent.

At the time of this writing, however, the general rate for F.S.T. is 13.5 percent. Beer is taxed at 19 percent. A lower rate (of 9 percent) applies to many building materials, though paint and light fixtures are taxed at 13.5 percent. Nails are subject to 9 percent F.S.T., but thumbtacks come in at 13.5 percent.

Imported goods are taxed on values translated to Canadian currency.

If goods are dutiable, F.S.T. is calculated on the value of the items PLUS the duty, so duty is included in total value for the purposes of calculating F.S.T.

c. G.S.T.

Effective January 1991, all goods and many services are subject to the G.S.T., fixed at 7 percent.

Suddenly, goods bought outside of the country look a little more attractive (say 6.5 percent more attractive?). And many items now bought at home and not currently taxed might seem just a little more costly.

I'm not trying to justify looking outside of Canada for goods, but this book is about buying worldwide, so it makes buying by mail (and looking for bargains) a good deal more attractive, doesn't it?

A number of goods and services are not subject to the G.S.T. (nor, according to the government, are "those to which a 'zero' rate of tax applies"). These are exported products and services; most agricultural and fish products; certain major purchases by farmers and fishermen; basic groceries; prescribed medical devices; and prescription drugs.

Other items are G.S.T. exempt. These include: most education and financial services (including insurance); health and dental care services; long-term residential rents; and daycare services. A vocal group (and you should be part of it) is continuing to lobby the government to eliminate G.S.T. on books, so watch for developments on that front as election time draws near.

The federal government tells us that the prices of domestically produced high-ticket items, such as cars, washers, dryers and televisions will actually go down in price, once the G.S.T. is in place. Other goods will rise in price, enough to make the overall consumer price index increase by about 1.25 percent.

For toll-free information anywhere in Canada about the G.S.T. and the rules for applying it, call 1-800-267-6620 and remember the time change if you're out West. French-language explanations are accommodated by dialling 1-800-267-6640, and information for the hearing impaired is at 1-800-267-6650.

d. Shipping Out of Province

As mentioned (in passing) above, goods bought in another province and shipped to you, or bought in your home province and shipped elsewhere, are P.S.T. exempt. Often you'll find that the cost of shipping goods is offset by the savings in sales taxes you'll realize by employing this little sleight-of-hand. That's why savvy Canadian shoppers travelling within Canada will often have bulky purchases shipped home to save themselves the hassle of packing and carting the items around. Sometimes you even come out ahead.

One obvious advantage to shipping out of province is that, within Canada, your purchases are still subject to the same consumer protection legislation that serves us all. So if you have a problem with a shopping source in Alberta and you live in New Brunswick, you can still contact your local office of Consumer and Corporate Affairs for help if you've gotten nowhere on your own. Be sure to keep documentation of all transactions, dates, and even notes about telephone conversations.

Be sure you understand shipping deadlines and allow the supplier to account for any delays in shipment. Meanwhile, if I hear that "mudslide at Boston Bar" story one more time, I'll scream!

8. RESTRICTED ITEMS

Generally, Customs makes a distinction between "prohibited" and "restricted" items. Some things simply can't be legally imported into Canada; others may be, but not until you've engaged in a lengthy process of forms and permits.

a. Illicit Drugs

There are a number of items and substances that may not be brought into Canada. Obviously, you are not permitted to import illegal street drugs, such as marijuana, cocaine or heroin.

b. Pornography

This category includes books, video tapes, photographs and so on, all of which are strictly illegal in Canada — which makes one wonder how those tapes get to the "adult" video store. Never mind: the point here is that individual consumers are sure to get hassled if they bring these items into Canada.

c. Health Cures

Certain health remedies are not permitted in Canada. These include seven specific amino acids, some herbs and oils derived from herbs, "unapproved drugs," and some very potent drugs, such as AZT. In the case of AZT, even when it was still unapproved, supplies could be obtained from the U.S. and were legal to import under the supervision of a Canadian doctor, via a humanitarian provision of the Food and Drug Act known as "emergency drug release."

In the case of laetrile (a reputed anti-cancer treatment), although it is still not acknowledged as a legitimate cancer cure in Canada, a court ruling in Oklahoma about five years ago helped to set the precedent for authorizing its use in 38 U.S. states, so again, it can be imported into Canada in small, personal-use quantities.

Generally speaking, the U.S. government gets involved in policing the use of an unapproved drug only if the substance is being transported across state lines. Canadian authorities monitor drugs being imported, so check with your local office of the Federal Health Protection Branch before ordering any health cures by mail.

According to Croft Woodruff, a nutrition researcher and consultant, and the president of the Canadian Health Food Association, health and drug manufacturing is highly profit-driven, so there is a push to bring new "discoveries" to market quickly, which often doesn't suit the monitoring authorities in Canada and the U.S. He points out: "The Canadian Health Protection Branch is very strict, and I think they do a much better job of monitoring health foods, pharmaceuticals and food products than they do in the U.S." Woodruff says that a number of substances are available by mail order from the States and that individuals may bring in about three months' supply of any non-controlled substance (anything that is not outright illegal, that is) without being hassled by the Canadian authorities. But there have been problems.

Recently there was a controversy over the use of contaminated Tryptophan, one of 21 amino acids in vogue as a health product. Tryptophan is metabolized in the brain into niacin and subsequently produces serotonen, a natural enzyme that helps people sleep. In other words, it results in a naturally produced substance as a safe alternative to sedatives or prescription drugs, which can be dangerous and habit-forming. The contaminated Typtophan has resulted in at least 19 deaths in the U.S. attributed to the contaminant, which contributed to a condition known as Eosinophilia Myalgia Syndrome (E.M.S.), an inflammation of the muscles. Of 100 brands of Tryptophan marketed in the U.S., only 10 or 12 were found to contain the contaminant, and only a few specific lot numbers of those, for that matter. "However," Woodruff emphasizes, "no one should be buying it over the counter or by mail order. It should only be bought by prescription." So it's not always wise to circumvent Canadian restrictions by buying from U.S. or off-shore sources.

The Canadian government initially banned all amino acids, but, after a thorough review in 1987, all but seven of them were released for general use.

Some common herbs are carefully monitored, such as wormwood (its oil is toxic, but wormwood tea, which is vile tasting anyway, cannot be taken in quantities large enough to harm you). Another herb under government scrutiny is comfrey, which, when taken as a tea, is well-known among midwives as a cure for mastitis in nursing mothers. Large quantities as additives in health compounds, on the other hand, may apparently cause a toxic reaction and liver damage.

My general advice on buying health cures, and even vitamins, by mail is to check with your local Health Protection Branch before ordering.

d. Counterfeits, Replicas and Genuine Art

It appears the rules for bringing in counterfeit watches to Canada are much less strict than the rules in the U.S. are. In the States (the land of free enterprise), much more protection is given to trademarks and copyrights, so fake Rolex and Piaget watches are routinely confiscated. In the years I've been researching this book, however, I've been unable to obtain a clear ruling on this issue from Canada Customs. The rule of thumb seems to be that if you're bringing in one or two of these "fabulous fakes" for your own use or that of your friends, fine. If you try to import 200 replicas, you're in trouble.

There's a story going the rounds that a major manufacturer of fine watches is approached once in awhile by consumers who are looking for "replacement batteries." The catch is that the brand in question doesn't incorporate batteries in its watches! However, so conscious are these particular watchmakers of good customer relations, that they will now actually provide replacement batteries for the obvious counterfeits. The mark of a counterfeit watch, by the way, is often (in the case of Rolexes, for example) that the second hand does not sweep, but instead clicks through the seconds as it moves, indicating a quartz movement (not mechanical works, as are found in the expensive timepieces).

Fake works of art are another matter. Artwork, if it is "original," is duty-free. You may need a certificate of authenticity to import such items free. Anything that has a functional use is not considered art.

Original paintings and limited edition prints are tax- and duty-free. Having the prints numbered and signed makes all the difference in the world.

A vase or piece of ceramic pottery, however artistic, is not considered "artwork" under the tariff regulations.

Counterfeit works of art are dutiable. Non-original works of art are classified as "pictures" and are subject to 11.3 percent duty and 13.5 percent F.S.T. Ditto for mass-produced posters, however "uptown" they might appear.

e. Antiques

Genuine antiques must be 100 years old to be exempt of duty and tax. Items between 50 and 99 years old are duty-free but not F.S.T.-exempt.

Wines and spirits are articles that cannot be entered as antiques, even though they might be 100 years old or more.

f. Agricultural No-no's

There are tight controls on the importation of livestock, pets, meat and meat products, plants, fresh fruit and vegetables. For specific information on any of these items, please write to Food Production and Inspection Branch, Agriculture Canada, Ottawa, Ontario K1A 0C5.

These folks can be quite helpful and supportive on some imports (and some meats can be brought in if the quantities are small enough), but other rules are inflexible, such as restrictions on pine trees, which could carry diseases harmful to our forests.

Neither bees nor turtles may be imported into Canada.

g. Endangered Species
It is illegal to import some types of snakeskin and most kinds of genuine ivory, reptile skin (such as African alligator), or tortoiseshell. Other items that need inquiry are products made of fur, skin, feathers or bone. Check first with Convention Administrator, Canadian Wildlife Service, Environment Canada, Ottawa, Ontario K1A 0E7.

h. Dangerous Items
It is illegal to import some firearms, especially fully automatic rifles and machine guns. Check with local police or Customs officials to determine restrictions. Customs has a booklet, "Importing a Firearm or Weapon into Canada," which may prove helpful.

Other offensive weapons include switchblade knives, throwing stars, nunchaku sticks, mace, spiked wristbands, blowguns, brass knuckles and silencers for guns.

Explosives, fireworks and ammunition are tightly controlled and can only be imported with a special permit. For details, write Chief Inspector of Explosives, Energy, Mines and Resources, 580 Booth Street, Ottawa, Ontario K1A 0E4.

i. Used Motor Vehicles
Customs law prohibits the entry of used or second-hand vehicles that are not of the current model year. New vehicles may be imported, with duties paid. The booklet "Importing a Motor Vehicle into Canada" is available from Customs.

j. CB Radios
CB radios must meet Canadian standards. To determine if one you wish to import does so, contact your nearest office of the Federal Department of Communications for information.

k. "Grey Market" Goods
It is technically illegal to bring in electrical items that have not been CSA approved. Please read the chapter on Grey Market goods (next) for a fuller explanation.

9. THE GREY MARKET

The "Grey Market" must surely be one of the major "grey areas" in Canada. It's odd, but when I started researching this book, I knew about the term, yet it seemed most people I asked thought it referred to marketing goods and services to Golden Agers. In fact, that's not what it means at all.

Grey market goods are perfectly normal goods (usually electronics, watches, cameras or perfumes) that have originated from an offshore source. They are quite legal, first-line goods, manufactured by the well-known companies whose names they bear. Grey marketing is also known as "parallel importation" and is meant to take advantage of the uneven pricing of products made by multinational manufacturers.

According to a *Globe and Mail* report, "Parallel importers buy well-known, brand-name products in countries with weaker currencies, and sell them to retailers in other countries at prices below those [which] domestic, authorized suppliers can offer."

The item goes on to say: "The practice usually involves high-value, low-weight goods such as cameras, batteries and even condoms and occurs most often when currencies change value substantially and quickly."

The major difference between grey market goods and domestic ones (besides the fact that they cost much less than local merchandise) is that they may not be warranteed by the companies that made them in the same way the items meant for the Canadian retail market are.

So, if you buy a Pentax camera through a Hong Kong discount store, or if your brother-in-law knows someone at Sony in the U.S. who can get you goods at "cost plus 10 percent," you may wind up with a big problem if the warranty doesn't cover your wonderful piece of equipment in Canada. You might also find out that the only product info and instructions in your possession are in a (very) foreign language.

A number of Canadian retailers play the grey market game, too, and sometimes you don't even know you're buying goods of this nature.

According to the *Financial Times of Canada*, when Seiko refused to let Consumers Distributing sell its watches through its catalogues in the early 1980s, Consumers simply went around the company and bought the watches through grey market sources. Seiko sued for trademark infringement, lost, appealed and lost again before the Supreme Court of Canada. But the ruling also gave Seiko the right to nullify the warranty.

Most electronics items must be C.S.A. approved to benefit from warranty coverage in Canada or, in fact, to be legal to own and operate in Canada.

If you buy a plug-in phone at The Sharper Image in Lake Tahoe, you may be surprised to find you can't bring it into Canada at all! That's not to cast aspersions on The Sharper Image, of course. The rules are in effect at our borders and when they're enforced, you may be caught in the "grey tape."

All these electronic items really need is a Canadian Standards Association sticker, which proves they have been tested for electrical safety. Either the CSA sticker or the equivalent provincial inspection sticker is required by Canadian law for all electrical goods sold in this country, except for those operated by batteries.

In a *Vancouver Sun* newspaper account last year, B.C.'s Mark Startup, of the Retail Merchants Association, was quoted on the practice of selling grey market goods in regular stores: "I would say that's a very common pattern in Canadian retailing. It's a reflection of the fact that Canadian manufacturers must be more competitive. I couldn't give you any names of retailers doing this — the practice of merchandising in the retail trade is probably the most coveted aspect of the business."

According to Dr. David Tse, Professor of Marketing at U.B.C., some distributors purposely change model numbers for different countries to attempt to outsmart grey-marketeers. If a distributor is caught dealing in grey market goods and the manufacturer decides to prosecute, says Tse, the distributor could lose its licence.

One other fact you should be aware of is that certain products (unless specifically made for export to Canada) are not compatible with Canadian systems. Examples are television sets and VCR equipment (including camcorders) for use in Asia or Great Britain, where the lineage and actual system of transmission is competely different from ours. Even where these units are battery-operated, they cannot decode our signals and will not work in this country.

If you are in doubt about an item you want to buy via mail order, check with your nearest branch of the Canadian Standards Association, which has offices in Winnipeg, Edmonton, Vancouver, Toronto, Moncton and Montreal.

Their inspection is not cheap! You must ship the item in question (if you've already bought it) to their office. Inspection costs $100 per hour, and it takes 8 to 12 weeks just for approval time. Whew! Provincial inspection is often cheaper and it still takes about six weeks. Their tests are not usually as comprehensive as the CSA's.

On the other hand, read the fine print on your home insurance and you may discover there is a clause about using certified electrical equipment. If an item in your home is not CSA approved and there's any hint that it started a fire, your insurance might not cover you. Sound scary? Maybe you should stick to grey market cameras.

Here's a possible out: if the unit plugs in through an adapter, that may be all you need to send in for the inspection.

Oh, and by the way, if it's an answering machine in question, that has to go for approval to the D.O.C. — the Department of Communications. Big Brother, where are you when we need you?

The last word on grey market goods goes to the Consumers' Association of Canada, which is in favour of grey market products. Ontario branch president Joan Huzar says it's a simple matter of competition and choice, but she believes that customers should be told that their purchase didn't reach the store with the manufacturer's blessing.

Should you buy grey market goods? Of course, if you're buying offshore electronics at a discount, you already know the risks and where the item came from, so it's a decision you have to make for yourself.

10. "PRICE QUOTES" AND TELEPHONE SERVICE

The practice of "price quoting" is fairly commonplace in the mail order business. Some firms either don't produce catalogues at all, produce catalogues with model numbers but no prices, or produce only descriptive material of the products and no price lists at all.

Price quotes are particularly common with discount and liquidation companies where the exact model number and size may never again appear in stock.

Some camera discounters (like the famous 47th St. Cameras in NYC) ONLY do price quotes, and though it may seem like a nuisance to the novice buyer, it's really a very efficient way to do business for all concerned.

What happens is that you ring up the store and quote the item, model number (and size, if that's appropriate) and they will give you a price. Sometimes you can wheedle a slight discount. Once the price is agreed upon (or if you're shopping around, say "I'll get back to you," then remember to do so), and take the name of the clerk who quoted to you. Usually, you have a limited amount of time to purchase at the quoted price; anything from a few days to 15 days is common. If the item is offered at a special price, delaying too long may mean it's sold out when you're ready to buy.

If you are not a regular account customer, you will generally call back, make the deal (remember to determine shipping costs and taxes, if any) and bill the item to a credit card. Regular account customers may complete the deal by faxing the store a purchase order, and they are billed upon shipping. Very rarely, you can have the item shipped C.O.D. and pay then. Most companies discourage C.O.D. (except to places of business, and long-standing customers, at that) because it's so risky for them.

Price quotes are a good way to compare prices quickly. It's also been my experience that you sometimes get different quotes from different clerks, so you can use the Revenue Canada approach, which is to keep calling for advice until you hear the answer you want, then write down the advisor's name and keep it handy ("Hey, you can't deduct that!" "Oh? Well, I talked to a Mr. Hank Bankley at your office on October 23, 1990, and he said I could deduct it as long as it was only used on alternate Tuesdays").

You will find the price quote option mentioned here and there in the source listings.

Other telephone mail order service usually requires payment by credit card or through established credit with the source.

Fax machines are also useful for ordering, reviewing available choices and keeping track of purchases. Please also read Chapter Four concerning telephone and fax orders.

11. MINIMUM ORDERS

Sometimes a merchant will insist on a minimum order. This is fully understandable where a credit card transaction is taking place, but most often it's a silly policy, particularly when the seller is likely to win your repeat business by first selling you a little knick-knack and satisfying your urge to buy "something."

On the other hand, when you're dealing with wholesalers or factories directly, their business is geared up to selling in bulk, and taking the time to remove a couple of items from their large inventory, wrap them up, label them and ship them can take away from their first priority to serve retailers and large-order purchasers.

Occasionally in the text, you will find reference to minimum orders. Most of these are fairly well established, so I caution you to observe these sources' wishes.

I often ask bargain hounds to tread carefully when dealing with wholesale sources, because we don't want to barge in, irritate these great "finds" and spoil the fun for those who come after us.

12. CONSUMER SATISFACTION

a. Can't Get No. . .

To start with, you must understand that there is a certain risk inherent in buying by mail. First, you are agreeing to purchase goods, sight unseen, from people with whom you have no prior experience. For all we know, the company may have changed hands and Martians could have taken over the shop, altering all the rules of fair play we Earthlings have come to know and love.

Secondly, these space invaders might have no intention of sending you the goods you ordered. They could very well run out and cash your cheque and blast off for Andromeda.

They could send you a defective or broken item. You know for certain that they're ripping you off if the broken bits are individually wrapped in tissue paper.

Paranoid fantasies aside (where ARE those closet organizers I ordered?), there are some very real problems that can develop out there in Mailorderland and the solutions are not a mere hop and skip down the Yellow Brick Road, either.

b. Who Can't (or Won't) Help

Many consumer protection agencies in Canada simply don't have the legislative clout to do much about consumer fraud.

The Better Business Bureau does its best, but sometimes consumers make false reports to "get even" with a store against which they have a personal grudge. Sometimes the complaints are legitimate enough, but unprovable. And the most the BBB can usually do in any case is to publicize the company's failure to treat customers fairly.

Provincial consumer authorities are likewise hamstrung. Many complaints they receive are out of their jurisdiction.

Newspaper "help lines" are dying out, NOT because of consumer apathy, but quite the opposite; there's a great need, but these services are very expensive operations to maintain and these complaints are often nearly impossible to resolve. Again, bad publicity is usually their only weapon.

Once in awhile a newspaper (often the tabloid style papers are the most interested) will take up the cudgel for the victim of a particularly offensive consumer hoax, but these causes are one-offs; you won't often be able to use the newspaper as a reliable knight in shining armour.

c. What to Do

Allow enough time to elapse to be certain the company is not going to send you what you've ordered. If your cheque has been cashed or the charge appears on your credit card statement, and you've still not received the goods, act at once.

If you've paid by cheque, write or call the company directly and outline, in reasonable terms, what you expected, what you got (nothing, broken, defective, whatever), and what you would like the company to do now to resolve your problem.

In the case of payment by credit card, immediately contact the issuing bank or financial institution, and again, in pleasant and reasonable terms, let them know the situation. If the company appears to be cheating you, chances are the credit card company will reverse the charge and go after the offending merchant/space invader directly.

Should the mail order source be in another country, you might also write (be polite but firm) authorities (such as a trade or tourist council — they hate bad press) and request assistance.

You can also write to me. Although I can't sort out your problem, I can certainly check the facts for myself and leave those scam-artists out of the next edition, to save another guy some grief.

d. Who CAN Help

When it becomes clear you are not going to achieve satisfaction on your own, turn to those who can assist you. Provincial and state authorities have certain mandates, and if your problem falls into their jurisdiction, they can help.

If your goods are being sent to a point in the U.S., American mail order laws (which are a little more stringent than ours) will apply.

If the company has advertised an item to you in a misleading fashion, Canada's Consumer and Corporate Affairs (Federal) can help you, and they will want all the documentation you can give them. If the goods have been misrepresented to you (the patio furniture you paid $400 for turned out to be suitably scaled for Barbie's doll-sized cabana, for instance), they can get the merchant for misleading advertising.

If the item you want is continually advertised and continually out-of-stock, something is wrong, and Consumer Affairs will want to know about it.

Once charges have been laid, Consumer Affairs makes public its cases, through its quarterly "Misleading Advertising Bulletin", which any interested individuals can obtain free by writing to:

Marketing Practices Branch
Consumer and Corporate Affairs Canada
Ottawa, Ontario
Canada K1A 0C9. (819) 997-4282

This publication is free, as I said, and is a useful way of keeping track of the cheaters and misleaders among our retailers and suppliers. Remember, Consumer Affairs' jurisdiction only covers Canada, so complaints outside of the country can't be handled by them.

Next, if the outfit is Canadian, check to see if it is a member of the Direct Marketing Association, which is working to self-police its members. The association will go to bat for you and even refund your money directly if it believes a member company has wronged you. This organization is really helping to upgrade domestic mail ordering, and in fact, *TV Guide* will accept mail order ads only from DMA members.

Write to: Canadian Direct Marketing Association
1 Concorde Gate, Suite 607
Don Mills, Ontario
M3C 3N6 (416) 391-2362

Canadian Advertising Standards Council can be approached if advertising codes of ethics have been breached.

The Consumers' Association of Canada may be able to offer help and advice. There are branches across Canada for the Association and the Council.

e. Unsolicited Merchandise

This is one of my favourite facts: under Canada's Consumer Protection Act, if something arrives at your home addressed to you, and neither you nor any member of your family ordered it, IT IS A GIFT! Don't pay for it. The company just GAVE it to you, isn't that nice?

However, what often happens is that most people have unwittingly "ordered" the item by not reading the fine print or by forgetting they ordered it in the first place.

One common ploy of solicitation is to send people a notice saying, "We can't believe you don't want this wonderful crushed velvet dog bed. Please return the enclosed acknowledgement form and you'll win a prize, but don't forget to check the box indicating your free gift." Then, in teeny-tiny print it says, "And we'll send your expensive 'Doggie-dreamer' by chauffeur-driven limousine/courier."

These schemes and scams are getting trickier by the minute. And if I had a dollar for every time I'd "won" something in the last few years, I'd be a millionaire without the lottery.

f. Bait and Switch

A common ploy among disreputable retail firms, this is the practice of offering one item for sale at a very cheap price, but never actually selling it. Such goods are referred to as "nailed down," and one nasty, nasty national electronics retailer in Canada is said to penalize its commissioned salesmen for the cost of the item if he actually sells that "loss-leader" to you! When you come into the store or try to buy the item by mail, you're told by the salesperson that it's (a) out of stock or (b) "that one's no good, this one is better." The hustled item is more expensive, of course. This practice comes under the Competition Act in Canada. It's hard to prove, so my best advice is caveat emptor—let the buyer beware.

"Upselling" is a similar (albeit not quite so shoddy) method, whereby the salesperson wins your trust and then hustles you into buying something more expensive. The usual tack is: "You'll wear out three of these cheapies before this supercalifragalistic model is out of date." Beware, beware, beware.

g. Standard Returns Procedures

The usual routine when returning something unsatisfactory is to first contact the company with whom you're doing business and find out how they want the goods returned. Sometimes there is a stated policy in their catalogue or mail order material that explains how the item should be wrapped, insured, sent, and so on, and within what time frame they uphold their claims of freshness, perfect condition, or what have you.

Almost all mail order sources will expect you to pay postage, courier, freight or shipping, when returning unsuitable merchandise.

Some places accept returned goods with an "unconditional" guarantee, but they will often want to know (for future planning of their product line, for instance) why you were dissatisfied. Often "unsuitable" is sufficient explanation, without going into great detail about how the ham didn't match your drapes.

If you're not sure you will keep an item, be certain to hang onto all the original wrapping material. If there is styrofoam in the package, try to keep it intact as you remove the contents.

If there is visible breakage when I open the parcel, my personal trick is to take a quick snapshot of the contents, just for my records. I've only once ever had to send the photo (and the company didn't want their smashed honey jars back, since the photo was "evidence" enough; they sent a replacement at once), but it's reassuring to know you can prove your claim. My camera has a "dateback" feature that burns a permanent record of the calendar date into the edge of the negative, and that helps keep things straight, too.

Remember that if you order from a U.S. company for delivery into the States, you may have more consumer protection than you do within Canada, particularly if you experience long delays in consumer satisfaction after a complaint. I usually allow six to eight weeks for the problem to be resolved, and then I start writing gentle reminder letters at two-week intervals, increasing the noise level until I get what I want.

As a general guideline, I cut the family-run operations a little more slack, expecting professional expediency from the major mail order houses, which is as it should be.

Remember, most goods are not sent by mail order "on approval." If you get into the habit of returning items in great numbers, you may find some of the best sources will refuse your business in the future. Again, this is a matter of caveat emptor, and consider-before-you-buy tactics.

h. Size Conversions

Part of knowing what you want is being able to order the correct size for your needs. Sophisticated clothing sources include detailed measurement charts with their catalogues or price lists. Places in Hong Kong, Scandinavia and Great Britain are particularly good at this, but just in case, here's a complete list of all the size conversions you might need. Note that Hong Kong sizing *for their market* is in British sizing, but if the goods are meant for export, sizes will be Canadian/U.S.

Women's Dresses, Skirts, Jackets and Coats

Canadian/U.S.	3	5	7	9	11	12	13	14	15	16	18
Continental	36	38	38	40	40	42	42	44	44	46	48
British/HK	8	10	11	12	13	14	15	16	17	18	20

Women's Sweaters and Blouses

Canadian/U.S.	10	12	14	16	18	20
Continental	38	40	42	44	46	48
British/HK	32	34	36	38	40	42

Women's Hosiery

Canadian/ British/U.S.	8	8½	9	9½	10	10½
Continental	1	2	3	4	5	6

Women's Shoes

Canadian/ HK/U.S.	5	6	7	8	9	10
Continental	36	37	38	39	40	41
British	3½	4½	5½	6½	7½	8½

Some children's clothing from the U.K. (e.g., Mothercare) is sized in Continental measures, which has always driven me crazy. Hong Kong sizing for children is the same as U.S. and Canadian sizes. Remember to buy larger sizes of anything from offshore suppliers if the garment is made of 100 percent cotton, because they aren't into preshrunk cottons as much as are American and Canadian manufacturers.

Children's Clothing

Canadian	3	4	5	6	6x
Continental	98	104	110	116	122
British	18	20	22	24	26

Children's Shoes

Canadian	8	9	10	11	12	13	1	2	3
Continental	24	25	27	28	29	30	32	33	34
British	7	8	9	10	11	12	13	1	2

Men's Shirts

Canadian and British sizes for men's shirts are the same. It's safe to buy men's short-sleeved shirts as small (approx. 15); medium (approx. 16-1/2); and large (approx. 18). Again, consider shrinkage in cotton, if it's a tight fit. Most Hong Kong and U.S. suppliers use only pre-shrunk cotton, particularly sportswear sources, such as Lands' End or J. Crew, who are fussy about quality and good fit in men's shirts.

Canadian	14½	15	15½	16	16½	17	17½	18
Continental	37	38	39	41	42	43	44	45

Men's Suits

Again, British and Canadian standards are the same. Remember to request fabric swatches anytime you order suits by mail — and hang onto your sample to compare it with the finished garment for colour and "hand" (how it feels) .

Canadian	34	36	38	40	42	44	46	48
Continental	44	46	48	50	52	54	56	58

Men's Shoes

Canadian	7	8	9	10	11	12	13
Continental	39½	41	42	43	44½	46	47
British	6	7	8	9	10	11	12

Men's Hats

If you live near a branch of Tilley's Endurables, drop in to see their hat-sizing machine at work. You can even measure a man's hat without his head in it, to determine the correct size.

Canadian	6⅞	7⅛	7¼	7⅜	7½	7⅝
Continental	55	56	58	59	60	61
British	6¼	6⅞	7⅛	7¼	7⅜	7½

Weird, isn't it? You'll find gloves are usually marked in all sizes, regardless of their country of origin. Rings are generally sized with those little pieces of cardboard with cut-outs marked for each size and into which you fit your finger till you find one that's just right. Virtually every company selling rings by mail will send you this type of card, so you can't go wrong.

Remember to consider differences in measurement between metric and the old imperial measures, especially when ordering from the U.S. It might be a wise investment to purchase a cloth tape measure with millimetres on one side and inches on the other, just to be on the safe side.

13. DISCOUNT OPERATIONS

When is a bargain really a bargain? When it costs less than anywhere else, right?

Or is it better a year later when it's sold at clearance prices?

When making this sort of decision, you always have to weigh how much use and enjoyment you'll get from the item you buy "now" and how much can be deferred till "later."

We live in a consumer-driven "now" society. But life isn't just things. Acquire everything your heart desires, and soon your possessions will own you. Personally, I like to mull things over a little. Sometimes I miss out on some beauties of deals; sometimes I "win big."

Mail order shopping runs by the same rules. Much of what we want is dictated by lifestyle, security, convenience and aesthetic considerations. Not everything is a bargain.

Discount operations in this book are of two basic kinds: there are North American-style discounters who offer mass-produced goods at clear-out prices, reduced because the overhead costs of stocking and displaying these goods nicely in expensive shops is eliminated; then there are third-world sources that rely on cheap material costs and cheap labour to produce ethnic, funky, wholesome-looking goods we can buy up inexpensively.

A seasoned retailer friend of mine gave me a lecture about "price points," a concept that was new to me at the time. She said that in the world of business, the cliché is that "everyone has his or her price." In the world of retail, she claims, "we all have our price-point," or a value at which we can no longer resist buying a particular item. Then, and only then, in our minds, is it a bargain.

My friend runs a designer discount chain in Canada. She regularly sells designer lines at between 40 and 60 percent off retail. I browse in her stores, but I rarely buy. She holds a sale and offers me a 100 percent silk jacket (albeit unlined) for $10. Do I buy it? You bet.

I resist buying for most of the time at her store because I travel abroad so often that I've become spoiled by the availability of really inexpensive merchandise. But a $10 silk jacket right in my home town? Are you kidding? I might be spoiled, but I'm not stupid.

That's "price point." Obviously, I can be bent around for a $10 silk jacket.

And that's a discount operation. "Bargain" is a relative term, so decide where your price point is and go for it.

I hope that explains what it means in the listings when I talk about "great bargains."

14. CATALOGUE COSTS AND REBATES

Many mail order merchants now charge a fee for their catalogues. Sometimes this is to offset the very high costs of printing fancy, colour publications. Other times, it's to test the market, so that more "qualified" (means: committed to actually buying from them) customers will be attracted to them.

In many instances, the source will refund the cost of the catalogue by shipping for free, or by crediting the cost of the catalogue against your first order from it. Some sources include a discount coupon for use with future orders, and sometimes that coupon is worth even more than you paid for the catalogue itself.

I've tried to include in the listings as full a description as possible about what is free and what isn't, and what you'll get for your money if you must pay.

A word of warning (though I've said this elsewhere already): please try to send paper money for small-denomination catalogue fees, especially when sending it to the U.K. or Scandinavia. In those countries, cashing your cheque can cost even more than the amount for which you've written it. Since loonies are so obvious and bulky to mail, a supply of U.S. one-dollar bills may be put aside for the purpose of sending modest amounts of cash through the mail. Please don't send large amounts of cash by post, but I'm sure one or two dollars will be small enough to risk for the wonders of a foreign "shopping spree," don't you?

15. SPECIAL DEALS AND GIFT SERVICES IN THE LISTINGS

We've noted in each listing where there are special deals for readers of this book. Often all that is required of you is to write the merchant and mention you saw it in *Shopping the World*. You might also mention my name, if you think that will help, especially where a foreign language might cause confusion. Usually the "special deal" is that the mail order source offers a free catalogue instead of charging you for it, but sometimes there's a gift or premium instead, or as well.

In addition, there are a great many sources who will make your gift-sending occasions simpler by sending items to your friends directly and enclosing a gift card with your wishes. The closer to home those suppliers are, the more likely they'll get your greetings right.

If your gifts originate from abroad, most of them will come into this country or the U.S. duty-free. If you're sending items from U.S. sources to American friends, often the cost of shipping is free, too. Sometimes bold discounts are offered if you buy all your gifts from one source. Again, all those details are noted in the individual source listings.

In the text, we refer to some credit cards by abbreviations. VISA is still VISA, of course. M/C means MasterCard; Amex means American Express and the others are spelled out in full. IMO means International Money Order and is also used to indicate the acceptance of regular postal money orders when the source is in Canada or the U.S.

SUBJECT INDEX

Food and Drink
Cakes and Cookies

Candy

108 Grand Finale Confections
Buttercream caramels, dessert sauces, chocolate coated caramel candy bars
116 Hanover House
Gifts, novelties, cookware, furnishings, clothing
117 Harbor Sweets
Hand-made chocolates
118 Harrods
Gourmet food, apparel, gifts and furniture
124 Heritage Canada Gift Collection
Newfoundland hand-knit woollens, Christmas cards, posters, Inuit silk scarf, journals, honey, baskets, placemats and gifts
144 Jaffe Bros. Inc.
Organically grown foods
180 Marks & Spencer Hampers
Gift packs, gourmet foods and wine
181 Marshall's Fudge
Hand-made fudge and candies
189 Minerva Street Chocolate
Truffles
196 Mr. Romance
Romantic books, ideas, gifts and novelties; new line of custom, Victorian lingerie and bridal gowns
197 Mr. Spiceman
Spices in one-pound sizes
215 Paprikas Weiss Importer
Herbs and spices; coffee and teas; imported specialty foods
219 Paron Chocolatier
Unique chocolate products
220 Pecan St. Sweets
Gourmet pecan candies
226 The Popcorn Factory
Fancy popcorn, mints, cookies, gummy bunnies, Rachel's brownies, popping supplies, gift tins
236 Robinson's Maple Products
Maple syrup, candy and specialty items
238 Roger's Chocolates
Exquisite chocolate confections known as "Victoria Creams"
245 Sears Canada Inc
Major mail order supplier of clothing, household goods and gifts
249 Select Origins Inc.
Herbs, spices, various specialty cooking ingredients
257 Simpson and Vail
Teas, coffee, specialty foods
261 Specialty Food Shop
Foods for special restricted diets
264 Spiegel
Upmarket clothing, gifts, home furnishings, executive toys
270 Sultan's Delight Inc.
Middle-Eastern foods
281 The Postilion
Plum pudding, cognac hard sauce, chocolate sauces, yule logs, gift packages
318 The Wisconsin Cheeseman
Cheese, meats, candy and gift packs

Nuts

10 American Spoon Foods
Fruit products, chestnuts, dried fruit
43 Camparte's of California
Candies, hand-dipped chocolates, dried fruit and nuts

Gourmet Foods

Chocolate decadence and Northwest raspberry purée among other specialty desserts

94 Frederick & Nelson
Gifts, clothing, toys, gift packs, lingerie and executive toys

100 Gauntlett Fey Inc., Cheese Outlet
Cheese, cheesecakes

102 Gazin's
Cajun-Creole gourmet foods

107 Grand Finale
Factory close-outs on gifts, linens, furniture, toys, china, apparel and cookware

108 Grand Finale Confections
Buttercream caramels, dessert sauces, chocolate-coated caramel candy bars

116 Hanover House
Gifts, novelties, cookware, furnishings, clothing

117 Harbor Sweets
Hand-made chocolates

118 Harrods
Gourmet food, apparel, gifts and furniture

124 Heritage Canada Gift Collection
Newfoundland hand-knit woollens, Christmas cards, posters, Inuit silk scarf, journals, honey, baskets, placemats and gifts

145 Jake's Famous Products, Inc.
Gourmet foods and seafoods

177 M.M. Poonjiaji & Co.
Mango chutneys, mango and fruit pickles, curry powder and paste are the specialties here

180 Marks & Spencer Hampers
Gift packs, gourmet foods and wine

183 Maury Island Farming Company
Jams, jellies, preserves, toppings

189 Minerva Street Chocolate Truffles

191 Moon Shine Trading Co.
Honeys, nut butters, chocolate-nut spreads

196 Mr. Romance
Romantic books, ideas, gifts and novelties; new line of custom, Victorian lingerie and bridal gowns

208 Neiman-Marcus
Gifts, cookware, clothing and executive toys

215 Paprikas Weiss Importer
Herbs and spices; coffee and teas; imported specialty foods

219 Paron Chocolatier
Unique chocolate products

220 Pecan St. Sweets
Gourmet pecan candies

226 The Popcorn Factory
Fancy popcorn, mints, cookies, gummy bunnies, Rachel's brownies, popping supplies, gift tins

236 Robinson's Maple Products
Maple syrup, candy and specialty items

241 Rowena's and Captain Jaap's Jam & Jelly Factory
Gourmet jams, jellies, sauces and cakes

242 S.E. Rykoff & Co.
Gourmet foods and cookware

245 Sears Canada Inc.
Major mail order supplier of clothing, household goods and gifts

249 Select Origins Inc.
Herbs, spices, various specialty cooking ingredients

257 Simpson and Vail
Teas, coffee, specialty foods

263 Sphinx Date Ranch
Medjool dates and dried fruit

Practical Foods and Spices

and shears, garden books, dessert sauces and gourmet foods, hammocks, garden furniture and tools

299 Victoria International Knives Ltd.
Knives, cutlery, scissors, razors and English darts

313 Williams-Sonoma
Cooks' catalogue

318 The Wisconsin Cheeseman
Cheese, meats, candy and gift packs

Cooking and Foods

3 The Added Touch
Gift baskets, novelties, gardening supplies, closet organizers

10 American Spoon Foods
Fruit products, chestnuts, dried fruit

31 Bloomingdale's
All kinds of high-end clothing, home furnishings, cosmetics and gifts

51 Chalif Inc.
Gourmet condiments (mustards, sauces, mayonnaises)

82 El Paso Chili Co.
Southwestern chili products

87 The Executive Chef
Gift baskets, gourmet foods

94 Frederick & Nelson
Gifts, clothing, toys, gift packs, lingerie and executive toys

100 Gauntlett Fey Inc., Cheese Outlet
Cheese, cheesecakes

102 Gazin's
Cajun-Creole gourmet foods

108 Grand Finale Confections
Buttercream caramels, dessert sauces, chocolate-coated caramel candy bars

124 Heritage Canada Gift Collection
Newfoundland hand-knit woollens, Christmas cards, posters, Inuit silk scarf, journals, honey, baskets, placemats and gifts

134 Ikea Mail Order
Home furnishings, cookware, toys, knock-down furniture, shelving, office furniture, decor accents

144 Jaffe Bros. Inc.
Organically grown foods

145 Jake's Famous Products, Inc.
Gourmet foods and seafoods

177 M.M. Poonjiaji & Co.
Mango chutneys, mango and fruit pickles, curry powder and paste are the specialties here

180 Marks & Spencer Hampers
Gift packs, gourmet foods and wine

183 Maury Island Farming Company
Jams, jellies, preserves, toppings

197 Mr. Spiceman
Spices in one-pound sizes

215 Paprikas Weiss Importer
Herbs and spices; coffee and teas; imported specialty foods

236 Robinson's Maple Products
Maple syrup, candy and specialty items

241 Rowena's and Captain Jaap's Jam & Jelly Factory
Gourmet jams, jellies, sauces and cakes

242 S.E. Rykoff & Co.
Gourmet foods and cookware

245 Sears Canada Inc.
Major mail order supplier of clothing, household goods and gifts

249 Select Origins Inc.
Herbs, spices, various specialty cooking ingredients

Cookbooks

Cookware

4 Alive Health Centre
Health products and vitamins
8 American Express Canada, Inc.
Limited edition prints, plates and coins
30 Best Products
Housewares, electronics, furniture, toys, sporting goods, jewelry, watches
31 Bloomingdale's
All kinds of high-end clothing, home furnishings, cosmetics and gifts
46 Canadian Tire Corporation Ltd.
Sporting, camping, hardware, auto, pool, plumbing, gardening, and handyman supplies, plus toys
48 Carrousel of Ideas
Gift items, novelties, toys, watches, chatchkas
49 Casselryds Gla o Porselin
China and crystal
55 Clothcrafters
Aprons, totes, yard goods, mats, sheets, curtains, cookware, parchment paper, terry towels, insect netting, chef's hats and more
94 Frederick & Nelson
Gifts, clothing, toys, gift packs, lingerie and executive toys
102 Gazin's
Cajun-Creole gourmet foods
107 Grand Finale
Factory close-outs on gifts, linens, furniture, toys, china, apparel, and cookware
110 Gump's Mail Order
Crystal, silver, linen, contemporary gifts, jewelry and apparel
113 Hammacher Schlemmer
Unique household, recreation, personal care, gardening and electronic products
116 Hanover House
Gifts, novelties, cookware, furnishings, clothing
118 Harrods
Gourmet food, apparel, gifts and furniture
122 Hedonics
Electronics, specialty gifts and novelties
131 Horchow Catalogue
Gifts, clothing, furnishings
134 Ikea Mail Order
Home furnishings, cookware, toys, knock-down furniture, shelving, office furniture, decor accents
137 Industrial Revolution
Closet organizers, cookware, linens and towels, office supplies, furniture, lamps, etc.
146 Jay Norris Select
Novelties, chatchkas, clothing and gifts
159 L.L. Bean, Inc.
Outdoor goods and apparel
166 Lao Song Handicrafts
Christmas ornaments, stuffed animals, craft items
171 Lillian Vernon Corporation
Giftware
187 Merlo's Cutlery
Knives, cutlery and utensils
208 Neiman-Marcus
Gifts, cookware, clothing and executive toys
210 New Roots Nutrition
Discount quality vitamins and hypo-allergenic formulas
215 Paprikas Weiss Importer
Herbs & spices; coffee & teas; imported specialty foods

Clothing
Women's

39 C. Kennedy & Sons, Ltd.
Wool sweaters, Irish linens, tweed jackets

41 Cabela's
Sportswear, camping, hunting, fishing, outdoors gear

42 The Cambrian Factory
Tweed clothing and accessories for ladies and gentlemen; knitwear

48 Carrousel of Ideas
Gift items, novelties, toys, watches, chatchkas

54 Cleo Ltd.
Woven and hand-knitted outerwear in natural fibres

55 Clothcrafters
Aprons, totes, yard goods, mats, sheets, curtains, cookware, parchment paper, terry towels, insect netting, chefs' hats and more

63 D & A Merchandise Co.
Underwear, foundations, lingerie, hosiery, socks, pantyhose

79 Eddie Bauer Outdoor Outfitters
Outdoors apparel

80 The Edinburgh Woollen Mill
Topcoats, sweaters, skirts and jackets of 100-percent wool

89 The Faith Mountain Company
Home accessories, apparel, flowers

94 Frederick & Nelson
Gifts, clothing, toys, gift packs, lingerie and executive toys

95 Frederick's of Hollywood
Lingerie, dresses, sportswear, swimwear, hosiery and boots

105 Golden Carp
Bags, handbags, wallets, belts, all made from "fishskin leather"

107 Grand Finale
Factory close-outs on gifts, linens, furniture, toys, china, apparel and cookware

110 Gump's Mail Order
Crystal, silver, linen, contemporary gifts, jewellery and apparel

113 Hammacher Schlemmer
Unique household, recreation, personal care, gardening and electronic products

115 Handart Embroideries
Source of embroidered tablecloths, bedspreads, kimonos, pillow shams, blouses, cloisonné souvenirs, bracelets and more

116 Hanover House
Gifts, novelties, cookware, furnishings, clothing

118 Harrods
Gourmet food, apparel, gifts and furniture

124 Heritage Canada Gift Collection
Newfoundland hand-knit woollens, Christmas cards, posters, Inuit silk scarf, journals, honey, baskets, placemats and gifts

131 Horchow Catalogue
Gifts, clothing, furnishings

133 Icemart Mail-order Department
Icelandic knits

139 Iroqrafts Ltd.
Native art and sculpture, particularly from the Iroquois

140 J. Crew
"Understated flair," stylish sportwear, active-wear, swimwear, business clothes

146 Jay Norris Select
Novelties, chatchkas, clothing and gifts

259 Socks Galore & More
Socks for men, women and children, sold at a discount

260 Song Smai Charoenkrung Collection
Made-to-order or ready-made men's and women's clothing

264 Spiegel
Upmarket clothing, gifts, home furnishings, executive toys

266 Stanley Market
Linens, sweaters, embroideries, Chinese jackets and Chinese arts and crafts

273 Taiga Works
Outdoor gear, camping, hunting, fishing, hiking gear and apparel

279 The Garden
Sundials, garden accessories, watering cans, pruning saws and shears, garden books, dessert sauces and gourmet foods, hammocks, garden furniture and tools

288 Touch of Gems
Thai silk, reproduction jewellery

291 Tweeds Inc.
Funky sportswear and accessories

280 The Paragon
Household goods, some clothing

300 Victoria's Secret
Lingerie, underwear and nightgowns

304 W.S. Robertson (Outfitters) Ltd.
Scottish knitwear, especially Pringles of Scotland and Lyle & Scott sweaters, sold in cashmere, lamb's-wool and Botany wool

308 Westaway and Westaway
Harris tweeds, sweaters, shirts, kilts, wool skirts, cashmeres, Shetland knits

313 Williams-Sonoma
Cooks' catalogue

Men's

1 A. Andrews and Co.
Sporting goods, electronics, fancy table linens, souvenirs

3 The Added Touch
Gift baskets, novelties, gardening supplies, closet organizers

11 The American Traveller
Gift items, executive toys, watches, language tapes, electronics

12 Amnesty International
Novelties, pens, posters, keychains

15 The Arctic Trading Company
Authentic native products

18 Ascot Chang Co. Ltd.
Custom-made men's and ladies shirts, robes and pyjamas

21 Banana Republic
Men's and women's sportswear

28 Ben Lee Co.
Linens, embroidered items, sweaters, Chinese art, oil paintings and chops

31 Bloomingdale's
All kinds of high-end clothing, home furnishings, cosmetics and gifts

39 C. Kennedy & Sons, Ltd.
Wool sweaters, Irish linens, tweed jackets

41 Cabela's
Sportswear, camping, hunting, fishing, outdoors gear

42 The Cambrian Factory
Tweed clothing and accessories for ladies and gentlemen; knitwear

167 Laurel Burch, Inc.
Art prints, jewellery, novelties
168 Le Baron Outdoor Products Ltd.
Outdoors equipment and apparel
169 Le Tricoteur
Fishermen's sweaters
171 Lillian Vernon Corporation
Giftware
174 Local House Co. Ltd.
Folk art and handicrafts
175 Louis Chock
Underwear, pyjamas, pantyhose, robes
179 Mark's Work Wearhouse
Work wear, sportswear, boots, rain gear
195 Mountain Equipment Co-op
Outdoors, hiking, climbing, hunting, fishing and camping gear, backpacks, tents, sleeping bags and apparel
198 Museum of Fine Arts, Boston
Museum reproductions, art, posters, jewellery
206 The Nature Co.
Nature-theme products
208 Neiman-Marcus
Gifts, cookware, clothing and executive toys
209 New Big Man Company
Custom tailoring (Shanghai style)
213 Oriental Pacific
Sweaters for men, women and children, vests
221 Peter Jones
Yard goods, linens, china, crystal and silver
229 Pur et Simple Inc.
Environment-friendly products
231 Rama Trade
Anything that can be found in Thailand and legally imported into Canada
232 Rammagerdin h.f.
Icelandic woollen goods and souvenirs
239 Romshops, Treasures of the ROM
Museum reproductions, art, posters, books, Christmas decorations, sculpture, games, jewellery
245 Sears Canada Inc.
Major mail order supplier of clothing, household goods and gifts
255 The Sharper Image
Executive toys, electronics, gadgets, luggage, novelties and gifts
256 Shinawatra
Silk yard goods and handicrafts
259 Socks Galore & More
Socks for men, women and children, sold at a discount
260 Song Smai Charoenkrung Collection
Made-to-order or ready-made men's and women's clothing
264 Spiegel
Upmarket clothing, gifts, home furnishings, executive toys
266 Stanley Market
Linens, sweaters, embroideries, Chinese jackets and Chinese arts and crafts
273 Taiga Works
Outdoor gear, camping, hunting, fishing, hiking gear and apparel
279 The Garden
Sundials, garden accessories, watering cans, pruning saws and shears, garden books, dessert sauces and gourmet foods, hammocks, garden furniture and tools
280 The Paragon
Household goods, some clothing
287 Tilley Endurables Adventure Clothing
Travel and adventure gear and apparel

Children's

152 Kathleen's Aran Knits
Aran hand-knit sweaters, tweeds, throws
155 Kings Slap Shop
L.A. Kings hockey team souvenirs and sports paraphernalia from other teams
156 The Knitwear Architects
Hand-knitting kits
159 L.L. Bean, Inc.
Outdoor goods and apparel
164 Lands' End Direct Merchants
Clothing, sportswear, luggage, children's clothes
166 Lao Song Handicrafts
Christmas ornaments, stuffed animals, craft items
167 Laurel Burch, Inc.
Art prints, jewellery, novelties
168 Le Baron Outdoor Products Ltd.
Outdoors equipment and apparel
169 Le Tricoteur
Fishermen's sweaters
174 Local House Co. Ltd.
Folk art and handicrafts
194 Mothercare by Mail
Items for expectant mothers and children to age eight
195 Mountain Equipment Co-op
Outdoors, hiking, climbing, hunting, fishing and camping gear, backpacks, tents, sleeping bags and apparel
206 The Nature Co.
Nature-theme products
208 Neiman-Marcus
Gifts, cookware, clothing and executive toys
213 Oriental Pacific
Sweaters for men, women and children, vests
229 Pur et Simple Inc.
Environment-friendly products
231 Rama Trade
Anything that can be found in Thailand and legally imported into Canada
232 Rammagerdin h.f.
Icelandic woollen goods and souvenirs
239 Romshops, Treasures of the ROM
Museum reproductions, art, posters, books, Christmas decorations, sculpture, games, jewellery
245 Sears Canada Inc.
Major mail order supplier of clothing, household goods and gifts
250 Seva Foundation, c/o Seva Service Society
Third-world crafts, paper products
256 Shinawatra
Silk yard goods and handicrafts
259 Socks Galore & More
Socks for men, women and children, sold at a discount
264 Spiegel
Upmarket clothing, gifts, home furnishings, executive toys
266 Stanley Market
Linens, sweaters, embroideries, Chinese jackets and Chinese arts and crafts
273 Taiga Works
Outdoor gear, camping, hunting, fishing, hiking gear and apparel
279 The Garden
Sundials, garden accessories, watering cans, pruning saws and shears, garden books, dessert sauces and gourmet foods, hammocks, garden furniture and tools
280 The Paragon
Household goods, some clothing

Shoes and Boots

Family Outerwear

home furnishings, cosmetics and gifts
39 C. Kennedy & Sons, Ltd.
Wool sweaters, Irish linens, tweed jackets
41 Cabela's
Sportswear, camping, hunting, fishing, outdoors gear
42 The Cambrian Factory
Tweed clothing and accessories for ladies and gentlemen; knitwear
54 Cleo Ltd.
Woven and hand-knitted outerwear in natural fibres
79 Eddie Bauer Outdoor Outfitters
Outdoors apparel
80 The Edinburgh Woollen Mill
Topcoats, sweaters, skirts and jackets of 100-percent wool
94 Frederick & Nelson
Gifts, clothing, toys, gift packs, lingerie and executive toys
116 Hanover House
Gifts, novelties, cookware, furnishings, clothing
133 Icemart Mail-order Department
Icelandic knits
139 Iroqrafts Ltd.
Native art and sculpture, particularly from the Iroquois
140 J. Crew
"Understated flair," stylish sportwear, active-wear, swimwear, business clothes
142 The J. Peterman Company
Unique, hard-to-find items with a "factual romance"
146 Jay Norris Select
Novelties, chatchkas, clothing and gifts
155 Kings Slap Shop
L.A. Kings hockey team souvenirs and sports paraphernalia from other teams
159 L.L. Bean, Inc.
Outdoor goods and apparel
164 Lands' End Direct Merchants
Clothing, sportswear, luggage, children's clothes
168 Le Baron Outdoor Products Ltd.
Outdoors equipment and apparel
171 Lillian Vernon Corporation
Giftware
179 Mark's Work Wearhouse
Work wear, sportswear, boots, rain gear
194 Mothercare by Mail
Items for expectant mothers and children to age eight
195 Mountain Equipment Co-op
Outdoors, hiking, climbing, hunting, fishing and camping gear, backpacks, tents, sleeping bags and apparel
206 The Nature Co.
Nature-theme products
208 Neiman-Marcus
Gifts, cookware, clothing and executive toys
245 Sears Canada Inc.
Major mail order supplier of clothing, household goods and gifts
273 Taiga Works
Outdoor gear, camping, hunting, fishing, hiking gear and apparel
286 Tibetan Refugee Self-Help Centre
Carpets, tapestries, hand-made crafts, sweaters, coats, caps, mufflers, gloves, socks, boots and artifacts
287 Tilley Endurables Adventure Clothing
Travel and adventure gear and apparel
291 Tweeds Inc.
Funky sportswear and accessories

Specialized Clothing (Sports, Fishing, etc.)

208 Neiman-Marcus
Gifts, cookware, clothing and executive toys
222 Pied Piper Catalog
Items for gifted children
245 Sears Canada Inc.
Major mail order supplier of clothing, household goods and gifts
255 The Sharper Image
Executive toys, electronics, gadgets, luggage, novelties and gifts
264 Spiegel
Upmarket clothing, gifts, home furnishings, executive toys
273 Taiga Works
Outdoor gear, camping, hunting, fishing, hiking gear and apparel
287 Tilley Endurables Adventure Clothing
Travel and adventure gear and apparel
304 W.S. Robertson (Outfitters) Ltd.
Scottish knitwear, especially Pringles of Scotland and Lyle & Scott sweaters, sold in cashmere, lamb's-wool and Botany wool

Shawls and Sweaters

3 The Added Touch
Gift baskets, novelties, gardening supplies, closet organizers
15 The Arctic Trading Company
Authentic native products
17 Artland
Table linens, embroidery arts, handicrafts, beaded evening tops, women's apparel
28 Ben Lee Co.
Linens, embroidered items, sweaters, Chinese art, oil paintings and chops
31 Bloomingdale's
All kinds of high-end clothing, home furnishings, cosmetics and gifts
39 C. Kennedy & Sons, Ltd.
Wool sweaters, Irish linens, tweed jackets
41 Cabela's
Sportswear, camping, hunting, fishing, outdoors gear
42 The Cambrian Factory
Tweed clothing and accessories for ladies and gentlemen; knitwear
48 Carrousel of Ideas
Gift items, novelties, toys, watches, chatchkas
54 Cleo Ltd.
Woven and hand-knitted outerwear in natural fibres
60 Creagen Ltd.
Sweaters
79 Eddie Bauer Outdoor Outfitters
Outdoors apparel
80 The Edinburgh Woollen Mill
Topcoats, sweaters, skirts and jackets of 100-percent wool
89 The Faith Mountain Company
Home accessories, apparel, flowers
94 Frederick & Nelson
Gifts, clothing, toys, gift packs, lingerie and executive toys
107 Grand Finale
Factory close-outs on gifts, linens, furniture, toys, china, apparel and cookware
113 Hammacher Schlemmer
Unique household, recreation, personal care, gardening and electronic products

291 Tweeds Inc.
Funky sportswear and accessories

304 W.S. Robertson (Outfitters) Ltd.
Scottish knitwear, especially Pringles of Scotland and Lyle & Scott sweaters, sold in cashmere, lamb's-wool and Botany wool

308 Westaway and Westaway
Harris tweeds, sweaters, shirts, kilts, wool skirts, cashmeres, Shetland knits

Clothing for the Handicapped

146 Jay Norris Select
Novelties, chatchkas, clothing and gifts

SHELTER
Furniture

16 Art Resources
Sculpture, art reproductions, decor accents, lamps, carpets, jewellery, antiques

19 Atfield Fine Arts
Carpets, Jim Thompson silk upholstery fabrics

20 B.C. Playthings
Educational toys, games, children's furniture and books, at discount prices

30 Best Products
Housewares, electronics, furniture, toys, sporting goods, jewellery, watches

31 Bloomingdale's
All kinds of high-end clothing, home furnishings, cosmetics and gifts

46 Canadian Tire Corporation Ltd.
Sporting, camping, hardware, auto, pool, plumbing, gardening and handyman supplies, plus toys

59 The Country Loft
Country/primitive furniture and accessories

71 Dick Blick Company
Art and craft supplies

83 The Elephant House
Burmese lacquerware

89 The Faith Mountain Company
Home accessories, apparel, flowers

99 Gardener's Eden
Gardening "extras"

101 The Gazebo of New York
High-end home accessories

107 Grand Finale
Factory close-outs on gifts, linens, furniture, toys, china, apparel and cookware

110 Gump's Mail Order
Crystal, silver, linen, contemporary gifts, jewellery and apparel

113 Hammacher Schlemmer
Unique household, recreation, personal care, gardening and electronic products

116 Hanover House
Gifts, novelties, cookware, furnishings, clothing

118 Harrods
Gourmet food, apparel, gifts and furniture

131 Horchow Catalogue
Gifts, clothing, furnishings

134 Ikea Mail Order
Home furnishings, cookware,

Do-It-Yourself Supplies

245 Sears Canada Inc.
Major mail order supplier of clothing, household goods and gifts
252 Shaker Workshops
Reproductions of Shaker furniture in kits or assembled and finished
256 Shinawatra
Silk yard goods and handicrafts

Wall Coverings and Curtains

7 American Discount Wallcoverings
Wall coverings, window treatments, fabrics and accessories: any and all major brands
30 Best Products
Housewares, electronics, furniture, toys, sporting goods, jewellery, watches
31 Bloomingdale's
All kinds of high-end clothing, home furnishings, cosmetics and gifts
46 Canadian Tire Corporation Ltd.
Sporting, camping, hardware, auto, pool, plumbing, gardening and handyman supplies, plus toys
55 Clothcrafters
Aprons, totes, yard goods, mats, sheets, curtains, cookware, parchment paper, terry towels, insect netting, chefs' hats and more
57 Colorel Corporation
Mini-blinds, verticals, pleated shades
107 Grand Finale
Factory close-outs on gifts, linens, furniture, toys, china, apparel and cookware
110 Gump's Mail Order
Crystal, silver, linen, contemporary gifts, jewellery and apparel
113 Hammacher Schlemmer
Unique household, recreation, personal care, gardening and electronic products
115 Handart Embroideries
Source of embroidered tablecloths, bedspreads, kimonos, pillow shams, blouses, cloisonné souvenirs, bracelets and more
116 Hanover House
Gifts, novelties, cookware, furnishings, clothing
118 Harrods
Gourmet food, apparel, gifts and furniture
131 Horchow Catalogue
Gifts, clothing, furnishings
134 Ikea Mail Order
Home furnishings, cookware, toys, knock-down furniture, shelving, office furniture, decor accents
137 Industrial Revolution
Closet organizers, cookware, linens and towels, office supplies, furniture, lamps, etc.
146 Jay Norris Select
Novelties, chatchkas, clothing and gifts
166 Lao Song Handicrafts
Christmas ornaments, stuffed animals, craft items
208 Neiman-Marcus
Gifts, cookware, clothing and executive toys
221 Peter Jones
Yard goods, linens, china, crystal and silver

Floor Coverings

146 Jay Norris Select
Novelties, chatchkas, clothing and gifts
166 Lao Song Handicrafts
Christmas ornaments, stuffed animals, craft items
171 Lillian Vernon Corporation
Giftware
208 Neiman-Marcus
Gifts, cookware, clothing and executive toys
221 Peter Jones
Yard goods, linens, china, crystal and silver
231 Rama Trade
Anything that can be found in Thailand and legally imported into Canada
245 Sears Canada Inc.
Major mail order supplier of clothing, household goods and gifts
254 Shanghai Silk-Knit Carpet Factory
Hand-made silk carpets
264 Spiegel
Upmarket clothing, gifts, home furnishings, executive toys
278 The Barn
Custom woven rugs and specialty decorative items
286 Tibetan Refugee Self-Help Centre
Carpets, tapestries, hand-made crafts, sweaters, coats, caps, mufflers, gloves, socks, boots and artifacts

Bedding, Linen and Towels

1 A. Andrews and Co.
Sporting goods, electronics, fancy table linens, souvenirs
3 The Added Touch
Gift baskets, novelties, gardening supplies, closet organizers
17 Artland
Table linens, embroidery arts, handicrafts, beaded evening tops, women's apparel
28 Ben Lee Co.
Linens, embroidered items, sweaters, Chinese art, oil paintings and chops
30 Best Products
Housewares, electronics, furniture, toys, sporting goods, jewellery, watches
31 Bloomingdale's
All kinds of high-end clothing, home furnishings, cosmetics and gifts
48 Carrousel of Ideas
Gift items, novelties, toys, watches, chatchkas
55 Clothcrafters
Aprons, totes, yard goods, mats, sheets, curtains, cookware, parchment paper, terry towels, insect netting, chefs' hats and more
91 Fatima Self Help Center
Smocked dresses, Christmas ornaments and craft items
94 Frederick & Nelson
Gifts, clothing, toys, gift packs, lingerie and executive toys
101 The Gazebo of New York
High-end home accessories
107 Grand Finale
Factory close-outs on gifts, linens, furniture, toys, china, apparel and cookware
110 Gump's Mail Order
Crystal, silver, linen, contemporary gifts, jewellery and apparel

Closet Accessories

46 Canadian Tire Corporation Ltd.
Sporting, camping, hardware, auto, pool, plumbing, gardening and handyman supplies, plus toys
48 Carrousel of Ideas
Gift items, novelties, toys, watches, chatchkas
94 Frederick & Nelson
Gifts, clothing, toys, gift packs, lingerie and executive toys
101 The Gazebo of New York
High-end home accessories
107 Grand Finale
Factory close-outs on gifts, linens, furniture, toys, china, apparel and cookware
110 Gump's Mail Order
Crystal, silver, linen, contemporary gifts, jewellery and apparel
113 Hammacher Schlemmer
Unique household, recreation, personal care, gardening and electronic products
116 Hanover House
Gifts, novelties, cookware, furnishings, clothing
131 Horchow Catalogue
Gifts, clothing, furnishings
134 Ikea Mail Order
Home furnishings, cookware, toys, knock-down furniture, shelving, office furniture, decor accents
137 Industrial Revolution
Closet organizers, cookware, linens and towels, office supplies, furniture, lamps, etc.
146 Jay Norris Select
Novelties, chatchkas, clothing and gifts
171 Lillian Vernon Corporation
Giftware
208 Neiman-Marcus
Gifts, cookware, clothing and executive toys
245 Sears Canada Inc.
Major mail order supplier of clothing, household goods and gifts
255 The Sharper Image
Executive toys, electronics, gadgets, luggage, novelties and gifts
264 Spiegel
Upmarket clothing, gifts, home furnishings, executive toys
280 The Paragon
Household goods, some clothing
305 Waymarc
Office, store, warehouse, institutional shelving, storage, filing and electronics items

Wood Stoves, Portable Heaters and Windmills

30 Best Products
Housewares, electronics, furniture, toys, sporting goods, jewellery, watches
41 Cabela's
Sportswear, camping, hunting, fishing, outdoors gear
46 Canadian Tire Corporation Ltd.
Sporting, camping, hardware, auto, pool, plumbing, gardening and handyman supplies, plus toys
81 Efstonscience Inc.
Gadgets, everything scientific, maps, books, magnifiers
113 Hammacher Schlemmer
Unique household, recreation,

Hot Tubs and Saunas

Lamps and Lighting Fixtures

89 The Faith Mountain Company
Home accessories, apparel, flowers

94 Frederick & Nelson
Gifts, clothing, toys, gift packs, lingerie and executive toys

101 The Gazebo of New York
High-end home accessories

107 Grand Finale
Factory close-outs on gifts, linens, furniture, toys, china, apparel and cookware

110 Gump's Mail Order
Crystal, silver, linen, contemporary gifts, jewellery and apparel

113 Hammacher Schlemmer
Unique household, recreation, personal care, gardening and electronic products

116 Hanover House
Gifts, novelties, cookware, furnishings, clothing

131 Horchow Catalogue
Gifts, clothing, furnishings

134 Ikea Mail Order
Home furnishings, cookware, toys, knock-down furniture, shelving, office furniture, decor accents

137 Industrial Revolution
Closet organizers, cookware, linens and towels, office supplies, furniture, lamps, etc.

146 Jay Norris Select
Novelties, chatchkas, clothing and gifts

171 Lillian Vernon Corporation
Giftware

208 Neiman-Marcus
Gifts, cookware, clothing and executive toys

231 Rama Trade
Anything that can be found in Thailand and legally imported into Canada

245 Sears Canada Inc.
Major mail order supplier of clothing, household goods and gifts

255 The Sharper Image
Executive toys, electronics, gadgets, luggage, novelties and gifts

264 Spiegel
Upmarket clothing, gifts, home furnishings, executive toys

279 The Garden
Sundials, garden accessories, watering cans, pruning saws and shears, garden books, dessert sauces and gourmet foods, hammocks, garden furniture and tools

280 The Paragon
Household goods, some clothing

Hardware

3 The Added Touch
Gift baskets, novelties, gardening supplies, closet organizers

14 Anything Left Handed Limited
Goods, utensils and novelties for left-handed people

30 Best Products
Housewares, electronics, furniture, toys, sporting goods, jewellery, watches

41 Cabela's
Sportswear, camping, hunting, fishing, outdoors gear

46 Canadian Tire Corporation Ltd.
Sporting, camping, hardware, auto, pool, plumbing,

Doodads (Weather Vanes, Lawn Decorations and Small Hardware)

26 Beadworld
Jewellery findings, beads, necklaces, earrings and bracelets

35 Bouquet Enterprises
Wooden decorative accessories and dolls

46 Canadian Tire Corporation Ltd.
Sporting, camping, hardware, auto, pool, plumbing, gardening and handyman supplies, plus toys

48 Carrousel of Ideas
Gift items, novelties, toys, watches, chatchkas

53 Church Goods Co.
Religious items, curios, novelties

59 The Country Loft
Country/primitive furniture and accessories

93 Foster-Trent Inc.
Lawn ornaments

101 The Gazebo of New York
High-end home accessories

104 Ginger Schlote
Mail order only of economy jewellery, mountings, findings, rings and accessories

113 Hammacher Schlemmer
Unique household, recreation, personal care, gardening and electronic products

122 Hedonics
Electronics, specialty gifts and novelties

134 Ikea Mail Order
Home furnishings, cookware, toys, knock-down furniture, shelving, office furniture, decor accents

146 Jay Norris Select
Novelties, chatchkas, clothing and gifts

158 L.H. Selman Ltd.
Gift items, paperweights

171 Lillian Vernon Corporation
Giftware

173 Little Switzerland
A source for perfume, fine china, watches, crystal and objets d'art

198 Museum of Fine Arts, Boston
Museum reproductions, art, posters, jewellery

202 Nat Schwartz
China, crystal, silver, giftware, name brands, discounts

228 Public Broadcasting Service
Mugs, sweatshirts, totebags, books and videos

239 Romshops, Treasures of the ROM
Museum reproductions, art, posters, books, Christmas decorations, sculpture, games, jewellery

245 Sears Canada Inc.
Major mail order supplier of clothing, household goods and gifts

250 Seva Foundation, c/o Seva Service Society
Third-world crafts, paper products

252 Shaker Workshops
Reproductions of Shaker furniture in kits or assembled and finished

255 The Sharper Image
Executive toys, electronics, gadgets, luggage, novelties and gifts

270 Sultan's Delight Inc.
Middle-Eastern foods

279 The Garden
Sundials, garden accessories, watering cans, pruning saws and shears, garden books, dessert sauces and gourmet foods, hammocks, garden furniture and tools

LIFESTYLES AND LEISURE
Hobbies, General

182 Mary Maxim
Needlework, crafts, knitting supplies, kits, patterns
195 Mountain Equipment Co-op
Outdoors, hiking, climbing, hunting, fishing and camping gear, backpacks, tents, sleeping bags and apparel
204 National Public Radio
Mail order National Public Radio cassette tapes
206 The Nature Co.
Nature-theme products
214 P.G.N. Sales
Berol England paints, art supplies, inks, lettering supplies
222 Pied Piper Catalog
Items for gifted children
223 Pierre Deux
French provincial floral print fabrics, clothing, pillows and upholstery
224 Players Chess & Game Showroom
Chess paraphernalia, board games, backgammon sets
230 Radio Shack
Electronics and gadgets
234 Regal Gifts & Greetings
Gifts, greeting cards, catalogue sales
245 Sears Canada Inc.
Major mail order supplier of clothing, household goods and gifts
279 The Garden
Sundials, garden accessories, watering cans, pruning saws and shears, garden books, dessert sauces and gourmet foods, hammocks, garden furniture and tools
299 Victoria International Knives Ltd.
Knives, cutlery, scissors, razors and English darts

Photography

30 Best Products
Housewares, electronics, furniture, toys, sporting goods, jewellery, watches
81 Efstonscience Inc.
Gadgets, everything scientific, maps, books, magnifiers
88 47th St. Photo
Photo equipment, watches, electronics, computers
113 Hammacher Schlemmer
Unique household, recreation, personal care, gardening and electronic products
130 Honest Photo & Audio Supplies
Cameras and tape recorders
309 Western Canada Wilderness Committee
Calendars, books, posters and postcards
317 Winsource Camera & Video Co.
Cameras, tape recorders, video equipment

Needlework

1 A. Andrews and Co.
Sporting goods, electronics, fancy table linens, souvenirs
6 Amazon Drygoods
19th-century reproductions, clothing and patterns
14 Anything Left Handed Limited
Goods, utensils and novelties for left-handed people
17 Artland
Table linens, embroidery arts, handicrafts, beaded evening tops, women's apparel

Travel

273 Taiga Works
Outdoor gear, camping, hunting, fishing, hiking gear and apparel
293 Unicef Canada
Games, Christmas and greeting cards, cookbooks, posters, coffee mugs, collectors' plates, pop-up books and personalized stationery
301 Village Books
Books, maps, posters, cards and guidebooks
312 Wide World Books & Maps
Travel books, maps and accessories

Seeds and Plants

2 Abundant Life Seed Foundation
Seeds
37 Burpee
Seeds and garden supplies
38 Butterbrooke Farm
Heirloom and "ole standard" veggie seeds
40 C.A. Cruickshank Ltd.
Seeds
62 Culpeper Limited
Herbal products
74 Dominion Seed House
Seeds and gardening supplies
99 Gardener's Eden
Gardening "extras"
116 Hanover House
Gifts, novelties, cookware, furnishings, clothing
119 Harrowsmith
Nature videos, how-to books (gardening)
124 Heritage Canada Gift Collection
Newfoundland hand-knit woollens, Christmas cards, posters, Inuit silk scarf, journals, honey, baskets, placemats and gifts
150 John Deere
Household and garden equipment and "big" toys
186 Mellinger's Inc.
A huge assortment of gardening supplies, seeds, bulbs, live plants and green thumb conveniences
237 Rockwood Gardens Ltd.
Seeds, bulbs and plants
243 San Francisco Herb Co.
Pot-pourri, spices and teas
245 Sears Canada Inc.
Major mail order supplier of clothing, household goods and gifts
251 Seventh Generation
Recycling materials, natural household and garden products
269 Stokes Seeds
Seeds, gardening supplies
276 Territorial Seeds (Canada) Ltd.
Seeds, gardening books, season extenders
279 The Garden
Sundials, garden accessories, watering cans, pruning saws and shears, garden books, dessert sauces and gourmet foods, hammocks, garden furniture and tools
284 Thompson & Morgan Ltd.
Seeds
285 Thompson & Morgan, U.S.
Seeds
306 Weall & Cullen Gardeners Supply Inc.
Gardeners' supplies, Sheffield handtools, faucets, sundials, Tilley Endurable hats, Barbour clothing and greenhouses

Books, Records, Tapes, Videos and Magazines

124 Heritage Canada Gift Collection
Newfoundland hand-knit woollens, Christmas cards, posters, Inuit silk scarf, journals, honey, baskets, placemats and gifts
130 Honest Photo & Audio Supplies
Cameras and tape recorders
135 Impact Publications
Career and travel books
146 Jay Norris Select
Novelties, chatchkas, clothing and gifts
154 King Sound
Tape recorders
157 Knowledge Bookstore
Books, cassettes, records, VHS tapes
160 L.M. Media Marketing
Free films and videos
170 Learning at Home
Educational materials
188 Metropolitan Museum of Art
Museum reproductions, jewellery, art, sculpture, gifts
198 Museum of Fine Arts, Boston
Museum reproductions, art, posters, jewellery
199 Museum of Modern Art
Museum-quality posters, books, cards
200 Music for Little People
Musical instruments, tapes
203 National Geographic Society
Maps, books, globes, magazine subscriptions
204 National Public Radio
Mail order National Public Radio cassette tapes
205 National Wildlife Federation
Wildlife magazines and audio/visual teaching aids
206 The Nature Co.
Nature-theme products
208 Neiman-Marcus
Gifts, cookware, clothing and executive toys
214 P.G.N. Sales
Berol England paints, art supplies, inks, lettering supplies
222 Pied Piper Catalog
Items for gifted children
224 Players Chess & Game Showroom
Chess paraphernalia, board games, backgammon sets
228 Public Broadcasting Service
Mugs, sweatshirts, totebags, books and videos
229 Pur et Simple Inc.
Environment-friendly products
233 The Reader's Catalog
Books, gifts
239 Romshops, Treasures of the ROM
Museum reproductions, art, posters, books, Christmas decorations, sculpture, games, jewellery
245 Sears Canada Inc.
Major mail order supplier of clothing, household goods and gifts
251 Seventh Generation
Recycling materials, natural household and garden products
255 The Sharper Image
Executive toys, electronics, gadgets, luggage, novelties and gifts
258 Smithsonian Institution
Museum exhibit related gifts
264 Spiegel
Upmarket clothing, gifts, home furnishings, executive toys
276 Territorial Seeds (Canada) Ltd.
Seeds, gardening books, season extenders
278 The Barn
Custom woven rugs and specialty decorative items
279 The Garden
Sundials, garden accessories,

Stamps and Coins

Art

sweaters, Chinese art, oil paintings and chops
31 Bloomingdale's
All kinds of high-end clothing, home furnishings, cosmetics and gifts
35 Bouquet Enterprises
Wooden decorative accessories and dolls
59 The Country Loft
Country/primitive furniture and accessories
89 The Faith Mountain Company
Home accessories, apparel, flowers
106 Good Impressions
Victorian and decorative rubber stamps
110 Gump's Mail Order
Crystal, silver, linen, contemporary gifts, jewellery and apparel
113 Hammacher Schlemmer
Unique household, recreation, personal care, gardening and electronic products.
116 Hanover House
Gifts, novelties, cookware, furnishings, clothing
118 Harrods
Gourmet food, apparel, gifts and furniture
124 Heritage Canada Gift Collection
Newfoundland hand-knit woollens, Christmas cards, posters, Inuit silk scarf, journals, honey, baskets, placemats and gifts
131 Horchow Catalogue
Gifts, clothing, furnishings
138 International Bank of Asia
High-end leather goods, ties, watches, electronics, coins, jewellery, executive toys and gifts
139 Iroqrafts Ltd.
Native art and sculpture, particularly from the Iroquois
167 Laurel Burch, Inc.
Art prints, jewellery, novelties
173 Little Switzerland
A source for perfume, fine china, watches, crystal and objets d'art
188 Metropolitan Museum of Art
Museum reproductions, jewellery, art, sculpture, gifts
198 Museum of Fine Arts, Boston
Museum reproductions, art, posters, jewellery
199 Museum of Modern Art
Museum-quality posters, books, cards
206 The Nature Co.
Nature-theme products
231 Rama Trade
Anything that can be found in Thailand and legally imported into Canada
239 Romshops, Treasures of the ROM
Museum reproductions, art, posters, books, Christmas decorations, sculpture, games, jewellery
258 Smithsonian Institution
Museum exhibit related gifts
264 Spiegel
Upmarket clothing, gifts, home furnishings, executive toys
266 Stanley Market
Linens, sweaters, embroideries, Chinese jackets and Chinese arts and crafts
309 Western Canada Wilderness Committee
Calendars, books, posters and postcards

Antiques

Canadiana and Americana

59 The Country Loft
Country/primitive furniture and accessories

82 El Paso Chili Co.
Southwestern chili products

89 The Faith Mountain Company
Home accessories, apparel, flowers

101 The Gazebo of New York
High-end home accessories

103 Gimbel & Sons Country Store
Collectables, thimbles, porcelain dolls and miniatures

106 Good Impressions
Victorian and decorative rubber stamps

116 Hanover House
Gifts, novelties, cookware, furnishings, clothing

124 Heritage Canada Gift Collection
Newfoundland hand-knit woollens, Christmas cards, posters, Inuit silk scarf, journals, honey, baskets, placemats and gifts

139 Iroqrafts Ltd.
Native art and sculpture, particularly from the Iroquois

142 The J. Peterman Company
Unique, hard-to-find items with a "factual romance"

188 Metropolitan Museum of Art
Museum reproductions, jewellery, art, sculpture, gifts

198 Museum of Fine Arts, Boston
Museum reproductions, art, posters, jewellery

206 The Nature Co.
Nature-theme products

226 The Popcorn Factory
Fancy popcorn, mints, cookies, gummy bunnies, Rachel's brownies, popping supplies, gift tins

234 Regal Gifts & Greetings
Gifts, greeting cards, catalogue sales

239 Romshops, Treasures of the ROM
Museum reproductions, art, posters, books, Christmas decorations, sculpture, games, jewellery

252 Shaker Workshops
Reproductions of Shaker furniture in kits or assembled and finished

258 Smithsonian Institution
Museum exhibit related gifts

264 Spiegel
Upmarket clothing, gifts, home furnishings, executive toys

274 Talheim Craftworks, c/o Joseph E. Wack, Prop.
Hand-carved hardwood kitchen implements

278 The Barn
Custom woven rugs and specialty decorative items

Pipes and Tobacco

15 The Arctic Trading Company
Authentic native products

94 Frederick & Nelson
Gifts, clothing, toys, gift packs, lingerie and executive toys

96 G. Smith and Sons, The Snuff Centre
Snuff, cigars, pipes, tobacco and "smokers' requisites"

116 Hanover House
Gifts, novelties, cookware, furnishings, clothing

118 Harrods
Gourmet food, apparel, gifts and furniture

Games, Toys and Dolls

94 Frederick & Nelson
Gifts, clothing, toys, gift packs, lingerie and executive toys
103 Gimbel & Sons Country Store
Collectables, thimbles, porcelain dolls and miniatures
107 Grand Finale
Factory close-outs on gifts, linens, furniture, toys, china, apparel, and cookware
111 Haddon Rocking Horse Ltd.
Manufacturers of wooden rocking horses
113 Hammacher Schlemmer
Unique household, recreation, personal care, gardening and electronic products
116 Hanover House
Gifts, novelties, cookware, furnishings, clothing
118 Harrods
Gourmet food, apparel, gifts and furniture
121 Hearthsong
Toys, books, art supplies and games
134 Ikea Mail Order
Home furnishings, cookware, toys, knock-down furniture, shelving, office furniture, decor accents
150 John Deere
Household and garden equipment and "big" toys
171 Lillian Vernon Corporation
Giftware
174 Local House Co. Ltd.
Folk art and handicrafts
194 Mothercare by Mail
Items for expectant mothers and children to age 8
198 Museum of Fine Arts, Boston
Museum reproductions, art, posters, jewelry
208 Neiman-Marcus
Gifts, cookware, clothing and executive toys
222 Pied Piper Catalog
Items for gifted children
224 Players Chess and Game Showroom
Chess paraphernalia, board games, backgammon sets
234 Regal Gifts and Greetings
Gifts, greeting cards, catalog sales
239 Romshops, Treasures of the ROM
Museum reproductions, art, posters, books, Christmas decorations, sculpture, games, jewelry
244 Saxkjaers
Giftware, crystal, china, figurines, jewelry
245 Sears Canada Inc.
Major mail order supplier of clothing, household goods and gifts
250 Seva Foundation, c/o Seva Service Society
Third-world crafts, paper products
251 Seventh Generation
Recycling materials, natural household and garden products
253 Shanghai Arts & Crafts
Wooden crafts and toys
255 Sharper Image, The
Executive toys, electronics, gadgets, luggage, novelties and gifts
258 Smithsonian Institution
Museum exhibit related gifts
262 Speilzeug-Rasch
Toys
264 Spiegel
Upmarket clothing, gifts, home furnishings, executive toys

Party Supplies

Erotica and Lingerie

24 Banyen Books
Metaphysical, occult, psychology, astrology books and paraphernalia
95 Frederick's of Hollywood
Lingerie, dresses, sportswear, swimwear, hosiery and boots
116 Hanover House
Gifts, novelties, cookware, furnishings, clothing
265 Stamford Hygienic Collection
Sexual aids and lingerie
300 Victoria's Secret
Lingerie, underwear and nightgowns

Occult, Religious, Self-help, Astrology, Meditation

24 Banyen Books
Metaphysical, occult, psychology, astrology books and paraphernalia
32 The Bodhi Tree
Metaphysical books and paraphernalia
127 Hollywood Magic, Inc.
Magic supplies
319 Worldwide Curio House
Items related to the mystic arts, occult, witchcraft and voodoo

Bicycles and Motorcycles

11 The American Traveller
Gift items, executive toys, watches, language tapes, electronics
30 Best Products
Housewares, electronics, furniture, toys, sporting goods, jewellery, watches
46 Canadian Tire Corporation Ltd.
Sporting, camping, hardware, auto, pool, plumbing, gardening and handyman supplies, plus toys
79 Eddie Bauer Outdoor Outfitters
Outdoors apparel
81 Efstonscience Inc.
Gadgets, everything scientific, maps, books, magnifiers
94 Frederick & Nelson
Gifts, clothing, toys, gift packs, lingerie and executive toys
113 Hammacher Schlemmer
Unique household, recreation, personal care, gardening and electronic products
116 Hanover House
Gifts, novelties, cookware, furnishings, clothing
146 Jay Norris Select
Novelties, chatchkas, clothing and gifts
159 L.L. Bean, Inc.
Outdoor goods and apparel
195 Mountain Equipment Co-op
Outdoors, hiking, climbing, hunting, fishing and camping gear, backpacks, tents, sleeping bags and apparel
245 Sears Canada Inc.
Major mail order supplier of clothing, household goods and gifts
255 The Sharper Image
Executive toys, electronics, gadgets, luggage, novelties and gifts

Art Supplies

ACCESSORIES
Hand-Made Accessories

104 Ginger Schlote
Mail order only of economy jewellery, mountings, findings, rings and accessories

109 Guangzhou Decor Porcelain Factory
Hand-painted porcelain bowls, plates, tea sets, vases, jars, umbrella-holders

110 Gump's Mail Order
Crystal, silver, linen, contemporary gifts, jewellery and apparel

115 Handart Embroideries
Source of embroidered tablecloths, bedspreads, kimonos, pillow shams, blouses, cloisonné souvenirs, bracelets and more

116 Hanover House
Gifts, novelties, cookware, furnishings, clothing

120 Hayim Pinhas Kimyevi Ve Maden Mamulleri Ihracat Ve Ithalat As
Meerschaum pipes

124 Heritage Canada Gift Collection
Newfoundland hand-knit woollens, Christmas cards, posters, Inuit silk scarf, journals, honey, baskets, placemats and gifts

131 Horchow Catalogue
Gifts, clothing, furnishings

139 Iroqrafts Ltd.
Native art and sculpture, particularly from the Iroquois

149 Jim Thompson Silk Company
Silk clothing, accessories, ties, placemats, upholstery fabrics, jewellery boxes, pillow shams, and silk fabric

166 Lao Song Handicrafts
Christmas ornaments, stuffed animals, craft items

174 Local House Co. Ltd.
Folk art and handicrafts

231 Rama Trade
Anything that can be found in Thailand and legally imported into Canada

232 Rammagerdin h.f.
Icelandic woollen goods and souvenirs

239 Romshops, Treasures of the ROM
Museum reproductions, art, posters, books, Christmas decorations, sculpture, games, jewellery

244 Saxkjaers
Giftware, crystal, china, figurines, jewellery

250 Seva Foundation, c/o Seva Service Society
Third-world crafts, paper products

252 Shaker Workshops
Reproductions of Shaker furniture in kits or assembled and finished

253 Shanghai Arts & Crafts
Wooden crafts and toys

272 Sweater Market
Men's and women's hand-knit, 100% wool sweaters

274 Talheim Craftworks, c/o Joseph E. Wack, Prop.
Hand-carved hardwood kitchen implements

279 The Garden
Sundials, garden accessories, watering cans, pruning saws and shears, garden books, dessert sauces and gourmet foods, hammocks, garden furniture and tools

286 Tibetan Refugee Self-Help Centre
Carpets, tapestries, hand-made crafts, sweaters, coats, caps, mufflers, gloves, socks, boots and artifacts

High-Style Accessories

227 PT & P (Thailand) Co. Ltd.
PVC wallets, briefcases, address books, wedding registers

231 Rama Trade
Anything that can be found in Thailand and legally imported into Canada

239 Romshops, Treasures of the ROM
Museum reproductions, art, posters, books, Christmas decorations, sculpture, games, jewellery

244 Saxkjaers
Giftware, crystal, china, figurines, jewellery

264 Spiegel
Upmarket clothing, gifts, home furnishings, executive toys

266 Stanley Market
Linens, sweaters, embroideries, Chinese jackets and Chinese arts and crafts

267 Stecher's Limited
Duty-free goods, watches, perfumes, lighters, pens, crystal, leather goods, jewellery, and figurines

Wedding Supplies and Stationery

31 Bloomingdale's
All kinds of high-end clothing, home furnishings, cosmetics and gifts

56 Colonial Plates and Dolls
Collectables, plates, dolls, costume jewellery, David Winter cottages, miniatures

116 Hanover House
Gifts, novelties, cookware, furnishings, clothing

118 Harrods
Gourmet food, apparel, gifts and furniture

196 Mr. Romance
Romantic books, ideas, gifts and novelties; new line of custom, Victorian lingerie and bridal gowns

227 PT & P (Thailand) Co. Ltd.
PVC wallets, briefcases, address books, wedding registers

234 Regal Gifts & Greetings
Gifts, greeting cards, catalogue sales

264 Spiegel
Upmarket clothing, gifts, home furnishings, executive toys

266 Stanley Market
Linens, sweaters, embroideries, Chinese jackets and Chinese arts and crafts

Jewellery: Gemstones, Fabulous Fakes, Quality Goods

1 A. Andrews and Co.
Sporting goods, electronics, fancy table linens, souvenirs

8 American Express Canada, Inc.
Limited edition prints, plates and coins

13 Anabelle's Collection
Costume jewellery, antique reproductions, gifts

16 Art Resources
Sculpture, art reproductions, decor accents, lamps, carpets, jewellery, antiques

26 Beadworld
Jewellery findings, beads,

China and Crystal

Silver and Flatwear

52 Chiangmai Silverware
Silver jewellery and artifacts
94 Frederick & Nelson
Gifts, clothing, toys, gift packs, lingerie and executive toys
107 Grand Finale
Factory close-outs on gifts, linens, furniture, toys, china, apparel and cookware
110 Gump's Mail Order
Crystal, silver, linen, contemporary gifts, jewellery and apparel.
116 Hanover House
Gifts, novelties, cookware, furnishings, clothing
118 Harrods
Gourmet food, apparel, gifts and furniture
131 Horchow Catalogue
Gifts, clothing, furnishings
134 Ikea Mail Order
Home furnishings, cookware, toys, knock-down furniture, shelving, office furniture, decor accents
137 Industrial Revolution
Closet organizers, cookware, linens and towels, office supplies, furniture, lamps, etc.
171 Lillian Vernon Corporation
Giftware
173 Little Switzerland
A source for perfume, fine china, watches, crystal and objets d'art
178 Majestic Counterfeit Jewels
Fabulous fake jewellery in 14K gold
187 Merlo's Cutlery
Knives, cutlery and utensils
188 Metropolitan Museum of Art
Museum reproductions, jewellery, art, sculpture, gifts
202 Nat Schwartz
China, crystal, silver, giftware, name brands, discounts
208 Nieman-Marcus
Gifts, cookware, clothing and executive toys
221 Peter Jones
Yard goods, linens, china, crystal and silver
240 Ross-Simons Jewelers
Jewellery, china, crystal and sterling
244 Saxkjaers
Giftware, crystal, china, figurines, jewellery
245 Sears Canada Inc.
Major mail order supplier of clothing, household goods and gifts
264 Spiegel
Upmarket clothing, gifts, home furnishings, executive toys
267 Stecher's Limited
Duty-free goods, watches, perfumes, lighters, pens, crystal, leather goods, jewellery and figurines
275 Tere Hagan Flatware Matching Service
Flatware pattern-matching service
299 Victoria International Knives Ltd.
Knives, cutlery, scissors, razors and English darts

BUSINESS
Stationery and Office Supplies

14 Anything Left Handed Limited
Goods, utensils and novelties for left-handed people

Computers

11 The American Traveller
Gift items, executive toys, watches, language tapes, electronics
69 Dell Computer Corporation
Computer hardware and 50 most-popular software packages
76 800-SOFTWARE
Resell microcomputer software and hardware accessories for PCs and Macs
81 Efstonscience Inc.
Gadgets, everything scientific, maps, books, magnifiers
88 47th St. Photo
Photo equipment, watches, electronics, computers
113 Hammacher Schlemmer
Unique household, recreation, personal care, gardening and electronic products
122 Hedonics
Electronics, specialty gifts and novelties
130 Honest Photo & Audio Supplies
Cameras and tape recorders
138 International Bank of Asia
High-end leather goods, ties, watches, electronics, coins, jewellery, executive toys and gifts
154 King Sound
Tape recorders
192 Moore Business Supplies
Computer supplies, stationery and printing
230 Radio Shack
Electronics and gadgets
245 Sears Canada Inc.
Major mail order supplier of clothing, household goods and gifts
255 The Sharper Image
Executive toys, electronics, gadgets, luggage, novelties and gifts
317 Winsource Camera & Video Co.
Cameras, tape recorders, video equipment

Books (Business)

25 Barnes & Noble Bookstores, Inc. (Canada sales)
Discount books, videos, records and tapes
76 800-SOFTWARE
Resell microcomputer software and hardware accessories for PCs and Macs
184 Maxwell's Artists Materials Ltd.
Stationery and art supplies

Shelving

30 Best Products
Housewares, electronics, furniture, toys, sporting goods, jewellery, watches
46 Canadian Tire Corporation Ltd.
Sporting, camping, hardware, auto, pool, plumbing, gardening and handyman supplies, plus toys
134 Ikea Mail Order
Home furnishings, cookware, toys, knock-down furniture, shelving, office furniture, decor accents
137 Industrial Revolution
Closet organizers, cookware,

Office Furniture

Clip Art, Promotional and Printing Services

HEALTH AND BEAUTY
Cosmetics

31 Bloomingdale's
All kinds of high-end clothing, home furnishings, cosmetics and gifts
33 The Body Shop
All-natural cosmetics, not tested on animals
48 Carrousel of Ideas
Gift items, novelties, toys, watches, chatchkas
118 Harrods
Gourmet food, apparel, gifts and furniture
146 Jay Norris Select
Novelties, chatchkas, clothing and gifts
194 Mothercare by Mail
Items for expectant mothers and children to age eight
217 Parfumerie Catherine
French perfumes and cosmetics
310 The Whiteheart Company
Perfumes, pot-pourri, soaps and cosmetics

Vitamins

4 Alive Health Centre
Health products and vitamins
61 Croft's Health Products
Full line of health products, vitamins and preparations
210 New Roots Nutrition
Discount quality vitamins and hypo-allergenic formulas
245 Sears Canada Inc.
Major mail order supplier of clothing, household goods and gifts
302 The Vitamin Experts
Vitamins, supplements, amino acids, enzymes and minerals

Perfume

31 Bloomingdale's
All kinds of high-end clothing, home furnishings, cosmetics and gifts
33 The Body Shop
All-natural cosmetics, not tested on animals
94 Frederick & Nelson
Gifts, clothing, toys, gift packs, lingerie and executive toys
141 J. Floris Ltd.
Perfumes and toiletries
178 Majestic Counterfeit Jewels
Fabulous fake jewellery in 14K gold
217 Parfumerie Catherine
French perfumes and cosmetics
245 Sears Canada Inc.
Major mail order supplier of clothing, household goods and gifts
264 Spiegel
Upmarket clothing, gifts, home furnishings, executive toys
267 Stecher's Limited
Duty-free goods, watches, perfumes, lighters, pens, crystal, leather goods, jewellery, and figurines
310 The Whiteheart Company
Perfumes, pot-pourri, soaps and cosmetics

Wigs

27 Beauty by Spector, Inc.
Hairpieces, wigs, falls, braids and other hair-goods, sold at discount prices, for both men

Eyeglasses and Hearing Aids

Supplies and Services for the Handicapped

THE UNUSUAL
Objets d'Art

contemporary gifts, jewellery and apparel

111 Haddon Rocking Horses Ltd.
Manufacturers of wooden rocking horses

113 Hammacher Schlemmer
Unique household, recreation, personal care, gardening and electronic products

118 Harrods
Gourmet food, apparel, gifts and furniture

131 Horchow Catalogue
Gifts, clothing, furnishings

138 International Bank of Asia
High-end leather goods, ties, watches, electronics, coins, jewellery, executive toys and gifts

139 Iroqrafts Ltd.
Native art and sculpture, particularly from the Iroquois

166 Lao Song Handicrafts
Christmas ornaments, stuffed animals, craft items

173 Little Switzerland
A source for perfume, fine china, watches, crystal and objets d'art

178 Majestic Counterfeit Jewels
Fabulous fake jewellery in 14K gold

188 Metropolitan Museum of Art
Museum reproductions, jewellery, art, sculpture, gifts

198 Museum of Fine Arts, Boston
Museum reproductions, art, posters, jewellery

199 Museum of Modern Art
Museum-quality posters, books, cards

208 Nieman-Marcus
Gifts, cookware, clothing and executive toys

231 Rama Trade
Anything that can be found in Thailand and legally imported into Canada

239 Romshops, Treasures of the ROM
Museum reproductions, art, posters, books, Christmas decorations, sculpture, games, jewellery

252 Shaker Workshops
Reproductions of Shaker furniture in kits or assembled and finished

256 Shinawatra
Silk yard goods and handicrafts

258 Smithsonian Institution
Museum exhibit-related gifts

264 Spiegel
Upmarket clothing, gifts, home furnishings, executive toys

274 Talheim Craftworks, c/o Joseph E. Wack, Prop.
Hand-carved hardwood kitchen implements

286 Tibetan Refugee Self-Help Centre
Carpets, tapestries, hand-made crafts, sweaters, coats, caps, mufflers, gloves, socks, boots, and artifacts

298 Victoria & Albert Museum
Museum gifts and Victoriana

316 Winner Trading Co.
Jewellery, jewellers' tools, faux gems, display stands

Clothing (Unusual and Exotic)

6 Amazon Drygoods
19th-century reproductions, clothing and patterns

10 American Spoon Foods
Fruit products, chestnuts, dried fruit

Gifts

Snuff, cigars, pipes, tobacco and "smokers' requisites"

107 Grand Finale
Factory close-outs on gifts, linens, furniture, toys, china, apparel and cookware

109 Guangzhou Decor Porcelain Factory
Hand-painted porcelain bowls, plates, tea sets, vases, jars, umbrella-holders

110 Gump's Mail Order
Crystal, silver, linen, contemporary gifts, jewellery and apparel

111 Haddon Rocking Horses Ltd.
Manufacturers of wooden rocking horses

113 Hammacher Schlemmer
Unique household, recreation, personal care, gardening and electronic products

115 Handart Embroideries
Source of embroidered tablecloths, bedspreads, kimonos, pillow shams, blouses, cloisonné souvenirs, bracelets and more

120 Hayim Pinhas Kimyevi Ve Maden Mamulleri Ihracat Veithalat As
Meerschaum pipes

123 Hepting and Farrer Ltd., The Jewellers
Retail jewellery in silver or gold

124 Heritage Canada Gift Collection
Newfoundland hand-knit woollens, Christmas cards, posters, Inuit silk scarf, journals, honey, baskets, placemats, and gifts

131 Horchow Catalogue
Gifts, clothing, furnishings

138 International Bank of Asia
High-end leather goods, ties, watches, electronics, coins, jewellery, executive toys and gifts

141 J. Floris Ltd.
Perfumes and toiletries

145 Jake's Famous Products, Inc.
Gourmet foods and seafoods

146 Jay Norris Select
Novelties, chatchkas, clothing and gifts

151 John Lobb Ltd., Bootmaker
Hand-made shoes and boots, made to measure to a last made exclusively for your foot

153 Kendal Playing Card Sales
Unusual, beautiful, decorative playing cards

158 L.H. Selman Ltd.
Gift items, paperweights

159 L.L. Bean, Inc.
Outdoor goods and apparel

168 Le Baron Outdoor Products Ltd.
Outdoors equipment and apparel

171 Lillian Vernon Corporation
Giftware

173 Little Switzerland
A source for perfume, fine china, watches, crystal and objets d'art

177 M.M. Poonjiaji & Co.
Mango chutneys, mango and fruit pickles, curry powder and paste are the specialties here

180 Marks & Spencer Hampers
Gift packs, gourmet foods and wine

183 Maury Island Farming Company
Jams, jellies, preserves, toppings

186 Mellinger's Inc.
A huge assortment of gardening supplies, seeds, bulbs, live plants and green thumb conveniences

188 Metropolitan Museum of Art
Museum reproductions, jewellery, art, sculpture, gifts

314 Wing Sung Pen Factory
Cloisonné pens
318 The Wisconsin Cheeseman
Cheese, meats, candy and gift packs
319 Worldwide Curio House
Items related to the mystic arts, occult, witchcraft and voodoo

THE OUTDOORS

Hunting Supplies

41 Cabela's
Sportswear, camping, hunting, fishing, outdoors gear
46 Canadian Tire Corporation Ltd.
Sporting, camping, hardware, auto, pool, plumbing, gardening and handyman supplies, plus toys
79 Eddie Bauer Outdoor Outfitters
Outdoors apparel
159 L.L. Bean, Inc.
Outdoor goods and apparel
168 Le Baron Outdoor Products Ltd.
Outdoors equipment and apparel
195 Mountain Equipment Co-op
Outdoors, hiking, climbing, hunting, fishing and camping gear, backpacks, tents, sleeping bags and apparel
245 Sears Canada Inc.
Major mail order supplier of clothing, household goods and gifts
273 Taiga Works
Outdoor gear, camping, hunting, fishing, hiking gear and apparel

Fishing Equipment

41 Cabela's
Sportswear, camping, hunting, fishing, outdoors gear
46 Canadian Tire Corporation Ltd.
Sporting, camping, hardware, auto, pool, plumbing, gardening and handyman supplies, plus toys
79 Eddie Bauer Outdoor Outfitters
Outdoors apparel
159 L.L. Bean, Inc.
Outdoor goods and apparel
168 Le Baron Outdoor Products Ltd.
Outdoors equipment and apparel
195 Mountain Equipment Co-op
Outdoors, hiking, climbing, hunting, fishing and camping gear, backpacks, tents, sleeping bags and apparel
245 Sears Canada Inc.
Major mail order supplier of clothing, household goods and gifts
273 Taiga Works
Outdoor gear, camping, hunting, fishing, hiking gear and apparel

ALPHABETICAL LIST OF SOURCES

1 A. ANDREWS AND CO.
38-44, D'Aguilar Street, 1/F
GPO Box 2983
Hong Kong
(852) 5-266471

Just because A. Andrews is in all the tourist guides doesn't mean you should snub them. They sell electronics, souvenirs, toys, sporting goods and housewares, but their best prices are on embroidered table linens. Their extensive catalogue costs $5 by mail. Payment is accepted with VISA or bank draft only.

✔ Mail orders accepted
✔ Good bargain-hunting
Minimum order: no minimum
Shipping method: air or surface mail
Shipping time: 2-6 weeks
Returns policy: refunds made (but reluctantly)
Established since 1962

2 ABUNDANT LIFE SEED FOUNDATION
P.O. Box 772
Port Townsend, WA
U S A 98368
(206) 385-5660

If awards were given for art direction in seed catalogues, this one would be the hands-down winner. And if you are easily persuaded by lavish illustrations, easy indexing and tremendous assortments, you'd better not send for this one! Started by seedsman Forest Shomer, Abundant Life has earned a great reputation for unusual varieties, hard-to-find seeds and warm customer service. The (gorgeous) catalogue is free. Payment is accepted with IMO or cheques (drawn in U.S. funds, please).

✔ Mail orders accepted
Minimum order: no minimum
Shipping method: mail or UPS
Shipping time: 2 weeks
Returns policy: all goods guaranteed

3 THE ADDED TOUCH
132 Trafalgar Road
Oakville, Ontario
Canada L6J 9Z9
(416) 845-5032; fax: (416) 845-0989; Can. toll-free: (800) 268-5060

This shop, which is well known in the Oakville area, does a brisk mail-order business, too. Included in their goods are executive toys, gourmet goodies (sauces, pickled olives, wild rice, fruit cakes, gift packs), gardening supplies, men's items, travel items, hand-knit Kuchi socks, sundials, closet organizers, aprons, cookware, weathervanes, baskets, rugs, fireside accessories, quilts and fancy spices. Catalogues are published seasonally and are free. Payment is accepted by credit card, IMO or cheque by mail, or by VISA or M/C only if you wish to place phone orders. Ontario residents add 8 percent P.S.T.

✔ Mail orders accepted
✔ Phone orders accepted
Minimum order: no minimum
Shipping method: Canada Post, via "insured parcel delivery"
Shipping time: 1-2 weeks
Returns policy: all goods guaranteed

4 ALIVE HEALTH CENTRE

271 Oakridge Centre
650 West 41st Ave.
Vancouver, B.C.
Canada V5Z 2M9
(604) 263-3235

Alive Health Centres sell vitamins, minerals, supplements, juicers, yogurt makers, herbs, books, "cleansing programs" and the like, all by price-quote by phone. They stock thousands of products and do not produce a price list or catalogue. They also carry many hard-to-find European products. Payment is accepted with Visa, M/C, Amex, IMO or cheque.

✔ **MAIL ORDERS ACCEPTED**
✔ Phone orders accepted
✔ Good bargain-hunting
Minimum order: no minimum
Shipping method: Canada Post, postage paid on large orders
Shipping time: 1 week most locations in Canada
Returns policy: all goods guaranteed; return unused portion

5 ALL NIGHT MEDIA, INC.

Box 10607
San Rafael, CA
U S A 94901
(415) 459-3013

All Night Media was the brainchild of California artist Robert Bloomberg, whose "fan club" includes B. Kliban, M.K. Brown, Marv Newland, and cartoonists, animators, filmmakers and regular weirdos worldwide. His company sells rubber stamps that are inventive and tasteful and make great impressions — literally. Everything else you could need for creative rubber stamping is available at realistic prices through All Night Media. They have powder you can dust on and heat for a sparkly embossed effect and much more to personalize your creations. They also sell the definitive textbook on rubber stamping, *101 Ways to Stamp Your Art Out*. The catalogue is available for $2 (U.S. funds). They're published every June, plus there are seasonal flyers. Payment by VISA, M/C ($20 minimum purchase), IMO or cheques (U.S. funds only).

✔ Special offer to readers
✔ Mail orders accepted
✔ Phone orders accepted
Minimum order: No minimum
Shipping method: mail or UPS
Shipping time: 2 weeks from receipt of order
Returns policy: return flawed goods for exchange or refund

6 AMAZON DRYGOODS
2218 East 11th St.
Davenport, IA
U S A 52803-3760
(319) 322-6800

Janet Burgess has a background in historic costume and has been an interior designer and clothing designer for years. She is passionate about the past and is currently restoring a house built in 1854. Her collection of antique costumes, patterns, how-to's and reproductions must surely be unsurpassed in the world. Her catalogues (and there are many) feature antique dress patterns, memorabilia, millinery supplies, hats, dry goods, laces, heirloom crochet designs, Hallowe'en costume patterns, Victoriana, Americana, greeting cards, books, facsimile catalogues (my personal passion), antique cookbook reprints, needlework and knitting patterns, antique colouring books and anything you can imagine "for discriminating clientele who appreciate service and craftsmanship 100 years behind the times." Catalogues are priced as follows: the "small" catalogue is $2 (80 pages packed with illustrations and a zillion items to buy); the "authentic patterns from the past" catalogue is $4 (another 80 large-format pages, crammed full); and a small pattern selection is $1.50. Readers of this book may request a free copy of the new "Mailbox Magic" catalogue of modern gift, household and accessory items. Payment is accepted (U.S. funds only, please) by VISA, M/C, Amex, IMO or cheque.

- ✔ Mail orders accepted
- ✔ Phone orders accepted
- ✔ Good bargain-hunting

Minimum order: no minimum
Shipping method: mail or UPS
Shipping time: 2 weeks
Returns policy: inspection privilege of 3 days; all guaranteed
Established since 1975
Member of Victorian Society of America

7 AMERICAN DISCOUNT WALLCOVERINGS

1411 Fifth Ave.
Pittsburgh, PA
U S A 15219
(412) 471-6941; fax: (412) 471-3347;
Can./U.S. toll-free: (800) 245-1768 or (800) 777-2737 (both work)

Wow! This is a sensational find! This U.S. discounter sells every major brand of wall coverings and window treatments available, and all at savings of 32 percent or more off list. Please note that all prices are quoted in U.S. dollars. All their goods are fully guaranteed, but since some are shipped straight from the manufacturer, they ask that you open the package and inspect it carefully before cutting wallpaper or fabrics. A questionnaire is enclosed for you to fill out if you must return the goods for any reason. Not only do they unconditionally guarantee everything they sell, but they will also accept overages (within 20 days) if you've ordered too much wallpaper, for example, and they'll credit the pro-rated amount back to you. They offer even greater discounts on volume orders and they are known for their great customer service! They do not have a regular catalogue, but they'll send you product information on any items you want (and they stock everything); they can send you a listing of their lines and price quote anything you want by phone on their international toll-free lines. If all that weren't enough, they will send readers of this book free booklets about how to measure or how to hang wall coverings or many other topics. Most of their Canadian customers pay by credit card (there's a $5 service charge for cheques drawn on foreign banks) and most of us prefer to ship by air, for speed and convenience. All their goods are shipped free to U.S. addresses, by the way. Although they don't send gifts on your behalf to your friends, they do have gift certificates available. Credit cards accepted are VISA, M/C, Amex and Discover, and they'll take IMOs, too.

- ✔ Special offer to readers
- ✔ Mail orders accepted
- ✔ Phone orders accepted
- ✔ Good bargain-hunting

Minimum order: no minimum
Shipping method: mail, UPS or shipped by air freight
Shipping time: order filled same day received
Returns policy: all goods guaranteed (see text for details)
Established in 1977
Member: Better Business Bureau

8 AMERICAN EXPRESS CANADA, INC.

P.O. Box 3300
Postal Station "F"
Scarborough, Ontario
Canada M1W 9Z9
(416) 477-9666; Can. toll-free: (800) 387-9666

American Express in Canada offers a variety of goods to its card members on an exclusive basis (which means these offers are not available to non-members). Among the offerings are limited edition art prints, minted coins, collectors' plates, executive toys, luxury gifts, watches and the like. Glossy flyers are published periodically and sent to members free of charge. The privilege of membership is not without a price, however, and varies according to the type of card you have (green, gold, etc.). It is billed automatically to the account. Naturally, payment is accepted only by Amex card.

✔ Mail orders accepted
✔ Phone orders accepted
Minimum order: no minimum
Shipping method: mail or UPS, prepaid (by them)
Shipping time: 3 weeks
Returns policy: 15 day trial; all returns refunded

9 AMERICAN FLAG & GIFT

737F Manuela Way
Arroyo Grande, CA
U S A 93402
(805) 473-0395; U.S. toll-free: (800) 448-FLAG

This source sells flags and flag accessories, flagpoles, etc. They have state flags, country flags, ones for religious groups, holidays, historical flags, and more. Catalogue is published once a year and costs $2. Payment is accepted with VISA, M/C, IMO or cheque (U.S. funds, please).

✔ Mail orders accepted
✔ Phone orders accepted
✔ Good bargain-hunting

Minimum order: no minimum
Shipping method: mail or UPS
Shipping time: 10 days
Returns policy: all goods guaranteed

10 AMERICAN SPOON FOODS

P.O. Box 566
Petoskey, MI
U S A 49770
(616) 347-9030; U.S. toll-free: (800) 222-5886

Working from the recipes of Chef Larry Forgione and "forager" Justin Rashid, this company has earned a reputation for producing the finest preserves, sauces, jellies and specialty gourmet items in America today. Chef Forgione and his restaurant have won numerous awards, including the Ivy Award as one of the top ten restaurants in North America and the Chef of the Year Award (1988). American Spoon Foods have put Petoskey, Michigan, on the map. Included in their fine fare for mail order are wild and domestic nuts (hickory, pecans, black walnuts, chestnuts), no-sugar gift packs, conserves, fruit cakes, birch-bark baskets, Michigan maple syrup, dried exotic mushrooms, Chef Forgione's peanut sauce and his barbecue sauce, cherry gooseberry chutney, sourdough bread, Jalapena Cowboy caviar (and the original Cowboy caviar vegetable paté), pasta sauces, olives, Genovesi dried tomatoes, Neva Betta crackers, sausages, relishes, vinegars and catsups. There are also novelty clothing items, such as ASF aprons, baseball caps and T-shirts, Jonathan Simons' hand-carved, wild cherry wood utensils, "ugli" baskets (made from heavy poplar bark) and books about food and foraging. Their motto: "We capture and preserve what nature makes perfect." Illustrated catalogues are printed for spring/summer and winter and are free. Payment is accepted by VISA, M/C, Discover card and IMO.

✔ Mail orders accepted
✔ Phone orders accepted
Minimum order: $10 (U.S.)
Shipping method: mail only
Shipping time: 2-4 days
Returns policy: satisfaction guaranteed
Established in 1981

11 THE AMERICAN TRAVELLER

3825 West Green Tree Road
P.O. Box 17001
Milwaukee, WI
U S A 53217
(414) 352-0425; U.S. toll-free: (800) 237-5900

The American Traveller shares the same great gift catalogue with other in-flight marketing schemes (see U.S. Air's entry). You'll find executive toys, electronics, luggage, language tapes, novelties and gifts, and some hard-to-find gadgets, such as ski-bags, sporting gear and even a laptop and other electronics. Unfortunately, they will mail or ship goods only to U.S. addresses. Payment is accepted with VISA, M/C, Amex or Diners Club.

Minimum order: no minimum but will ship only to U.S. addresses
Shipping method: U.S. Postal Service or UPS (U.S. destinations only)
Shipping time: 2-4 weeks
Returns policy: all goods guaranteed

12 AMNESTY INTERNATIONAL
Canadian Section (English Speaking)
Ste. 900, 130 Slater St.
Ottawa, Ontario
Canada K1P 6E2
(613) 563-1891

Amnesty International is known to all of us, but the secret is they sell a variety of gift items and novelties by mail, such as lapel pins, posters, greeting cards, tote bags, records, pens, giftwrap, T-shirts, craft items for third-world countries; they even offer hand-blown glass. The catalogue is published once a year and is available free. Payment is accepted with VISA, M/C, IMO or cheque.

✔ Mail orders accepted
Minimum order: no minimum
Shipping method: Canada Post
Shipping time: 2-4 weeks, depending on season
Returns policy: all goods guaranteed

13 ANABELLE'S COLLECTION
TST P.O. Box 97544
Kowloon
Hong Kong
(852) 526-6284; fax: (852) 5-845-5977

Annabelle dropped one "n" from her name for this business, and her prices are reduced, too. She sells brass bracelets, costume jewellery, snakeskin belts, decor accents, silver necklaces and more. She has a price list only, but if you're after something in particular, send her a clipping and she might be able to match it, at a very low price. Payment is accepted with VISA, M/C, IMO or cheques.

- ✔ Mail orders accepted
- ✔ Phone orders accepted
- ✔ Good bargain-hunting

Minimum order: no minimum
Shipping method: airmail
Shipping time: 2-3 weeks
Returns policy: all goods guaranteed

14 ANYTHING LEFT HANDED LIMITED

65 Beak Street
London W1R 3LF
England
(71) 437-3910

Anything you could imagine of use to the left-handed person is found in this shop in London. Owner Patrick Fletcher wrote me that they have a great many Canadian customers because there are so few Canadian sources for these goods. If you are left-handed, you know exactly the problems you encounter: scissors, knives, rulers, address books, even jar-openers and spatulas are designed for "righties." They must charge $5 (Cdn.) for their annual catalogue (which they'll send airmail at that price) but their prices (quoted in pounds sterling) are fairly reasonable. Their slogan: "Our Customers Are Seldom Right." Heh, heh. Their catalogue is published approximately once a year and costs £2 sterling (about $5 Cdn.). Payment via IMO or "pound sterling cheque payable at UK bank."

- ✔ Mail orders accepted

Minimum order: not required
Shipping method: air or surface mail
Shipping time: about 7 days
Returns policy: pledge to replace defective goods
Established in 1963

15 THE ARCTIC TRADING COMPANY

Box 910
Churchill, Manitoba
Canada R0B 0E0
(204) 675-8804; (204) 675-2164; Can. toll-free: (800) 665-0431

It seems right that a catalogue of northern native people's work should be prefaced in Inuit, and that sort of sets the tone for this nice, full-colour, annual publication. Goods include Inuit art, posters, artifacts and traditional moose-hair tufting kits, as well as fur parkas, mukluks, moccasins, fur mitts and gauntlets, books on Canada's north, peace pipes and some lovely Iroquois pieces, Canadiana and collector's spoons.

Items are all sold at wholesale prices, and sometimes even these are sale priced or reduced by about 10 percent. Shipping charge averages $4, and timing depends on whether they have what you want in stock. Though there's a charge for the catalogue, a free brochure is available to our readers for writing or calling the toll-free number. Payment is accepted with VISA, M/C, Amex, Diners Club card, a Canadian money order, or C.O.D. (Canadian addresses only). Manitoba residents add P.S.T.

✔ Mail orders accepted
✔ Phone orders accepted
Minimum order: no minimum
Shipping method: Canada Post
Shipping time: depends on what's ordered
Returns policy: please phone before returning goods
Established in 1978

16 ART RESOURCES
142/20 Soi Sueksavitaya
North Sathorn Road
Bangkok 10500
Thailand
(662) 235-4846; 235-4847; fax: (662) 237-1731;
telex: 22045 GIRLFRI TH

My favourite piece of reproduction Art Deco sculpture came from Art Resources, which is the retail outlet for a manufacturer of fine art reproductions, Art Nouveau lamps, decor accents and gorgeous jewellery, pottery and carpets. They sell authentic antiques and artifacts, as well. A catalogue is printed periodically and updated with price lists. It is free to our readers. Payment is accepted with VISA, M/C, Amex, Diners Club, IMO or cheques.

✔ Mail orders accepted
✔ Phone orders accepted
✔ Good bargain-hunting
Minimum order: no minimum
Shipping method: airmail, insured or surface mail
Shipping time: 2-6 weeks
Returns policy: all goods guaranteed

17 ARTLAND
Shop No. 38, 1/F, Admiralty Centre
18, Harcourt Road
Hong Kong
(852) 529-9639

This place retails, wholesales and exports linens, embroidered goods, pillow shams, handicrafts, women's apparel, beaded sweaters and imaginative, extravagantly beaded evening tops. They will send a free price list and sometimes have sales flyers. Payment is accepted with VISA, M/C, Amex or IMO.

✔ Mail orders accepted
✔ Good bargain-hunting
Minimum order: no minimum
Shipping method: airmail or surface post
Shipping time: 2-6 weeks
Returns policy: all goods guaranteed

18 ASCOT CHANG CO. LTD.
2 floor, block D
41 Man Yue St.
Hunghom, Kowloon
Hong Kong
(852) 364-4384

Ascot Chang is a well-known Hong Kong garment maker, providing custom silk or cotton shirts worldwide. They also make fine silk blouses for women, and robes, pyjamas and accessories, at very good prices by North American standards. Once they have your size on file, reorders are simplified. Shipping is extra, but they can make sending goods through Customs easier for you (inquire for details). Their price list is published once a year (in June). Payment accepted by VISA, M/C, Amex, IMO or cheque.

✔ Mail orders accepted
✔ Phone orders accepted
✔ Good bargain-hunting
Minimum order: 3 pieces (garments)
Shipping method: surface or airmail
Shipping time: 8 - 10 weeks
Returns policy: no returns

19 ATFIELD FINE ARTS
42A Hollywood Road
Central
Hong Kong
(852) 5-422138

Here's a source for antique Chinese carpets and the world-famous Jim Thompson silk upholstery fabrics. In fact, a travel writer (and veteran shopper) I know claims the silks in this Hong Kong shop are better than those available in Thompson's original store in Bangkok. A price list is available, but shipping is very slow for goods. Payment is accepted with VISA, M/C, Amex and IMO.

✔ Mail orders accepted
Minimum order: no minimum
Shipping method: surface mail (ship)
Shipping time: 6-8 weeks
Returns policy: no returns on cut fabrics; carpets guaranteed
Member of Hong Kong Tourist Association

20 B.C. PLAYTHINGS

1065 Marine Drive
North Vancouver, B.C.
Canada V7P 1S6
(604) 985-6968; (604) 986-4111; Can. toll-free: (800) 663-4477

Pat Gallaher was a preschool teacher and is the parent of three girls, aged 5, 10 and 14. He and his family (including his mom and his sister) run this wonderful retail/resource designed to bring the best quality playthings to families at the most reasonable cost. Pat operates on a fixed markup, so even though he could get $15 for a child's "animal lotto" game, he'll charge only $13.80 because that represents a fair profit for him, and a good deal for you. Almost all of B.C. Playthings' goods are discounted. Included in their stock are climbing equipment, educational toys, hand-made wooden toys, games, children's books, kids' furniture, swings, shelving, storage modules, art supplies, stuffed animals, dolls and teddy bears, and much more.The catalogue is published once a year, is generously illustrated with photos of all the items and is free. Payment is accepted by VISA, M/C, IMO or cheque, but first-time orderers must prepay if they aren't charging the order to a credit card. B.C. residents add 6 percent P.S.T.

✔ Mail orders accepted
✔ Phone orders accepted
✔ Good bargain-hunting
Minimum order: no minimum
Shipping method: mail or "rush" delivery
Shipping time: within 48 hours
Returns policy: call first; returns within 30 days
Established in 1976

21 BANANA REPUBLIC

9669 Little Santa Monica Blvd.
Los Angeles, CA
U S A
(213) 858-7900

If your style is "safari chic," Banana Republic is the place for you. Their catalogue stock is not unlike that of Abercrombie and Fitch, but much less costly. In addition to women's and men's sporty apparel, they have some durable leather and canvas totes. Catalogues (plus sales flyers) are published seasonally. Payment is accepted with Visa, M/C, Amex, Diner's Club, IMO or cheque.

✔ Mail orders accepted
✔ Phone orders accepted
✔ Good bargain-hunting
Minimum order: no minimum
Shipping method: UPS to U.S. points; or U.S. Mail
Shipping time: 2-4 weeks, depending on stock
Returns policy: all goods guaranteed; no returns on clearances

22 BANDBOXES
P.O. Box 74, 115 N. Market Street
Shreve, OH
U S A 44676
(216) 567-2889

Lindsay E. Frost has personally revived the art of bandboxes, having created and sold more than 12,000 herself. Shapes and sizes vary according to whether you plan to use them for jewellery or for storing large items such as blankets or quilts. Every box is labelled and numbered. Many museums have acquired them for exhibit or permanent collections, and Lindsay's bandboxes are even sold through a large Americana shop in Tokyo. Shipping costs approximately 8 percent of the order for these lovely 19th-century reproduction, wallpaper-covered bandboxes. A single, descriptive flyer is available free. Wallpaper swatches cost $2 for a selection (non-refundable). Payment by IMO only.

✔ Mail orders accepted
✔ Phone orders accepted
Minimum order: no minimum
Shipping method: mail or UPS
Shipping time: 3 to 6 weeks, depending on order
Returns policy: custom-made; no returns

23 BANGKOK DOLLS
85 Soi Rajatapan
Rajaprarop Road
Bangkok
Thailand
(662) 245-3008

This factory shop also houses a museum, where traditional Thai dolls representing various hill tribes and ethnic groups are displayed. These are ideal dolls for the collector. Price lists are available, free. Payment is accepted with VISA, M/C, Amex or IMO.

✔ Mail orders accepted
✔ Good bargain-hunting
Minimum order: no minimum
Shipping method: surface or airmail
Shipping time: 2-6 weeks
Returns policy: no returns

24 BANYEN BOOKS

2671 West Broadway
Vancouver, B.C.
Canada
V6K 2G2
(604) 732-7912

Banyen is one of the continuing successes of the hippie era (still alive and well on the West Coast, thank you), largely because it's still run by friendly, peaceful people who are really committed to the subject matter they stock. There are books on metaphysics, the occult, psychology, astrology, yoga, birthing, nutrition, massage, healing arts, relationships and all manner of esoterica. They also sell meditation cassettes and Tarot decks, among many other compatible items. Mail order has not been a big success for them, so they may be reluctant to continue with it, but they are such a unique source for materials that it would be a pity not to try them when you're seeking something unusual. The catalogue that is available now will not be revised, but it is still fairly current. It costs $3. Payment is accepted with Visa, M/C, IMO or cheque.

✔ Mail orders accepted
✔ Phone orders accepted
Minimum order: no minimum
Shipping method: UPS or Canada Post book rate
Shipping time: 1-3 weeks, depending on method
Returns policy: all goods guaranteed, if returned in mint condition
Established in 1969

25 BARNES & NOBLE BOOKSTORES, INC. (CANADA SALES)

c/o McIntyre & Dodd Marketing
279 Humberline Drive
Rexdale, Ontario
Canada M9W 5T6
(201) 767-6660; fax: (201) 767-6638

As the world's largest bookstore, Barnes & Noble has access to more books, more cheaply than anyone else. Their free catalogues are printed winter, spring, summer and fall and include thousands of books, records, videos and tapes sold at discounts of up to 80 percent off regular publishers' prices — and multiple copy orders may be reduced in cost by another 20 percent! Goods you select pass through a customs broker to Rexdale, and from there they are sent to you via Canada Post. Much of the material sold is exclusive to Barnes & Noble. At the present time, their business in Canada is strictly institutional (schools, libraries, hospitals and prisons) though they welcome orders from individuals if you prepay. If you're doing steady, volume business, eventually you can order by purchase order and be billed separately. A sample catalogue is free to our readers. They prefer payment in U.S. funds by cheque, IMO or bank draft. Please note they cannot accept orders at the number given in this listing. It is for customer inquiries only. Please write or fax your order to their postal address instead.

✔ Special offer to readers
✔ Mail orders accepted
✔ Phone orders accepted
✔ Good bargain-hunting
Minimum order: no minimum
Shipping method: from NYC to customs brokers; then via Canada Post
Shipping time: 4-6 weeks to Canada
Returns policy: unconditional guarantee on everything
Established in 1873
Member: U.S. Direct Marketing Association, American Library Association

26 BEADWORLD
#63, 560 Johnson Street
Victoria, B.C.
Canada V8W 3C6
(604) 386-5534

Beadworld claims to stock the largest selection of beads and jewellery findings in Canada. Included in their offerings are Indian seed beads, Indian and African trade beads, semi-precious stone beads, necklaces, earrings, bracelets and leather lacing supplies. They also carry amber, bone and crystal. Their colour brochure and price lists are free. Payment is accepted with Visa, M/C, Amex, IMO or cheque.

✔ Mail orders accepted
✔ Phone orders accepted
✔ Good bargain-hunting

Minimum order: no minimum
Shipping method: airmail or surface mail
Shipping time: 2 weeks
Returns policy: all goods guaranteed

27 BEAUTY BY SPECTOR, INC.
Dept APB-90
McKeesport, PA
U S A 15134-0502
(412) 673-3259

Myer Spector is so sure you'll like his hairgoods that he publishes his private number in his literature so "you can reach me personally...anytime between the hours of 5 p.m. and 8 p.m., Eastern time." His company sells hairpieces for men, and wigs, falls and glamour hair products by mail, discounted by up to 50 percent off comparable retail. Some of the hairgoods are 100 percent human hair, others are synthetic. Catalogues are free, four times yearly. They are used to dealing with Canadians, so they can make clearing Customs easier for you, too, if you inquire. Because of the possibility of transmitting infectious scalp diseases, these goods are not returnable. To custom-match your own hair colour, you'll be asked to send a snippet of your hair with your order. Men are asked to fill out an extensive (but not overly personal) questionnaire when ordering hairpieces. Catalogues are published seasonally (four times a year) and are free if you mention this book. Payment accepted via VISA, M/C, IMO or cheque.

✔ Special offer to readers
✔ Mail orders accepted
✔ Phone orders accepted
✔ Good bargain-hunting
Minimum order: no minimum
Shipping method: mail only
Shipping time: 10 days to 2 weeks
Returns policy: hairgoods not returnable for hygienic reasons

28 BEN LEE CO.
G/F, 21E Hankow Road
Kowloon, Hong Kong
G.P.O. Box 8757, H.K.
Hong Kong
(852) 739-2480

This is where I go in Hong Kong to buy chops, which are hand-carved and polished personal stamps, usually made in granite and featuring the animal representing the year of your birth. They also sell sweaters,

linens, embroidered goods, Chinese art and oil paintings and souvenirs. Price lists for specific items are available free, on request. Payment is best via IMO or bank draft.

✔ Mail orders accepted
✔ Phone orders accepted
✔ Good bargain-hunting
Minimum order: no minimum
Shipping method: surface or airmail; request "insured" for valuables
Shipping time: 4-6 weeks
Returns policy: difficult, but possible

29 BEROL LIMITED
Oldmeadow Road, King's Lynn
Norfolk PE30 4JR
England
0553-61221; telex: 817409

This family business has its roots in the mid-19th century, in the days before they incorporated the original Venus and Eagle pencils companies. They are generally considered among the best art material suppliers in the world. Their catalogues are teaching aids, with projects, information on the use of materials and a great deal of wisdom and guidance thrown in. Since there are a number of Berol Books, it is best to write to enquire about what is available and at what cost. The materials, although priced about the same as domestic versions, are higher quality and go much further than Canadian-made "equivalents." They are particularly good at paints, poster colours, glue, drawing materials and indelible fabric paints.

✔ Mail orders accepted
Minimum order: no minimum
Shipping method: air or surface mail
Shipping time: 4-6 weeks
Returns policy: all goods guaranteed satisfactory
Established in 1969

30 BEST PRODUCTS
P.O. Box 26303
Richmond, VA
U S A 23260
(804) 752-3129; U.S. toll-free: (800) 221-BEST

This group of mail order companies sells almost all its goods at a hefty discount, and those items are mostly name-brand, first-line products. They include housewares, sporting goods, tools, small electricals, cameras, watches, jewellery, toys and more. The catalogue is a full 500 pages (published in the fall) and costs $2. Payment on orders is accepted with VISA, M/C, IMO or cheque (U.S. funds only).

✔ Mail orders accepted
✔ Good bargain-hunting
Minimum order: no minimum
Shipping method: airmail or surface mail, UPS
Shipping time: 2-3 weeks
Returns policy: 30-day money-back guarantee
Established in 1957

31 BLOOMINGDALE'S

Catalog Department
1000 3rd Ave.
New York City, NY
U S A 10022
(212) 355-5900

Everybody knows "Bloomie's," but not everyone knows that you can get onto their catalogue mailing list for free and the catalogues are wonderful! Each is usually published for a specific product grouping, such as women's apparel, men's wear, home furnishings and to promote special sales. Goods are luxurious, including the best designer lines, perfumes, sportswear, evening apparel, cosmetics and high-end gifts. Every kind of credit card is accepted (Visa, M/C, Amex, Access, Carte Blanche, Choice, Diner's Club, Discover, Eurocard, etc.) plus they are fairly aggressive about marketing their own credit system, and they will accept IMOs and cheques in U.S. funds, but the latter will slow down your order's turn-around time.

✔ Mail orders accepted
✔ Phone orders accepted
Minimum order: no minimum
Shipping method: UPS, Fed Ex or U.S. mail
Shipping time: 1 week, if in stock
Returns policy: all goods unconditionally guaranteed
Established in 1900

32 THE BODHI TREE

8585 Melrose Ave.
Los Angeles, CA
U S A
(213) 659-1733

If you're searching for a volume on metaphysics, the occult, astrology, human potential, or an unusual deck of Tarot cards, the Bodhi Tree is practically an American institution. Like Banyen Books in Vancouver, they stock items practically impossible to find elsewhere in North America, and they are more than willing to seek out the unusual on your behalf. They also stock meditation cassettes, and the like. Price lists are available on request, or they will price-quote for you by phone. Payment is accepted with IMO or cheques in U.S. funds only.

✔ Mail orders accepted
✔ Phone orders accepted
✔ Good bargain-hunting
Minimum order: no minimum
Shipping method: UPS or U.S. Postal Service
Shipping time: 2 weeks
Returns policy: all goods guaranteed if returned in mint condition

33 THE BODY SHOP
15 Prince Andrew Place
Don Mills, Ontario
Canada M3C 2H2
(416) 441-3202

The Body Shop has an international reputation for excellence, and that should come as no surprise, since they are established in 350 stores around the world. Their unillustrated, modest catalogue lists every product they sell, but no prices or sizes are given, as these are subject to periodic change. The hallmark of Body Shop products is that nothing from the line is ever tested on animals, yet every item is natural, made from pure ingredients, and is guaranteed not to irritate or upset the balance of your skin. Included in the product line are cosmetics, soaps, facial treatments, men's toiletries, shampoos, bath items and accessories, aromatherapy items, scented oils, gift packs and makeup. They make a particularly good soothing eye gel, which is surprisingly inexpensive (a fact that is soothing in itself). The catalogue is mailed out free. Payment is accepted at retail outlets or by mail with VISA, M/C, IMO or cheques.

✔ Mail orders accepted
✔ Phone orders accepted
Minimum order: no minimum
Shipping method: Canada Post
Shipping time: 2 weeks
Returns policy: all goods 100 percent guaranteed

34 BORN TO LOVE
21 Potsdam Rd., No. 61
Downsview, Ontario
Canada M3N 1N3
(416) 663-7143

This specialized mail order service deals only in Canadian products for families and children. They have safety devices and infant carriers you won't find elsewhere, as well as cloth diapers, Babysnibbs, Nikky diaper covers, nursing bras and children's books. They also offer a list of other people's catalogues for baby gear and carry ads for other Canadian sources. The catalogue is free. Payment is accepted with VISA, M/C, IMO or cheques.

✔ Mail orders accepted
✔ SASE required
Minimum order: no minimum
Shipping method: Canada Post
Shipping time: 1-2 weeks
Returns policy: all goods guaranteed
Established in 1984

35 BOUQUET ENTERPRISES
233 Glasgow Ave.
Kellogg, MN
U S A 55945
(507) 767-4955; U.S. toll-free (800) 328-5598

This manufacturer of wooden novelties and dolls is a wholesaler, so you must buy a minimum amount of goods to deal with them. They make countrified wooden wall plaques with flower motifs, sayings or antique-looking advertising slogans and other decorative wooden accessories. There's also a big choice of soft dolls and teddy bears, and even some duck and rabbit dolls in the collection. Your first catalogue is free if you tell them you're our reader. Catalogues are published every January and June. Payment is accepted by VISA, M/C, Amex, IMO or C.O.D.s to U.S. addresses.

✔ Special offer to readers
✔ Mail orders accepted
✔ Phone orders accepted
✔ Good bargain-hunting
Minimum order: $50 (U.S.)
Shipping method: mail or UPS
Shipping time: 2 weeks
Returns policy: return goods for credit or refund

36 BRIERE DESIGN
229 N. Race St.
Stateville, NC
U S A 28677
(704) 872-3517

Ron and Greg Briere make an assortment of wonderful, hand-crafted, folk art pieces that are entirely original (which means you won't see them anywhere else). Some are authentic period reproductions, while others are whimsical. Every piece is completely hand-made and is signed and dated when finished. The catalogue is updated periodically and costs $2 (refundable on first order). Our readers, however, may request one catalogue free. Payment is accepted with VISA, M/C or IMO and C.O.D.s are possible to U.S. destinations.

✔ Special offer to readers
✔ Mail orders accepted
✔ Phone orders accepted
Minimum order: no minimum
Shipping method: mail or UPS
Shipping time: 4 weeks
Returns policy: returns made with approval (call or write first)

37 BURPEE
018192 Burpee Building
Warminster, PA
U S A 18974
(215) 674-4915

Probably the best-known name in American seeds, W. Atlee Burpee has a reputation for quality, and they back it up with a 100-percent money-back guarantee on everything they sell. Their current catalogue (200 pages and free) lists 30 different tomato varieties. There are 400 kinds of vegetables, 600 varieties of flowers, plus fruit trees (check with Agriculture Canada before ordering), bulbs, shrubs and garden supplies. Payment is accepted with IMO or cheques.

✔ Mail orders accepted
Minimum order: no minimum
Shipping method: mail or UPS
Shipping time: 2 weeks
Returns policy: "your money back if not completely satisfied"
Established in 1876

38 BUTTERBROOKE FARM
78 Barry Road
Oxford, CT
U S A 06483
(203) 888-2000

Tom Butterworth started this venture over a decade ago and his seed co-op has members in every state in the U.S. and every province in Canada. His motto is "seeds for people, not for profit" and he's been true to his word, selling only organically raised, "ole standard" varieties, which are becoming harder and harder to locate. There's also a variety of helpful gardening literature available and a two-hour video tape on gardening available for purchase or rent. A 15-percent discount on seeds is available to co-op members (membership costs only $7.50 U.S. a year). The catalogue is free if you send a long, self-addressed stamped envelope (or 50 cents for postage). Payment is by IMO or cheques payable in U.S. funds only.

✔ Mail orders accepted
✔ SASE required
Minimum order: no minimum
Shipping method: mail or UPS
Shipping time: same day order fulfillment
Returns policy: all goods guaranteed
Established in 1979

39 C. KENNEDY & SONS, LTD.
Ardara
Co. Donegal
Ireland
(075) 41106

Listen to this: "The mountains of Donegal sweep down to the shores of the wild Atlantic, and along these shores live the wives and the daughters of the farmers and fishermen in their beautiful whitewashed cottages — enchanting, rugged, and the most hospitable of places. It is here that the now world-famous 'Hills of Donegal' sweaters have come to life." Now, sure and you'd be wanting to buy some of these fine garments? I was so excited when I discovered Kennedy's that I wrote to them three separate times, but whether you call them Hills of Donegal, Kennedy of Ardana or just C. Kennedy, they turn out to be the folks who hand-knit the same goods you'll find at twice the price in Eaton's, Simpson's and the Bay. This is the wholesale source! You can buy, direct from them, those Irish sweaters (if Sally Maloney knit yours, her name will be on the label!), men's and women's Donegal tweed (hand-woven) jackets, Irish double damask tablecloths, coats, capes, crocheted hats, loomed scarves, lap

shawls and tartan blankets. As if that weren't enough, they'll send readers of this book their $2 catalogue (printed every January), free. Payment is accepted via VISA, M/C, Amex, Access, Diners Club, Eurocard, TOKYO, IMO and cheque.

✔ Mail orders accepted
✔ Phone orders accepted
✔ Good bargain-hunting
Minimum order: no minimum
Shipping method: airmail or surface mail
Shipping time: 10 - 21 days
Returns policy: refund in full if not satisfied
Established in 1946

40 C.A. CRUICKSHANK LTD.

1015 Mt. Pleasant Rd.
Toronto, Ontario
Canada M4P 2M1
(416) 488-8292

C.A. Cruickshank sells its "Garden Guild" seeds by mail, from a large assortment of fruits, vegetables, herbs and spices. The catalogue also includes gardening aids and supplies, and is published in the winter, leaving lots of time to decide on seeds before the warm weather sets in. The catalogue is free. Payment is via IMO or cheque.

✔ Mail orders accepted
Minimum order: no minimum
Shipping method: Canada Post
Shipping time: 2 weeks
Returns policy: all goods guaranteed satisfactory

41 CABELA'S

Sidney
Nebraska
U S A 69160
Can. toll-free: (800) 237-4444; toll-free customer service (Can.): (800) 237-8888

Cabela's is renowned for its effective insect repellent, but their catalogues are full of surprises, such as fashionable sportswear (men, women and kids); camping, hiking, hunting and fishing gear; outdoors supplies; tents; hurricane lamps; hiking boots; protective clothing; flotation vests; Gore-Tex rainwear; fishing lures; comfy moccasins; T-shirts and more. The 200-page, full-colour spring catalogue expires December 31, but by then you should have the fall edition, all free.

Payment is accepted by VISA, M/C or Amex only. If you want your goods shipped by air, call the toll-free number to find out how much more it will cost.

✔ Mail orders accepted
✔ Phone orders accepted
✔ Good bargain-hunting
Minimum order: no minimum
Shipping method: freight (truck), parcel post or Premium Air Services
Shipping time: depends on method
Returns policy: all goods unconditionally guaranteed
Established in 1962

42 THE CAMBRIAN FACTORY

Llanwrtyd Wells
Powys, Wales LD5 4SD
Great Britain
(05913) 211

Run as a sheltered workshop for the disabled, this factory makes exceptionally high-quality tweed garments for men and women. You might expect the styles to be stuffy and dated, but surprise: they're current, trendy and wonderfully well made. All the carding, spinning, dyeing and weaving is done on the premises with 100-percent Welsh wool. The original factory dates back to the 1820s, and the existing facility is one of the few working mills still left in the region. Good value for the dollar on all catalogue items. That catalogue is published once a year, usually in the spring and is free to our readers. Payment accepted by VISA, M/C, Amex, Access, and in Canadian currency "reluctantly."

✔ Special offer to readers
✔ Mail orders accepted
✔ Phone orders accepted
✔ Good bargain-hunting
Minimum order: no minimum
Shipping method: airmail or ship
Shipping time: if not in stock, 5-6 weeks
Returns policy: "if genuine reason for return is given, we accept"
Established in 1820s
Member: Powys County Council and Royal British Legion

43 CAMPARTE'S OF CALIFORNIA

925 Montana Ave.
Santa Monica, CA
U S A 90403
(213) 395-2297

Wonderful gift packs are the highlight of this offering, with yummies such as hand-dipped chocolates, dried (or chocolate-dipped) fruits, nut-stuffed fruit, peanut butter-grahams, chocolate-covered pretzels, all presented in reusable cedar boxes. A price list and illustrated brochure is free, by request. Payment is accepted with Visa, M/C, Amex, IMO or cheque (drawn in U.S. funds).

✔ Mail orders accepted
Minimum order: no minimum
Shipping method: UPS or mail
Shipping time: 1-2 weeks
Returns policy: foods are non-returnable but if spoiled, replaced
Established in 1950

44 CANADA POST CORPORATION

Stamp Travellers Club
P.O. Box 16000, Station "A"
Toronto, Ontario
Canada M5W 2V8
(416) 973-2433; Can. toll-free: (800) 565-CLUB

Canada Post operates the "Stamp Travellers Club," which is a great way to introduce children to the joys of collecting stamps. The kit comes with a magnifying glass, album, tweezers, stamp hinges, stamps and much more; as well, there are regular mailings to members. Membership costs $9.95 and is an easy and inexpensive gift for children from 7 to 15. As well, Canada Post sells an assortment of goodies from its free catalogue, such as collector's stamps, first-day covers, stamp sets, miniature toy mail trucks, Lego postal vans, coin packs and more, all through its Philatelic Centres, Canada-wide. My favourite is the toy savings bank that looks just like the standard postal boxes you see on street corners (not to be confused with the "Royal Mail" boxes that were all blown up years ago). Payment is accepted with cash or cheque.

✔ Mail orders accepted
✔ Phone orders accepted
Minimum order: no minimum
Shipping method: Canada Post, what else?
Shipping time: 2-3 weeks
Returns policy: all goods returnable, if faulty

45 CANADIAN BROADCASTING CORPORATION ENTERPRISES

Box 6440, Stn. "A"
Montreal, P.Q.
Canada H3C 3L4
(514) 597-4040

The C.B.C. markets tapes of its programs and special features and some other novelties, such as children's books and activity packages, teaching aids, and so on, but for some reason, the waiting period seems interminable. However, the catalogue is free. Payment is accepted by cheque or money order only. Quebec residents pay P.S.T.

✔ Mail orders accepted
Minimum order: no minimum
Shipping method: Canada Post, or mule train (very slow service)
Shipping time: a month or more
Returns policy: returns possible, but difficult

46 CANADIAN TIRE CORPORATION LTD.

Box 770, Station "K"
Toronto, Ontario
Canada M4P 2V8
(416) 480-3175; Can. toll-free: (800) 387-8803

I've included Canadian Tire just in case you're a Canadian with amnesia — or do you remember getting your catalogue at your door, after all? Scarcely a good Canuck living doesn't know Canadian Tire, but I thought I'd best mention them in the interests of being comprehensive. They sell sporting, camping, auto, pool, gardening and handyman supplies, plus plumbing, hardware and toys. Most of their sales are done from the catalogue, but fulfilled from one of their 400 stores coast to coast. If you live in an area not served by Canadian Tire directly, they will ship to you on a mail order basis, but they prefer to do this if you have a Canadian Tire credit card. Otherwise, payment is accepted with VISA, M/C or cheque.

✔ Mail orders accepted
✔ Phone orders accepted
Minimum order: no minimum
Shipping method: Canada Post or pick up at local branch
Shipping time: 2 weeks
Returns policy: all goods unconditionally guaranteed
Established in 1921

47 CAROL BLACK MINIATURES

"Sun Hill," Gt. Strickland, Penrith
Cumbria CA10 3DF
England
Hackthorpe (093-12) 330

Carol Black specializes in export orders and has customers around the world. She sells British miniatures (1/12th scale) and her full-colour catalogue, which is printed bi-annually, costs £3 sterling (£4 airmail to Canada). This is mitigated by a £1-discount voucher in the catalogue. Shipping is free for orders over £30. Payment is accepted by VISA, M/C or IMO payable only in U.S. funds (she won't accept Canadian).

✔ Mail orders accepted
✔ Phone orders accepted
Minimum order: no minimum
Shipping method: airmail
Shipping time: "by return post"
Returns policy: if goods well-packed within 5 days of receipt

48 CARROUSEL OF IDEAS

5934 Côte de Liesse Rd.
Town of Mount-Royal, P.Q.
Canada
H4T 2A5
(514) 737-4140; (514) 737-5810

Carrousel of Ideas is the catalogue published by Muralex Distribution, also known as Domestications, Inc. They import inexpensive giftware and novelties and sell them directly to you. Although some is standard junk mail-order fare, other items are actually bargain-priced and worth ordering, such as toys, pens, inexpensive watches, purses, housewares and cookware, costume jewellery, closet organizers, exercise equipment and ladies' sweaters and clothing. Catalogues are published six to seven times a year and are free. Telephone orders speed the process up considerably. Payment is accepted by VISA, M/C, cheques or C.O.D. (in Canada only).

✔ Mail orders accepted
✔ Phone orders accepted
✔ Good bargain-hunting
Minimum order: no minimum
Shipping method: Canada Post
Shipping time: 15 days
Returns policy: all goods guaranteed

49 CASSELRYDS GLA O PORSELIN
Box 158
Skarholmen, S 127 23
Sweden
(468) 7105116

One of the cheapest worldwide sources for Orrefors, Rosenthal crystal, Kosta Boda and other renowned lines of fine flatware, china and glasses, this place ships everything insured. It's an old family business, and what they lack in communication skills in English, they make up for in good service. The medium-sized catalogue is $2. Payment is accepted with VISA, M/C or Amex only.

✔ Mail orders accepted
✔ Good bargain-hunting
Minimum order: $50 (U.S.)
Shipping method: shipped insured
Shipping time: 5-8 weeks
Returns policy: all good guaranteed and shipped insured
Established in 1943

50 CATHY'S COLLECTIBLES
17/F, Block 31, Baguio Villa
550 Victoria Road
Hong Kong
(852) 875-0481

Cathy Chuang sells fabulous fakes and great-looking costume jewellery from her home, by appointment (or mail) only. If you're looking for a good copy of some designer bracelet, for example, search no farther. Send Cathy a magazine photo and she might be able to find something similar, at a fraction of the cost. A price list is available, or she'll price-quote a few items you might like. Payment is accepted with VISA, M/C, Amex, IMO, bank drafts or cheques in Canadian currency.

✔ Mail orders accepted
✔ Phone orders accepted
✔ Good bargain-hunting
Minimum order: no minimum
Shipping method: airmail, insured
Shipping time: 2 weeks
Returns policy: all goods guaranteed

51 CHALIF INC.
P.O. Box 27220
Wyndmoor, PA
U S A 19118
(215) 233-2023

Liz and Nick Thomas started this family-run business on a shoestring and have never looked back. Actually, the recipes are old family secrets dating back to the romantic escapades of Liz's aunt (who married Louis Chalif, a famous ballet dancer of the Czarist era in Russia). These days, Chalif has a different reputation, among the best gourmet condiments in the world. Included in the modest line are mustards, sauces and mayonnaises, all made with the highest quality ingredients and 100 percent natural and salt-free. The colour catalogue is updated once a year in August or September and is free. Plus, as one of our readers, you'll get a free recipe booklet as a bonus when you write. Volume purchasers can get a 5 to 10 percent discount. Payment must be received prior to shipping, via cheques or IMO payable in U.S. dollars.

✔ Special offer to readers
✔ Mail orders accepted
✔ Phone orders accepted
Minimum order: no minimum
Shipping method: mail or UPS
Shipping time: 1-2 weeks
Returns policy: all goods guaranteed
1981

52 CHIANGMAI SILVERWARE
62/10-11 Chiengmai-Sankampaeng Rd.
Chiangmai
Thailand
(053) 246-037

One of the largest silver factories in Thailand is located up in Chiangmai. Here, you'll find silver artifacts and hand-crafted jewellery, hammered silver bowls, necklaces, bracelets and earrings. A price list of goods available for export is free. Payment is accepted with VISA, M/C, Amex and IMO.

✔ Mail orders accepted
✔ Good bargain-hunting
Minimum order: no minimum
Shipping method: airmail
Shipping time: 2-3 weeks
Returns policy: goods guaranteed, but returns slow and difficult

53 CHURCH GOODS CO.
810 W. Jackson Blvd.
Chicago, IL
U S A 60607

This mail-order-only house appears to sell religious items, but in fact most of their stock is given over to potions (of the snake-oil variety, I fear), incense, curios, erotica, balms and even something called "lottery oil." There are also bibles, books interpreting dreams, exotic crosses and "Jinx removing powder," which I believe also works on fleas. Information flyer is free. Payment is via cheque or C.O.D. in the U.S. only.

✔ Mail orders accepted
Minimum order: no minimum
Shipping method: mail or C.O.D. (U.S. only)
Shipping time: 2-4 weeks
Returns policy: satisfaction guaranteed or your money back

54 CLEO LTD.
18 Kildare Street
Dublin 2
Ireland
(353 1) 761421

If your image of Irish hand-knits and woven fabrics stops at traditional Irish fishermen sweaters, are you in for a surprise from Cleo. I spotted a cape and a long, slim purple wool coat I would give a couple of my teeth for — just gorgeous! They also sell hand-knit vests, sweaters, multi-hued shawl/throw/lap rugs, billowy capes, caps and a fine men's jacket. They specialize in high quality clothes of their own design and sometimes have fabrics specially woven for them. The catalogue is produced once a year, as required, and though it normally costs $2, they'll send one free to our readers. They accept payment via VISA, M/C, Access card, IMO or cheque.

✔ Special offer to readers
✔ Mail orders accepted
✔ Phone orders accepted
✔ Good bargain-hunting
Minimum order: no minimum
Shipping method: surface or airmail
Shipping time: maximum time 2 months
Returns policy: "follow-up until customer is satisfied"
Established in 1936

55 CLOTHCRAFTERS

Elkhart Lake, WI
U S A 53020
(414) 876-2112; (414) 868-3366

Karen and John Wilson run this small family operation from their own Wisconsin home and offer their goods direct to you at factory wholesale prices (about 50 percent off comparable retail). They have some old-fashioned items you just can't find anymore. The hitch is that it costs them so much to mail to Canada, they'd rather send your order to a U.S. postal address for you. Otherwise, shipping charges are a little steep ($4 outside of U.S. unless your total order is under $15 so it's duty-free). Goods include aprons, totes, yard goods, mats, practical housewares, woodtotes, sheets, linens, curtains, terry towels, cookware, parchment paper, insect netting, chefs' hats, children's items and shower curtains. To offset their costs, please send an addressed, 6 x 9 envelope when requesting the catalogue. The catalogue is updated once a year, in September. Payment is accepted by VISA, M/C or IMO. Sending a cheque is acceptable, but it slows your order down.

✔ Special offer to readers
✔ Mail orders accepted
✔ Phone orders accepted
✔ Good bargain-hunting
✔ SASE required
Minimum order: no minimum
Shipping method: will mail, but prefers sending to U.S. address
Shipping time: 2 weeks, if paid by cheque
Returns policy: all goods guaranteed unconditionally
Established in 1978

56 COLONIAL PLATES AND DOLLS

7 Water Street, P.O. Box 305
St. Mary's, Ontario
Canada N0M 2V0
(519) 284-2807; Can. toll-free: (800) 265-4392

Doug and Claudia Forster run this service for plate and doll collectors, and they also stock wedding and shower gifts, Royal Doulton figurines, jewellery (fine and costume), David Winter and Lilliput cottages and other chatchkas. They are avid collectors themselves, and if they don't have what you're after right now, they'll vow to find it. A price list with photocopied photos of available plates is updated in newsletter style periodically and is free. Payment is accepted with VISA, M/C, IMO or cheques.

✔ Mail orders accepted
✔ Phone orders accepted
Minimum order: no minimum
Shipping method: Canada Post, insured
Shipping time: 2-4 weeks, if in stock
Returns policy: all goods guaranteed

57 COLOREL CORPORATION
8200 East Park Meadows Drive
Suite 8204
Littleton, CO
U S A 80124
(303) 792-3388; U.S. toll-free: (800) 877-4800;
fax: (303) 792-5846

This outfit sells major brand-name verticals, pleated shades and mini-blinds, plus custom-orders for odd-shaped windows, AND — they can fill your order in just one day! All goods are discounted (range is between 30 and 76 percent off retail) but the degree of discount depends on the item ordered. There are 60 colours available in their mini-blinds. Brochures and periodic catalogues are free. Payment is accepted with VISA, M/C, Discover card, IMO or cheques. Fax orders are accepted.

✔ Mail orders accepted
✔ Phone orders accepted
✔ Good bargain-hunting
Minimum order: no minimum
Shipping method: mail to Canada only
Shipping time: 1 day order-processing
Returns policy: all goods guaranteed
Established in 1982

58 COMMERCIAL ELECTRONICS
1305 Burrard St.
Vancouver, B.C.
Canada V6Z 1Z9
(604) 669-5525

All the brand names (Bang & Olufsen, NAD, QUAD, Revox, Pioneer, Advent, Lexicon and more) are sold here, where the professionals shop. They sell VCRs, televisions, CD players, speakers, amps, camcorders and any stereo components you can imagine. Free newsletters are published in spring and fall to advertise some of their lines, but prices change, so they prefer to price-quote on mail orders before you buy. Payment is accepted with VISA, M/C or Amex, but financing can also be arranged and trade-ins are welcome.

✔ Mail orders accepted
✔ Phone orders accepted
Minimum order: no minimum
Shipping method: UPS or Loomis
Shipping time: up to 2 weeks
Returns policy: all goods guaranteed
Member: Professional Audio Retailers Association

59 THE COUNTRY LOFT
South Shore Park
Hingham, MA
U S A 02043
(617) 749-7766; U.S. toll-free: (800) 225-5408

The Country Loft sells Americana, such as primitive furniture, Shaker tables (including some lovely drop-leafs), Windsor stools, home accessories, baskets, hand-made rugs, Santa Fe rugs, soft dolls, wooden candle holders, wooden signs, lamps, art, dried flowers, display shelves, hammocks, sundials, pillows, hurricane lamps, wooden cows and wooden duck decoys, to name but a few. Beautiful colour catalogues are produced three or four times a year, usually once each season. A two-year subscription for Canadians costs $3 (U.S.). However, our readers may write to request one free. Payment is accepted with VISA, M/C, Amex or IMO.

✔ Special offer to readers
✔ Mail orders accepted
✔ Phone orders accepted
Minimum order: no minimum
Shipping method: mail or UPS
Shipping time: 5 days
Returns policy: replacement/exchange or refund on any returns
Established in 1975

60 CREAGEN LTD.
Rm 3, 1/F, Admiralty Centre
18 Harcourt Road
Hong Kong
(852) 520-0168

This is the retail outlet for "Dorfit," a well-known Hong Kong manufacturer of sweaters for export. Actually, "manufacturer" is a bit of a misnomer because many of the sweaters are hand-knit as cottage industry items. Dorfit makes its goods under designer labels, so chances are you can find the same (or near equivalent) styles here for a quarter of the retail price at home. A price list is free, but is not much help if you don't get to see the garment, so it might work better if you send a magazine photo and inquire about costs. Most of the sweaters I've bought here cost less than $20 (Cdn.) — even for hand-knits! Payment is accepted with VISA, M/C or Amex.

✔ Mail orders accepted
✔ Good bargain-hunting
Minimum order: no minimum
Shipping method: airmail or surface mail
Shipping time: 2 weeks, if item is in stock
Returns policy: no returns

61 CROFT'S HEALTH PRODUCTS
6252 Fraser Street
Vancouver, B.C.
Canada
V5W 3A1
(604) 324-2121

Croft Woodruff is among the most knowledgeable health professionals in Canada, and this is his company. His catalogue is very detailed, and updated frequently. His prices are competitive and the excellent advice comes along with all purchases, free. Woodruff is a veteran radio broadcaster and frequent guest authority on health matters in Canada. Payment is accepted with Visa, M/C, IMO or cheque.

✔ Mail orders accepted
✔ Phone orders accepted
✔ Good bargain-hunting
Minimum order: no minimum but $25 orders and higher have postage included
Shipping method: Canada Post
Shipping time: same day shipping if in stock
Returns policy: all goods unconditionally guaranteed
Member: Canadian Health Food Association

62 CULPEPER LIMITED
Hadstock Road
Linton, Cambridge CB1 6NJ
England
(41) 223-891196; fax: (41) 223-893104

This source supplies herbal products of every description. They claim to be "established in 1927 and quite the best herbalist in the world." Their catalogue, usually costing a dollar, is free to you by surface mail if you mention this book (airmail still costs you a buck). Their catalogue is updated twice a year: once for spring (general listings) and once in the autumn (including Christmas items). Payment is preferred by credit card, which saves you money, since they will then charge you postage or shipping at cost. Accepted are VISA, M/C, Access, JCB and Amex.

✔ Special offer to readers
✔ Mail orders accepted
✔ Phone orders accepted
Minimum order: no minimum
Shipping method: airmail or surface mail
Shipping time: 1 week
Returns policy: all goods guaranteed
Established in 1927

63 D & A MERCHANDISE CO.
22 Orchard Street
New York, NY
U S A 10002
(212) 925-4766

Here's a place that carries all major U.S. brands of lingerie, underwear, foundations, socks and pantyhose, by makers such as Dior, Hanes, Jockey, Burlington, Bonnie Doon, Trimfit, Danskin, Playtex, Maidenform, Warner's, Lily of France, Christian Dior, BVD, and more. They are happy to price-quote on anything you want, so if you know the size and style, you can stock up. A brochure is available for $2 (Cdn.) but if you know what you want, you may not need one. Payment is accepted only with VISA or M/C and phone orders are welcome.

✔ Mail orders accepted
✔ Phone orders accepted
✔ Good bargain-hunting
✔ SASE required
Minimum order: no minimum
Shipping method: UPS or mail
Shipping time: 2-3 weeks
Returns policy: all unopened goods accepted for refund
Established in 1946

64 DANBURY MINT
47 Richards Ave.
Norwalk, CT
U S A 06857
Canada toll-free: (800) 243-4664

This is a source for collectors' plates and limited-edition china. Telephone lines are open late (an advantage to callers from the Western provinces) and they will send you a free brochure on anything you're looking for the same day you call. Payment is accepted with Visa, M/C, Amex, Diner's Club, IMO or cheque.

✔ Mail orders accepted
✔ Phone orders accepted
Minimum order: no minimum
Shipping method: airmail or surface mail only to Canada; UPS to U.S. points
Shipping time: averages 2-4 weeks
Returns policy: everything returnable within 30 days
Established in 1969

65 DANIEL SMITH

4130 1st Ave. South
Seattle, WA
U S A 98134
(206) 223-9599; U.S. toll-free: (800) 426-7923;
Wash.: (800) 426-6740

Daniel Smith offers savings of about 20 percent on all artists' supplies, and his prices are often the best available on everything he stocks — some 19,000 products in all. Many proprietary products are included. Goods include all fine art supplies, brushes, artists' paints, canvas, framing, fine art books, how-to books, easels, dry pigments, pastels, art paper, etching acid, litho inks, drawing inks, watercolours and painting knives. The 200-plus page annual catalogue, which lists all products, is printed for July and costs $5, and sale catalogues, which are free, are printed bi-monthly. Readers of this book may write for a free catalogue. Payment is accepted by VISA, M/C, IMO or cheque.

✔ Special offer to readers
✔ Mail orders accepted
✔ Phone orders accepted
✔ Good bargain-hunting
Minimum order: no minimum except $25 minimum on paper only
Shipping method: mail or UPS
Shipping time: shipped within 24 hours maximum
Returns policy: unconditional guarantee
Established in 1976

66 DEARBORN

1 Christopher Street
New York, NY
USA 10014
(212) 691-9153

NO LONGER IN BUSINESS

Creative packaging and gourmet qua[illegible]ght this product line from one of New York's trendiest so[illegible]cluded in the selection are pancake syrups, fancy desser[illegible] and toppings (such as "Bayou crunch"), classic sauces, so[illegible] called "dessert caviar" (which are chocolate-covered, crunc[illegible]s), chocolate-covered nuts, gift packs and a do-it-yourself c[illegible]truffle kit. The once-a-year catalogue is free. Payment is acc[illegible] Amex or IMO only.

- ✔ Mail [illegible]cepted
- ✔ Ph[illegible]rs accepted

[illegible] order: no minimum
[illegible]ng method: UPS to Canada only
[illegible]pping time: 3 weeks
Returns policy: no returns because they are food items

67 DEEPAK GEMS (HONG KONG)

TST P.O. Box 98283
Kowloon
Hong Kong
(852) 368-4686; fax: 3-724-1827

Gobind Mirpuri is from the old Deepak family of jewel-traders. They can find and sell you any type of unset gem you wish, at a fraction of the price you'd pay domestically — and these stones enter Canada duty-free (you do pay F.S.T. at port of entry). I like dealing with this family and have always gotten a good deal. Readers of this book are offered an additional 10 percent off quoted prices, and they pledge to meet anyone else's best price. I find it easier to buy from them than from India because refunds are possible from Hong Kong. Price lists and photos are available free. Payment is preferred with IMO or bank draft, but they will accept VISA or M/C.

- ✔ Special offer to readers
- ✔ Mail orders accepted
- ✔ Phone orders accepted
- ✔ Good bargain-hunting

Minimum order: no minimum
Shipping method: airmail, insured
Shipping time: 2 weeks
Returns policy: all goods guaranteed authentic and satisfactory

68 DEEPAK'S ROKJEMPERL PRODUCTS

61, 10th Khetwadi
Bombay 400004
India
(00-91)22-388031; (00-91)22-383644

Deepak's and its associated Shah's Rock Shop, Vijay World Traders, and Gemcraft India International deal mainly in wholesale gemstones. In 1988, because Canadian postal authorities would not compensate for lost insured parcel post shipments, the Indian government stopped accepting these goods for shipment out of India, if the parcels were bound for Canada. A sorry state of affairs, to be sure. Consequently, if you want to buy unset gems from India (which come into Canada duty-free), you must up the ante and buy a minimum of $500 U.S. at one time, to offset Deepak's much higher airfreight costs. Alternatively, if you have a U.S. mailing address, Deepak can ship there by surface for only a $50 (U.S.) minimum order. As well as diamonds, emeralds, rubies, sapphires, opals and many semi-precious stones, they sell carved bone, rosewood, handicrafts, sandalwood ornaments, beads, caste dolls and jeweller's tools, all at true wholesale prices. Since they are forbidden from refunding foreign currency, you should be certain before you order, since you'll only get replacement goods if you are dissatisfied. For fun, you can order a "beginner's special" for $25 (to the States) consisting of 300 grams each of rough garnets, amethyst, moonstones, diopside star, enstatite-cat's-eye, blue iolites and sunstones. Their catalogues are published two to three times a year, usually in February, June and December. They can accept Amex, but prefer payment in IMO or cheques (both in U.S. funds), or by bank draft. They promise a "special offer" to our readers, so please inquire.

✔ Special offer to readers
✔ Mail orders accepted
✔ Phone orders accepted
✔ Good bargain-hunting
Minimum order: yes, see text
Shipping method: air or surface mail
Shipping time: 1 to 2 weeks
Returns policy: replacement but government policy forbids refunds

69 DELL COMPUTER CORPORATION

2 East Beaver Creek
Richmond Hill, Ontario
Canada L4B 2N3
(416) 881-3513; Can. toll-free: (800) 387-5755

Michael Dell is an entrepreneurial whiz-kid who became so successful at mail ordering computers that he had to quit university to concentrate full-time on being a multi-millionaire. He began mail-ordering IBM-PC clones from a garage while he was a 19-year old student in Texas only a handful of years ago. His equipment was so good and his after-sales service so thorough that he has become kind of a legend both in the fields of marketing and in computers. In fact, *Inc. Magazine* in the U.S. just awarded him the "entrepreneur of the year" award. His company's sales topped $300 million in 1989, so it's doing something right! His Canadian operation sells computer hardware (IBM-compatable PCs), and he's recently started producing a high-performance laptop. Most of the business is done by phone, including service. The company is considered number one in customer satisfaction in the computer industry, resolving over 90 percent of customers' problems within six minutes of receiving the call. You talk directly to an engineer who can talk "lay" lingo to you, while understanding the inner workings of the computer and being able to remedy difficulties quickly; they back up their hardware as long as you own it. Almost all of their business is handled nowadays by salesmen in the field, but they will take phone orders and ship the goods to you (via UPS) anywhere in Canada. Catalogues are available only in the U.S. In Canada, they send you their detailed "fulfilling" package, which is updated for each product every week. They also stock and sell the 50 most popular software packages, including spreadsheets, word processing, and so on. Payment is accepted with VISA, Amex or by arranged credit terms and purchase orders.

✔ Phone orders accepted
✔ Good bargain-hunting
Minimum order: no minimum
Shipping method: UPS to Canadian addresses
Shipping time: depends on item ordered
Returns policy: all goods unconditionally guaranteed
Established in 1984

70 DIAMONDS BY RENNIE ELLEN

15 West 47th Street, Room 401
New York, NY
U S A 10036
(212) 869-5525

Rennie Ellen is a major character! She has a background as a consumers' advocate and got into the jewellery business almost by accident. Though she won't send goods directly into Canada (you must use a U.S. address), and it costs $10 for shipping and insurance, she is a diamond wholesale operation with factory-direct prices. You'll save 50 to

75 percent off retail on diamonds, engagement rings, earrings, pendants, and fine jewellery including sapphires, rubies and other precious stones. The modest 16-page catalogue costs $1 (refundable on first order). Payment is accepted only via IMO or bank teller cheques (bank draft) payable in U.S. funds.

✔ Mail orders accepted
✔ Phone orders accepted
✔ Good bargain-hunting
Minimum order: no minimum
Shipping method: mail to U.S. addresses only
Shipping time: 10-15 days
Returns policy: all goods guaranteed

71 DICK BLICK COMPANY

P.O. Box 1267
Galesburg, IL
U S A 61401
(309) 343-6181; U.S. toll-free: (800) 477-8192

This wholesaler of art and craft supplies sells everything the creative person could desire. They also sell framing supplies and some office furniture and accessories, such as lamps. Schools and other institutions get the best deals, with discounts increasing with the size of the order. A large catalogue is produced, which is $2. Payment on orders is accepted with VISA or M/C only.

✔ Mail orders accepted
✔ Phone orders accepted
✔ Good bargain-hunting
Minimum order: no minimum, but large orders get bigger discounts
Shipping method: airmail, surface mail or UPS
Shipping time: 2-4 weeks
Returns policy: money-back guarantee
Established in 1911

72 DILLETTANTE CHOCOLATES

2300 E. Cherry
Seattle, WA
U S A 98122
(206) 328-1530

While apprenticing in Budapest, Paris and Vienna, Master Pastry Chef Julius Rudolph Franzen learned the closely guarded secrets of the chocolate confectionery in the court of Franz Josef, Emperor of Austria.

Later, as Master Candymaker to Czar Nicholas II in St. Petersburg, Julius further perfected his craft. Just before the outbreak of World War I, he immigrated to the U.S., where he taught the old world formulas to his American brother-in-law, Earl Remington Davenport. Today, Earl's grandson, Dana Taylor Davenport, continues the family tradition by creating the most wonderful truffles, Rheingold, marzipan and buttercreams you can imagine — from the same secret recipes that pleased the crowned heads of Europe. Goods are sold from a small flyer, which is free. Payment is accepted via VISA, M/C, Amex or IMO (U.S. funds only, please).

✔ Mail orders accepted
Minimum order: no minimum
Shipping method: mail or UPS
Shipping time: 2 weeks
Returns policy: all goods guaranteed satisfactory

73 DOLLSVILLE DOLLS & BEARSVILLE BEARS
461 North Palm Canyon Dr.
Palm Springs, CA
U S A 92262
(619) 325-2241; (619) 325-3655; U.S. toll-free: (800) CAL-BEAR; CALIF only: (800) 447-5575

Cheryl and John McBride have created a Palm Springs store for collectors, and now they write from everywhere to buy their imported dolls and bears by mail. Included are the Steiff (button in ear) collection, Merrythoughts bears, teddy bears from House of Nesbet in England, and specially outfitted bears like Zsa Zsa Gabear (guaranteed not to slap your face), Wm. Shakesbear and Bearishnikov. Most of their stock is discounted regularly (e.g., Gorham dolls are discounted 20 percent). Although the monthly newsletter costs $5 for a yearly subscription (including a $10 discount coupon), they'll send you one free for mentioning this book (be sure to include a long, self-addressed envelope). Goods are guaranteed, but if you have a problem, you're asked to call within three days of receipt. Payment is accepted via VISA, M/C, Amex, Discover, IMO or cheques.

✔ Special offer to readers
✔ Mail orders accepted
✔ Phone orders accepted
✔ SASE required
Minimum order: no minimum
Shipping method: mail or UPS
Shipping time: same day if in stock
Returns policy: 3-day exchange on all goods (call if unsuitable)
Established in 1979

74 DOMINION SEED HOUSE

Georgetown, Ontario
Canada L7G 4A2
(416) 877-2801

Dominion Seed House offers "quality seeds for Canadian gardens," and much more in the way of advice, garden implements, compost rotting compounds, equipment and gadgets. If the address seems sparse, keep in mind that Dominion is the biggest operation in Georgetown — they don't need directions to find it! The catalogue is produced each winter and is free. Payment is accepted with IMO or cheque.

✔ Mail orders accepted
Minimum order: no minimum
Shipping method: Canada Post
Shipping time: 2-3 weeks
Returns policy: all goods guaranteed

75 DR. COOKIE, INC.

18706 No. Creek Parkway, Suite #104
Bothell, WA
U S A 98011
(206) 481-2447; U.S. toll-free: (800) 247-4259;
fax orders: (206) 487-2246

This line of gourmet cookies was developed by Marvin Wayne, MD, who wanted to create a great tasting snack that was actually good for people: low in cholesterol and salt, and high in fibre. Eventually, he was dubbed "Dr. Cookie," and his fellow physician, a cardiologist named Dr. Stephen Yarnell, was so impressed with the goodies that he joined his colleague. Now they make six varieties of healthful cookies and package them in unique red tins or gift boxes. There's also a Dr. Cookie Cookbook ($6.95 U.S., plus shipping) so you can make your own versions of these treats. Other gift items include aprons and the distinctive red Dr. Cookie sweatshirt. Note (offer for retailers and business-owners reading this book only): Dr. Cookie will send you a free sample PR packet if you send a written enquiry including your business card. Flyer and price list are published periodically, free to readers of this book. Payment by VISA, M/C, IMO or cheque.

✔ Special offer to readers
✔ Mail orders accepted
✔ Phone orders accepted
Minimum order: cookie tin of 28 cookies
Shipping method: UPS, courier, mail orders
Shipping time: orders filled same day received
Returns policy: refunds or free replacement — gladly
Established in 1985

76 800-SOFTWARE

918 Parker Street
Berkeley, CA
U S A 94710
(415) 644-4819; U.S. toll-free: (800) 888-4880

800-Software has the international reputation for having the most knowledgeable staff and most accurate shipping department in the industry. Add to this great prices and great service and you'd be crazy not to try them if you're into computers. They sell software, hardware, databases, buffers, printers, keyboards, mice, and accessories for memory expansion, desktop publishing, spreadsheets, word processing plus microcomputer gear for PCs and Macintosh. In addition, they run periodic specials on many items. Their catalogue is changed for summer and winter and is free. They prefer to give you current "price quotes" instead of relying only on catalogue prices. See introductory chapters for info on price quotes. If you're a qualified customer, they will ship on the strength of your purchase order. Otherwise, payment is accepted by VISA, M/C, Amex, IMO, cheques or C.O.D. in tbe U.S.

✔ Mail orders accepted
✔ Phone orders accepted
✔ Good bargain-hunting
Minimum order: no minimum
Shipping method: mail or UPS
Shipping time: same day shipping
Returns policy: "we stand by manufacturer's policy"

77 EARLY ADVANTAGE

47 Richards Ave.
Norwalk, CT
U S A 06857
Canada toll-free: (800) 367-4534

Here's a source for children's videos to help children learn. There are language courses and learning aids, some with animation and some live action. A free descriptive brochure is available by calling toll-free, anytime. Payment is accepted with Visa, M/C, Amex, Diner's Club, IMO or cheque.

✔ Mail orders accepted
✔ Phone orders accepted
Minimum order: no minimum
Shipping method: airmail or surface mail only to Canada; UPS to U.S. points
Shipping time: averages 2-4 weeks
Returns policy: everything returnable within 30 days
Established in 1969

78 THE EASTON PRESS
47 Richards Ave.
Norwalk, CT
U S A 06857
Canada toll-free: (800) 367-4534

The Easton Press specializes in educational videos for adults and children. Descriptive brochures are free for the asking — and the phone call is free, too, from anywhere in Canada, anytime. Payment is accepted with Visa, M/C, Amex, Diner's Club, IMO or cheque.

✔ Mail orders accepted
✔ Phone orders accepted
Minimum order: no minimum
Shipping method: airmail or surface mail only to Canada; UPS to U.S. points
Shipping time: averages 2-4 weeks
Returns policy: everything returnable within 30 days
Established in 1969

79 EDDIE BAUER OUTDOOR OUTFITTERS
P.O. Box 3700
Seattle, WA
U S A 98124-3700
(206) 885-5976; Can. toll-free: (800) 426-8020

Eddie is well known as "outdoors outfitters" in the U.S. and they've been expanding rapidly in Canada, with over a dozen stores already in B.C., Alberta and Ontario, and more opening even as we go to press. They sell outdoors, hunting, fishing, camping and hiking gear, great hats, boots and other supplies. The big, annual catalogue is supplemented by seasonal (and sale) flyers from Canadian stores, which will automatically put you on their mailing list if you write to the Seattle address. The catalogue is free. Payment is accepted with VISA, M/C, Amex, IMOs and cheques.

✔ Mail orders accepted
✔ Phone orders accepted
Minimum order: no minimum
Shipping method: mail, UPS or courier
Shipping time: 24-48 hours
Returns policy: all goods unconditionally guaranteed
Established in 1920

80 THE EDINBURGH WOOLLEN MILL
COC 1, Langholm
Dumfriesshire, DG 13 OBR
Scotland
541-80611; 541-80092

This catalogue outlet for a factory mill sells Lyle & Scott and Pringle knits, plus fine wool skirts, jackets, suits and topcoats. Prices are about 60 percent off Canadian retail (and a number of British woollen shops in this country carry the same lines). The colour catalogue is published annually and is free. Payment is accepted in VISA, M/C, Amex, Diners Club and IMO (pounds sterling, please).

✔ Mail orders accepted
✔ Phone orders accepted
✔ Good bargain-hunting
Minimum order: no minimum
Shipping method: airmail or sea mail
Shipping time: 2-6 weeks
Returns policy: refund if unsatisfactory; return for refund
Established in 1808

81 EFSTONSCIENCE INC.
3350 Dufferin St.
Toronto, Ontario
Canada M6A 3A4
(416) 787-4581 (orders); (416) 787-4585 (customer service)

Here's the source for all things scientific: books, maps, magnifiers (every magnification you can imagine), things for hobbyists, collectors, electrical doodads, gadgets and great ideas for family fun. There's a kit to create your own bumper-stickers, a clay you bake in the oven to a permanent hardness (I bought this stuff and used it for dozens of fun projects with my kids), biofeedback monitors, parabolic monitors and enough to fill a book, which is why their detailed colour catalogue costs $2. You'll get the next one free if you order something. Payment is accepted by VISA or M/C only, or by purchase order and billing, if you order from a recognized institution, such as a school.

✔ Mail orders accepted
✔ Phone orders accepted
✔ Good bargain-hunting
Minimum order: no minimum
Shipping method: Canada Post regular or Priority Post
Shipping time: faster by Priority Post (3 day)
Returns policy: all goods guaranteed 30 days or money back
Member: Canadian Direct Marketing Association and Better Business Bureau

82 EL PASO CHILI CO.
100 Ruhlin Court
El Paso, TX
U S A 79922
(915) 544-3434

Hot! If you crave Southwestern spices, such as chili, jalapenos, sauces, salsa, or Bar-B-Q, this is the place. Norma Kerr has carved out a big reputation for herself for authentic Mex-Tex gourmet fixings, and the packaging alone is so decorative you'll want to buy one of everything. We particularly like the Coyote nuts ("They're Howlin' Hot"). The Kerrs also sell Southwestern wreaths made from chilis or Indian corn or fragrant cinnamon. Norma writes: "El Paso has a very distinctive regional cuisine and of course we think it's the best." They use no fillers or preservatives, of course. The catalogue is published every spring and it's free. Payment is best by VISA, M/C, Amex or cheque.

✔ Special offer to readers
✔ Mail orders accepted
✔ Phone orders accepted
Minimum order: $15 U.S. minimum
Shipping method: mail or UPS
Shipping time: 5 to 10 days
Returns policy: no returns unless defective
Established in 1981

83 THE ELEPHANT HOUSE
67/12 Soi Phra Phinit, Soi Suan Phlu
Sathorn Tai Rd.
Bangkok
Thailand
(662) 286-5280

This place has wonderful artifacts and antiques, but their specialty is Burmese lacquerware, which they stock in great abundance. They do have a colour catalogue, but since stock turns over so rapidly, it's wise to write and tell them what you're looking for, then negotiate over price. Expect to save about 40 percent off what it would cost you locally — if you could even find the item, that is. Payment is accepted with VISA, M/C or Amex.

✔ Mail orders accepted
Minimum order: no minimum
Shipping method: crated and shipped
Shipping time: up to 4 months
Returns policy: all goods guaranteed, but awkward to return

84 ELOXITE CORPORATION
806 10th Street, Dept. 12
Wheatland, WY
U S A 82201
(307) 322-3050

This source is a rockhound's paradise: wholesalers of lapidary goods and hobby supplies. An exchange fee is levied if you return goods for which they were not in error, so be certain before ordering. Their fast, one-day service sets them apart from the competition. Prices do not include postage, which varies according to just how many rocks you order. Expect savings of about 35 percent off regular retail prices. Their catalogue is reprinted every September and costs 25 cents (non-refundable). Their catalogue is free if you mention this book, and orders are taken via VISA, Mastercard or International Money Order.

✔ Special offer to readers
✔ Mail orders accepted
✔ Phone orders accepted
✔ Good bargain-hunting
Minimum order: minimum is $10 U.S.
Shipping method: postal service or via UPS
Shipping time: same day shipment
Returns policy: goods guaranteed, especially items shipped in error

85 THE ENCHANTED DOLL HOUSE

Route 7
Manchester Center, VT
U S A 05255
(802) 362-1327 (customer service); (802) 362-3030 (mail orders)

There are miniatures and there are miniatures. Some are small for the sake of being small, while others have detail, substance and finesse. The Enchanted Doll House sells only the latter. There are dolls, stuffed animals, teddy bears, dollhouses, limited edition toys, marionettes (particularly Mickey and Minnie), Beatles dolls, nostalgia items, Gumby and Pokey, Bullwinkle, Howdy Doody, collector's dolls, doll buggies and cribs, toys, and of course, those incredibly detailed miniatures. Sale catalogues are mailed out occasionally. Our readers can get a free sample catalogue (the dolls, toys and playthings catalogue usually costs $2, and the dollhouses, miniatures and accessories one costs $3), if this book is mentioned. Payment is accepted via VISA, M/C, Discover card, IMO or cheque (U.S. funds).

✔ Special offer to readers
✔ Mail orders accepted
✔ Phone orders accepted
Minimum order: no minimum
Shipping method: mail or UPS
Shipping time: approximately 3 weeks
Returns policy: anything may be returned (sets returned as sets)
Established in 1963

86 ERAWAN BEE FARM
180 Moo 6, Chiengmai-Lampoon Rd.
Amphur Sarapee
Chiengmai
Thailand
(053) 321-544; 561-361; fax in Bangkok: (662) 433-0108

Here's a wholesale source for honey, especially if you need large quantities. Remember that it is illegal to import bees to Canada, by the way. Price lists are available, free. Payment is accepted only with IMO, cheques or bank drafts (Canadian currency is okay).

✔ Mail orders accepted
✔ Phone orders accepted
✔ Good bargain-hunting
Minimum order: no minimum
Shipping method: airmail or surface mail
Shipping time: 2-6 weeks
Returns policy: no returns (food)

87 THE EXECUTIVE CHEF
1780 West 3rd Avenue
Vancouver, B.C.
Canada V6J 4R6
(604) 731-3663

Lesley Stowe Hume invented a dessert featured in a number of Vancouver restaurants called "Death by Chocolate." That fact alone would grant her the title of "most popular caterer in town," but I've added to that the secret insight that Executive Chef catered the wedding party for her competition: caterer Deborah Roitberg! Lesley's Christmas gift baskets rival the best you can buy anywhere in the world. They might include California orange blossom honey, McStevens cappuccino cocoa, flower blossom vinegar, Poriloff Beluga caviar, Manitoba wild rice, sun-dried cherries, Sonoma sun-dried tomatoes, fancy mustards, jams, jellies, nut brittles or other gourmet foods. There's even one romantic getaway basket complete with Executive Chef roasted red peppers in rosemary olive oil. Wow! The catalogue is published every fall for Christmas gift-ordering and is free. Payment is accepted by VISA or cheque only.

✔ Mail orders accepted
✔ Phone orders accepted
Minimum order: no minimum
Shipping method: Canada Post or UPS ($10 delivery charge)
Shipping time: 1-3 weeks, depending on season
Returns policy: all goods guaranteed

88 47TH ST. PHOTO

36 East 19th Street
New York, NY
U S A 10003
(212) 260-4410; (212) 260-4415; U.S. toll-free: (800) 221-7774; (800) 221-5858

This place may have the best prices in North America for cameras, watches, computer equipment, electonics, answering machines and phones. It's always worth the cost of the call to check a local price against 47th Street's. They prefer to price-quote by phone anyway (get the name of the clerk who takes your call because I know people who have been quoted one price and charged another!). They do their mail orders out of this address even though it isn't on 47th Street, never fear. The 200-page-plus catalogue costs $2. Payment is accepted only with VISA, M/C or Amex, so phone ordering makes sense.

✔ Mail orders accepted
✔ Phone orders accepted
✔ Good bargain-hunting
Minimum order: $25 minimum (U.S. funds)
Shipping method: airmail or UPS
Shipping time: 1 week
Returns policy: 15- or 5-day return period (depends on goods)

89 THE FAITH MOUNTAIN COMPANY

P.O. Box 199
Sperryville, VA
U S A 22740
(703) 987-8521; U.S. toll-free: (800) 822-7238

This is a "lifestyle" catalogue of home furnishings and decorative touches, clothing (mainly women's), and gift items, such as wreaths, pottery, sculpture, garden ornaments, dolls, miniatures, picnic baskets, jewellery, straw hats, dried herbs and flowers, rugs and many hand-made and unique products. They sell "everything for a sophisticated country lifestyle." They offer their catalogue free to our readers, instead of the usual $3 fee. It is published three times a year, in July, September/October and January. Payment is accepted by VISA, M/C, Amex, IMO and cheque.

✔ Special offer to readers
✔ Mail orders accepted
✔ Phone orders accepted
✔ Good bargain-hunting
Minimum order: no minimum

Shipping method: mail or UPS
Shipping time: 1 day
Returns policy: anything returnable — no questions asked
Established in 1977

90 THE FAMOUS PACIFIC DESSERT COMPANY

420 E. Denny Way
Seattle, WA
U S A 98122
(206) 328-1950; U.S. toll-free: (800) 666-1950

This outfit creates specialty desserts that are made with the finest and freshest ingredients and packaged in beautiful gift boxes. The cakes will keep for three months refrigerated and a year when frozen. Included are chocolate decadence with Northwest raspberry purée, raspberry Linzer torte, a confection called "Chocolate Thunder-White Lightning," and macadamia pineapple cake. Their motto: "Eat dessert first. Life is uncertain." They sell aprons and T-shirts featuring their credo. Their periodic catalogue is free. Payment is accepted by C.O.D. (U.S. destinations), VISA, M/C, Amex and IMO.

✔ Mail orders accepted
✔ Phone orders accepted
Minimum order: no minimum
Shipping method: mail or UPS
Shipping time: 1 week
Returns policy: if correctly stored, they'll replace any product
Established in 1982

91 FATIMA SELF HELP CENTER

c/o Good Shepherd Sisters
17/65 Asoke Din Daeng Road
Bangkok
Thailand
(662) 245-0457

They make everything here, from pot-holders and placemats to wonderful rompers and smocked dresses for children. There are also Christmas ornaments and decorations and many other craft items. Sometimes a price list is available, other times, they are out of print. Payment is accepted only with IMO or international bank draft. Write to specify what you are seeking.

✔ Mail orders accepted
✔ Good bargain-hunting
Minimum order: no minimum

Shipping method: surface mail
Shipping time: up to 4 months
Returns policy: no returns

92 FESTIVAL RECORDS MAIL ORDER

Vancouver Folk Music Festival
3271 Main Street
Vancouver, B.C.
Canada V5V 2M6
(604) 879-2931

Here's where you can buy obscure (and mainstream) folk records and tapes. They are not necessarily bargain priced (though they sometimes have sale prices) but many of these recordings cannot be found elsewhere in Canada, and some are exclusive to the Folk Festival. Shipping (always by first class mail) costs $3 for the first LP ($1 each additional) or $1.25 for the first CD or cassette (75 cents each additional). In Vancouver, you can stop by to pick up your order to save shipping. The catalogue is published annually and updated frequently with flyers and sale-notices. The catalogue costs $1, but you get a free one with your order, and you'll be added to the mailing list. Payment is accepted with VISA, M/C, IMO or cheques, payable to "Festival Records," please.

✔ Mail orders accepted
Minimum order: no minimum
Shipping method: Canada Post, first class mail only
Shipping time: 1 week
Returns policy: all goods guaranteed
Established in 1974

93 FOSTER-TRENT INC.

2345 Post Road
Larchmont, NY
U S A 10538
(914) 632-3104

If you have ever wanted to fill your front lawn with two-foot-wide "country cows," this is the place to round 'em up. Why settle for pink flamingoes, I ask? Cows are only $6.88 each (six for $33) and are a great (albeit weird) gift idea. Flyers are free. Payment accepted with IMO or cheques only.

✔ Mail orders accepted
Minimum order: no minimum
Shipping method: mail
Shipping time: 3-5 weeks
Returns policy: 30-day home trial, no risk returns

94 FREDERICK & NELSON
5th & Pine
P.O. Box 12310
Seattle, WA
U S A 98111-4310
(206) 682-5500

Frederick & Nelson's catalogue is full-colour, glamorous and very appealing. Included in the Christmas book (their major catalogue) is men's apparel, women's clothing, gifts, toys, gorgeous lingerie, executive toys, gloves, fine perfumes, jewellery, sportswear, electronics, cookware, china, frames, silver flatware, crystal and gift packs. Payment is accepted with VISA, M/C, Amex and Frederick & Nelson card.

✔ Mail orders accepted
✔ Phone orders accepted
Minimum order: no minimum
Shipping method: mail or UPS
Shipping time: 2 weeks
Returns policy: "Customer satisfaction is first and foremost"

95 FREDERICK'S OF HOLLYWOOD
6606 Hollywood Boulevard
Los Angeles, CA
U S A 90028
(213) 469-7043 or (213) 466-5151; (213) 466-8506

A huge number of people to whom I mentioned this book asked if I would remember to include Frederick's of Hollywood, which means either (1) my friends are all into sexy undergarments, or (2) "Frederick's" is synonymous with "mail order." In any case, their full-colour catalogue features hundreds of examples of lingerie, sportswear, Spandex, swimwear, hosiery, sexy boots and even some men's items. The catalogue is $5. Payment is accepted by Visa, M/C or Amex.

✔ Mail orders accepted
✔ Phone orders accepted
Minimum order: no minimum
Shipping method: mail or UPS
Shipping time: 2-3 weeks
Returns policy: all goods guaranteed

96 G. SMITH AND SONS, THE SNUFF CENTRE
74 Charing Cross Road
London WC2H 0BG
England
(71) 836-7422

Smith's popular Fribourg and Treyer snuffs have been established since 1720, but their shop in Charing Cross has been operating for 150 years less, almost an adolescent by comparison. They sell a vast and very high quality selection of tobaccos "packed at the peak of perfection in air-tight tins," as well as fine pipes, cigars, snuff, distinctive pewter snuff boxes and "smokers' requisites." One of their information flyers even explains, step-by-step, how a gentleman takes snuff. Their literature is updated sporadically (since their stock doesn't change much) and is free. Payment is accepted with VISA, M/C, Amex, Access, Diners Club, Eurocard and IMO.

✔ Mail orders accepted
✔ Phone orders accepted
Minimum order: no minimum
Shipping method: airmail or surface mail
Shipping time: 14 days
Returns policy: guarantee "complete satsifaction"
Established in 1869

97 THE GALLERY COLLECTION
Prudent Publishing
341 Ormont Drive
Weston, Ontario
Canada M9L 1N8
(416) 746-3400

This firm is the Canadian branch of a New Jersey firm, which custom-imprints very high-quality (not to mention very costly) Christmas cards with your own special greeting. The cards are embossed, heavy card and sometimes highlighted with gold. They come with matching envelopes. Orders received by an early deadline receive a 40 percent discount. Three weeks later the discount dips to 20 percent, and after that it disappears altogether. There is an additional set-up charge, but the larger your order, the cheaper the unit price. The catalogue is free. Payment is via billing after you order, or from purchase order from established clients.

✔ Mail orders accepted
Minimum order: 25 cards
Shipping method: Canada Post
Shipping time: shipping date after order received
Returns policy: no returns unless their error

98 GARDEN SOURCE BOOKS
5133 Bursill Street
Vancouver, B.C.
Canada V5R 3Z4
(604) 435-5815

Mark Miller and Donald Sands have carved out a careful bit of territory, and they aim to be the best in their field, so you can be the best in your garden: they sell gardening books, and nothing else. They stock dozens of books on the subject, and their annual catalogue is free to readers of this book. As well, our readers will receive a 10-percent discount on their first order if they mention they read it here. Payment is accepted by VISA, M/C, Amex, IMO or cheque.

✔ Special offer to readers
✔ Mail orders accepted
✔ Phone orders accepted
✔ Good bargain-hunting
Minimum order: no minimum
Shipping method: Canada Post (4th class, book mail)
Shipping time: 6-8 weeks
Returns policy: 30-day money-back guarantee
Established in 1989

99 GARDENER'S EDEN
P.O. Box 7307
San Francisco, CA
U S A 94120-7307
(415) 421-4242

This is a gorgeous catalogue and selection of garden "extras." Some are indulgences, some are practical, but all are wonderful and unique. There are interesting pieces of outdoor furniture, accessories, garden lanterns, and more. The catalogue is free. Payment is accepted by Visa, M/C, Amex, IMO or cheques in U.S. funds.

✔ Mail orders accepted
Minimum order: no minimum
Shipping method: UPS
Shipping time: 2-3 weeks
Returns policy: all goods guaranteed

100 GAUNTLETT FEY INC., CHEESE OUTLET
398-400 Pine Street
Burlington, VT
U S A 05401
(802) 864-7271; (802) 863-3968; U.S. toll-free: (800) 447-1205

This outlet allows you to buy high-quality Vermont cheeses (and luscious cheescakes), but the problem is that you can have them sent only to a U.S. address. Obviously, because of the perishable nature of these goods, you'll want to be sure that your American friends are in town when the notice comes. The catalogue is published about once a year, as required to update it, and is free. Payment is accepted by VISA, M/C or cheque.

✔ Mail orders accepted
✔ Phone orders accepted
Minimum order: no minimum
Shipping method: mail only to U.S. drop points
Shipping time: 2 days
Returns policy: no returns because they are foods

101 THE GAZEBO OF NEW YORK
9627 Brighton Way
Beverly Hills, CA
U S A
(213) 274-6057

This place is expensive, but the quality shows, from the authentic-looking (and -costing) patchwork quilts, to rag rugs and enameled light-switch covers. The country look goes Beverly Hills, if you know what I mean. The catalogue is $4. Payment is accepted with Visa, M/C, Amex or IMO.

✔ Mail orders accepted
Minimum order: no minimum
Shipping method: UPS or U.S. Mail
Shipping time: 2-6 weeks, depending on season
Returns policy: all goods guaranteed

102 GAZIN'S
P.O. Box 19221
New Orleans, LA
U S A 70179
(504) 482-0302; U.S. toll-free: (800) 262-6410

Their opulent little catalogues are jammed with wonderful food and cookware, such as Cajun-Creole gourmet foods, sausages, ice-cream makers, cookbooks, preserves, gumbo (soup) pots, bread mixes, fancy rices, Paul Prudhomme's cookbooks, Brannan's New Orlean's Cookbook, sauces, mayonnaise, coffee (some blended with chicory), Bienville & Rockefeller sauce, shrimp remoulade, imported patés, wine racks, corkscrews, LeRuth's vanilla bean marinade, cast-iron skillets for making Cajun blackened fish, Spanish saffron, extra-hot cayenne, herb kits, mustards, pickled okra, a barbecue fish grill, pickles, wild mushroom caviar, French walnut oil, sun-dried tomatoes, recipes, vanilla sugar, pecan pralines, Vieux Carré chocolate sauce, Pierce Duff sorbet mixes and much more. Five catalogues appear: fall, Christmas, winter, spring and spring/summer, and each costs $1 (refundable with first order). Our readers may request one free. Discounts as high as 50 percent are sometimes offered on discontinued items. Payment is accepted by VISA, M/C, Amex or IMO.

✔ Mail orders accepted
✔ Phone orders accepted
Minimum order: $10 (U.S.)
Shipping method: mail
Shipping time: usually shipped within 24 hours
Returns policy: return for immediate refund or replacement

103 GIMBEL & SONS COUNTRY STORE
P.O. Box 57
Boothbay Harbor, MA
U S A 04538
(207) 633-5088

The Gimbel family (not associated with Gimbels Department Stores) operates a charming, white-shuttered country store in Maine, which looks like some of the places you see in "Murder She Wrote." Their specialty is porcelain dolls, miniatures, thimbles (thousands of them!) and other collectables, most sold at very reasonable prices. Occasionally, they'll discount some overstocked merchandise or offer low prices on special purchases. They most certainly have the largest thimble selection in the world (hence the slogan "Gimbels Thimbles"). Their free colour catalogue is published every September and December, and prices are honoured for one year. Payment is accepted only by VISA or M/C.

✔ Mail orders accepted
✔ Phone orders accepted
Minimum order: $25 (U.S.) in total
Shipping method: mail or UPS (latter to Ontario only)
Shipping time: 2-day turnaround time
Returns policy: all goods guaranteed
Established in 1961
Member: New England Mail Order Association

104 GINGER SCHLOTE
Box 19523W
Denver, CO
U S A 80219
Phone number available to steady customers only on request

Ginger runs her business at home on a very personal basis, but she does not do phone orders at all. She tells me she is very interested in expanding her business with Canadian customers and hopes the Free Trade Agreement will help. What she sells is a fascinating assortment of jewellery accessories, findings, chains, rings, semi-precious stones, lapidary supplies, earring posts and wires, pendants, chain and clasp repair items, hearts, crosses, stars, cowpoke motif items, cements, brooches, bola cords, tie tacks, keyrings, and collectors' spoons. Whew! The catalogue is reprinted and updated once or twice a year and costs $1 (refundable with first order). Payment is accepted via cheque or IMO only.

✔ Mail orders accepted
✔ Good bargain-hunting
Minimum order: no minimum
Shipping method: mail only
Shipping time: 1 day
Returns policy: all goods guaranteed for refund or replacement
Established in 1981

105 GOLDEN CARP
568/2 Ploenchit Road
Bangkok 10500
Thailand
(662) 250-0922

Golden Carp sells only "fishskin leather" goods, which, unlike some snakeskin or crocodile skin, is completely legal to import to Canada. They fashion handsome, "uptown"-style handbags, wallets, purses, leather belts and other accessories from this material in a wide range of colours and sizes. Fishskin leather is surprisingly durable, too. Colour brochure or flyers and price lists are all free. Prices are very cheap. They will take additional percentages off for large orders. Payment is accepted with VISA, M/C, Amex, IMO or bank draft.

✔ Mail orders accepted
✔ Good bargain-hunting
Minimum order: no minimum
Shipping method: airmail or surface mail
Shipping time: 2-6 weeks (depends on method)
Returns policy: all items guaranteed

106 GOOD IMPRESSIONS
P.O. Box 33
Shirley, WV
U S A 26434
(304) 758-4252

Here you'll find Victorian motif, decorative rubber stamps of all kinds, along with stamping supplies, ink (even food-safe ink) and up to 50 percent discount on selected items, such as unmounted rubber dies and bulk rubber. A free copy of their newsletter, The Shirley Star, is available to our readers. The catalogue costs $1 (refundable on first order) and is printed every fall. Payment is accepted via VISA, M/C, IMO or cheques in U.S. funds.

- ✔ Special offer to readers
- ✔ Mail orders accepted
- ✔ Phone orders accepted
- ✔ Good bargain-hunting

Minimum order: no minimum
Shipping method: mail or UPS
Shipping time: 2 - 5 days
Returns policy: guaranteed against defects: replacement/credit/refund
Established in 1985

107 GRAND FINALE
P.O. Box 620049
Dallas, TX
U S A 75262-0049
(214) 243-6200

This place is a clearance house for factory close-outs, mostly of high-quality, brand-name merchandise. Savings of 50-70 percent are not uncommon. You might find expensive jewellery, Limoges china, bed and table linens, imported tableware, cashmere sweaters, cookware, designer apparel (men's and women's), luggage and other leather goods, toys, or what-have-you. Catalogues are published seasonally and cost $3 (refundable on first purchase) for one year's worth. Payment is accepted with VISA, M/C, Amex, Discover card, IMO or cheques.

- ✔ Mail orders accepted
- ✔ Phone orders accepted
- ✔ Good bargain-hunting

Minimum order: no minimum
Shipping method: mail or UPS
Shipping time: 2-3 weeks
Returns policy: all goods 100-percent guaranteed; return for refund

108 GRAND FINALE CONFECTIONS
200 Hillcrest Rd.
Berkeley, CA
U S A 94705
(415) 655-8414; U.S. toll-free: (800) 748-6271

As far as they know, they are California's smallest licensed candy factory, but what they give up in quantity, they make up in quality. They sell only about 10 different gift items, but every one is a gem, which you'll appreciate all the more if you're a chocoholic like me. They use only natural ingredients for their luscious melt-in-the-mouth caramels, dessert sauces and dark chocolate-covered caramel bars. The truffles are also to die for. You have packaging choices, too. You can order two jars of dessert sauce in a hand-made wooden box, or the same two jars "in a cheap cardboard box," as they say. This is a great source of gifts to be mailed directly to American cousins, and everything's guaranteed. Orders over $500 are discounted 10 percent (perfect for corporate gifts). They sell a single (but great) cookbook,too. Their free catalogue is updated once a year, late in October and it's wonderfully descriptive, in persuasive, full colour. Payment may be made via VISA, M/C, Amex or C.O.D. to a U.S. address.

✔ Mail orders accepted
✔ Phone orders accepted
Minimum order: one catalogue item ($10.95)
Shipping method: mail or UPS
Shipping time: 1-2 weeks
Returns policy: - money refunded if customer unsatisfied

109 GUANGZHOU DECOR PORCELAIN FACTORY

660 Jiefang Road, North Guangzhou
Guangzhou
China
30986; cable: Guangzhou 3971

Though slow to fill orders, this factory outlet does incredible work, with detail, gold-filigree, hand-painting on porcelain. Styles include floral, dragons, brocade-look, and shapes include bowls, tea sets, dinner sets, vases, jars, umbrella-holders and plates. They will also create custom-designs to your specifications, or work on materials you supply. Tiny flyers are quite descriptive, considering their small size, and include colour photos. They are free. Payment is by IMO or bank draft only. Be sure to enquire about payment details before ordering, and specify how much you are willing to pay for packing, crating, shipping, etc., as these details can become fuzzy at such a great distance. Guangzhou, by the way, is the Chinese name for the old city of Canton, which is the southermost city in China, and thus the most "Westernized" (means: easier to deal here than with Beijing).

✔ Mail orders accepted
✔ Good bargain-hunting
Minimum order: no minimum
Shipping method: surface mail
Shipping time: 6-8 weeks
Returns policy: only on damaged or defective goods

110 GUMP'S MAIL ORDER
P. O Box 890910
Dallas, TX
USA75389
(415) 984-9409; U.S. toll-free: (800) 284-8677

Gump's is one of the most prestigious gift shops in San Francisco, with wonderfully high-quality goods of every description. Many are unique and unusual. Included in their vast selection are Limoges porcelain, Baccarat crystal, silver, linens, contemporary gifts, jewellery, apparel, objets d'art, sculpture, fine art, lamps, decor accents, paperweights, trivets, planters, glassware, napkins, placemats, china, frames, room screens and some exquisite porcelain flowers for which I plan to save. Five catalogues are published in full colour each year: January, March, May, July and September. Canadian subscriptions are $15 (U.S.) for four issues, but our readers may request one copy free. Payment is accepted via VISA, M/C, Amex, Carte Blanche, Diners Club, Gump's charge or cheque (U.S. funds).

✔ Mail orders accepted
✔ Phone orders accepted
Minimum order: no minimum
Shipping method: mail or Federal Express
Shipping time: 1-2 weeks
Returns policy: 30-day return policy on everything in catalogue
Established in 1861

111 HADDON ROCKING HORSES LTD.
Station Road, Wallingford
Oxfordshire OX10 OHX
England
0491-36165

This source offers a beautiful range of hand-built and finished wooden rocking horses with all the style and elegance of the Georgian and Victorian versions upon which this line is based. If anything, they have improved upon the originals by combining mahogany with glass fibre for greater strength and lighter weight. Horses are immaculately detailed, and some come complete with removable, hand-stitched leather bridle and padded saddle with brass fittings and stirrups. Otherwise, there is a compete range of accessories available by mail. Prices are high, but so is the quality. Their catalogue is published once every two years and is free. Payment is accepted by VISA, M/C, Amex, IMO, cheque, Access or Diners Club.

- ✔ Mail orders accepted
- ✔ Phone orders accepted
- Minimum order: no minimum
- Shipping method: ship or airmail
- Shipping time: 6 weeks outside of U.K.
- Returns policy: all goods are guaranteed satisfactory
- Established in 1971

112 HAMILTON CLASSICS

47 Richards Ave.
Norwalk, CT
U S A 06857
Canada toll-free: (800) 367-4534

Hamilton watches are sold here, complete with money-back guarantee and manufacturers' warranty. No catalogue is available, but a toll-free call will get you a free, colour brochure by return mail. Payment is accepted with Visa, M/C, Amex, Diner's Club, IMO or cheque.

- ✔ Mail orders accepted
- ✔ Phone orders accepted
- Minimum order: no minimum
- Shipping method: airmail or surface mail only to Canada; UPS to U.S. points
- Shipping time: averages 2-4 weeks
- Returns policy: everything returnable within 30 days
- Established in 1969

113 HAMMACHER SCHLEMMER

147 East 57th St.
New York, NY
U S A 10022
(212) 421-9000; (312) 664-8170; U.S. toll-free: (800) 543-3366; U.S. customer service: (800) 233-4800

Their reputation for stocking only the "best," "the only" and "the unexpected" is unsurpassed worldwide. Some of the catalogue items are surprisingly inexpensive, but most are luxuriously costly. Almost anything you could imagine is included, from a pet doorbell (yes, that's right, so Rover can ring for admission), to the snore-reducing pillow, to the golfer's instant replay video system, to the self-propelled pool cleaning robot, or my personal favourite: the Sonic 2000 rodent repeller. Wherever required, they supply free batteries and adaptors. If you decide you don't want something you've received, they will refund the complete purchase price (no questions asked), including your return shipping expenses. Needless to say, these folks are real pros, operating

out of Chicago and New York and producing 11 full, 64-page colour catalogues every four to six weeks, year-round. Catalogues are free. Payment is preferred by VISA, M/C, Amex, Carte Blanche or Diners Club.

✔ Mail orders accepted
✔ Phone orders accepted
Minimum order: no minimum
Shipping method: UPS or Federal Express to Canada only
Shipping time: 3-5 days
Returns policy: unconditionally guaranteed; full refund if required
Established in 1848
Member: U.S. Direct Marketing Association

114 HAMPSTEAD HOUSE BOOKS

Unit 7, 60 Doncaster Ave.
Thornhill, Ontario
Canada L3T 1L5
(416) 881-0607

Specializing in Canadian books and remainders (discontinued books), this source could save you 50 to 75 percent over regular retail. Included in the catalogue offerings are cookbooks, history tomes, novels, coffee-table books, hobby books and large print books, among others. About 10 catalogues are published periodically through the year (as well, there are special sale catalogues and clearances) and are free. Payment is accepted via VISA, M/C, Amex or cheque. Ontario residents pay P.S.T.

✔ Mail orders accepted
✔ Phone orders accepted
✔ Good bargain-hunting
Minimum order: no minimum
Shipping method: Canada Post, 4th class (book rate)
Shipping time: 2-3 weeks
Returns policy: all goods guaranteed
Member: Canadian Booksellers Association, Canadian Direct Marketing Association

115 HANDART EMBROIDERIES

106 Hing Wai Building
36 Queen's Road, Central
Hong Kong
(852) 523-5744; fax: (852)-5-8455174

Handart enjoys a worldwide reputation for fast, friendly service and reasonably priced goods. If you can't visit Hong Kong in person, this may be the next best choice — by mail. All quoted prices include

shipping by surface mail. For airmail, add $5 U.S. per order. Discounts are offered on a sliding scale, from 5 percent to 25 percent (the larger your order, the greater your discount). There is no time limit on exchanges or refunds. If you are ever dissatisfied, they will cheerfully refund your entire purchase price. They promise "special discounts" to readers of this book, so mention *Shopping the World* when you write. Included in their catalogue is every imaginable kind of embroidered item, from tablecloths and bedspreads to kimonos, silk pyjamas, shirts, blouses, even slippers. They will ship gift items to a third party with your card enclosed. Orders may also be sent by fax: (852-5-8455174). A flyer-style catalogue is published every January and colour pictures of specific items are sent to you free, on request. Payment is accepted by VISA, M/C, Amex, IMO, cheque, Access or Eurocard.

✔ Special offer to readers
✔ Mail orders accepted
✔ Phone orders accepted
✔ Good bargain-hunting
Minimum order: no minimum
Shipping method: airmail or boat mail
Shipping time: one day to process order
Returns policy: full refund for any reason, anytime
Established in 1952
Member: Hong Kong Trade Association

116 HANOVER HOUSE

Hanover, PA
U S A 17331
(717) 637-6000; U.S. toll-free: (800) 621-5800

If there's anything you've ever wanted by mail order, Hanover House (or one of the companies for which it is a rep) will have it. There are housewares, clothing, gifts, art prints, lingerie, novelties, seeds and plants, Americana, collectables, and more. When you write, be sure to specify the types of catalogues in which you are most interested. Not all catalogues are free. Payment is accepted with VISA, M/C, Amex, Carte Blanche, Diners Club, Discover card, IMO or cheques.

✔ Mail orders accepted
✔ Phone orders accepted
Minimum order: no minimum
Shipping method: mail or UPS
Shipping time: 2 weeks
Returns policy: 14-day refund period

117 HARBOR SWEETS
Palmer Cove
85 Leavitt St.
Salem, MA
U S A 09170-5546
(508) 745-7648; U.S. and Canada toll-free: (800) 225-5669

Harbor Sweets attempts to make "the best chocolates in the world" and they must come darn close. There are soft, creamy caramels and a pecan in dark chocolate (Sand Dollars), orange crunch in dark chocolate (Sweet Shells) and wonderful confections in milk chocolate, too. Ingredients are all natural and they use no preservatives. Each piece is individually wrapped in gold-foil and elegantly gift-packaged. Naturally, they can ship directly to your friends, including your sentiments on a gift card. They do a lot of business with Canada and never have a problem (in fact, a gift sent to me from a friend came through duty-free). Shipping into Canada costs an extra $3. A free, full-colour catalogue is published three times a year: fall/Christmas, pre-Valentine's Day and late spring. Payment is accepted by VISA, M/C or Amex.

✔ Mail orders accepted
✔ Phone orders accepted
Minimum order: no minimum
Shipping method: mail or UPS
Shipping time: 48 hours
Returns policy: free replacement if goods are not satisfactory

118 HARRODS
Brompton Road, Knightsbridge
London SW1X 7XL
England
(71) 730-1234

Every manner of department store item is included at Harrods, which has the distinction of being the best-known store in the world. The catalogues, published twice a year, are huge and inviting and cost $5 to Canada. Goods include cookware, apparel, gourmet foods, candy, glass, crystal, china, flatware, toys and much more. Payment is accepted by VISA, M/C, Amex, Diners Club, Eurocard, Harrod's charge, IMO or cheque.

✔ Mail orders accepted
Minimum order: no minimum
Shipping method: mail, airmail or UPS
Shipping time: 2-4 weeks, depending on season
Returns policy: 30-day money-back guarantee

119 HARROWSMITH
7 Queen Victoria Road
Camden East, Ontario
Canada K0K 1J0
(613) 378-6661; Can. toll-free: (800) 267-7833

Harrowsmith is a great Canadian success story in the magazine (and back-to-basics) field. So it follows that their modest 32-page illustrated catalogue and small Christmas supplement would reflect that homey, ecologically ethical stance, and they don't disappoint. Inside are gardening how-to books, helpful garden source material and nature videos, such as "Listening to the Loons." Both catalogues are free. Payment is accepted with VISA, M/C, IMO or cheque. Ontario residents add P.S.T. to purchases.

✔ Mail orders accepted
Minimum order: no minimum
Shipping method: Canada Post
Shipping time: 2 weeks
Returns policy: all goods returnable if not satisfied

120 HAYIM PINHAS KIMYEVI VE MADEN MAMULLERI IHRACAT VE ITHALAT AS
Tahtakale Yavasçasahin Sk. Kristal
Han Kat:3 no:305
P.O. Box 500-34460
Sirkeci-Istanbul-Turkey
(9.01) 528 69 51; (9.01) 522 93 02

Hayim Pinhas sells one thing only, and that's Meerschaum pipes. They've been selling "best pipes since 1939" and their benefit to you is that you are buying directly from the handcarver. Their catalogue has been unchanged for five years and is free to our readers. Shipping charge is an additional $5.50 (Cdn.) over costs of pipes. Be certain when ordering, as there is a no-returns policy. Goods may be purchased by cheque or IMO only (Canadian funds are acceptable).

✔ Special offer to readers
✔ Mail orders accepted
✔ Phone orders accepted
Minimum order: 2 pipes minimum
Shipping method: mail only
Shipping time: 15 days
Returns policy: no returns
Established in 1939

121 HEARTHSONG
P.O. Box B
Sebastapol, CA
U S A 95473-0601
(707) 829-1550 ; U.S. toll-free: (800) 325-2502

This funky source for quality toys, books, art supplies and games caters to families with small children. Their catalogue is free. Payment is accepted with Visa, M/C, IMO or cheques payable in U.S. funds.

✔ Mail orders accepted
✔ Good bargain-hunting
Minimum order: no minimum
Shipping method: UPS or mail
Shipping time: 2 weeks
Returns policy: all goods guaranteed

122 HEDONICS
302 Bridgeland Avenue
Toronto, Ontario
Canada M6A 1Z4
(416) 785-0262; Can. toll-free: 1 (800) 387-5533

Hedonics is Canada's answer to "the best, the unique and the most exclusive." Included is the Seiko "Kitchen Whiz" calculator, Sanyo bread maker, hearing amplifiers, a neon phone, a de-bugging device and more. Catalogues are published seasonally and are free. A new warehouse showroom has opened in Toronto, if you wish to shop in person. Otherwise, credit card orders are taken by phone and you may use cheques or money orders only for mail ordering. Accepted methods of payment are VISA, M/C, Amex, IMO and cheque. Ontario residents, add 8 percent P.S.T.

✔ Mail orders accepted
✔ Phone orders accepted
Minimum order: no minimum
Shipping method: Canada Post
Shipping time: 3-4 weeks
Returns policy: all goods guaranteed
Established in 1984
Member: Better Business Bureau

123 HEPTING AND FARRER LTD., THE JEWELLERS
7-11 Murray Place
Stirling, Scotland
FK8 1DH
(0786) 50382

These traditional family jewellers produce a fine catalogue of retail jewellery in silver or gold. You can expect savings of 10 percent on quantity orders, or during their January sale. Their catalogue is renewed every November and is free. Payment is accepted with VISA, M/C, Amex, Access and Diners Club.

✔ Mail orders accepted
✔ Phone orders accepted
✔ Good bargain-hunting
Minimum order: no minimum
Shipping method: air or surface mail
Shipping time: 1 week if article in stock
Returns policy: all goods guaranteed

124 HERITAGE CANADA GIFT COLLECTION
P.O. Box 1358, Station "B"
Ottawa, Ontario
Canada K1P 5R4
(613) 237-1066; (613) 237-1867; Can. toll-free: (800) 267-6670

Heritage Canada presents a small but unique collection of Christmas gifts, including Inuit-print silk scarves signed in Inuktitut by the artists, Newfoundland cottage-craft (hand-knit) woollens, Christmas cards and decorations, posters, posh journals and datebooks, honey, jams, Quebec maple syrup, Micmac Indian authentic black ash baskets from P.E.I., Staddle Broomsquire cornbrooms from Arden, Ontario, native flower seeds, silk ties, books, and B.C.'s own Rogers' Victoria creams. The colour catalogue is free.

✔ Mail orders accepted
✔ Phone orders accepted
Minimum order: no minimum
Shipping method: Canada Post; shipping costs start at $4
Shipping time: by phone: 2-3 days; reg.: 2-3 weeks
Returns policy: all goods guaranteed against defects

125 THE HERITAGE CLUB
47 Richards Ave.
Norwalk, CT
U S A 06857
Canada toll-free: (800) 367-4534

This is a source for books of all kinds, particularly reference, educational and history. There is no catalogue, but price lists and brochures are available, by calling toll-free during Eastern time zone business hours. Payment is accepted with Visa, M/C, Amex, Diner's Club, IMO or cheque.

✔ Mail orders accepted
✔ Phone orders accepted
Minimum order: no minimum
Shipping method: airmail or surface mail only to Canada; UPS to U.S. points
Shipping time: averages 2-4 weeks
Returns policy: everything returnable within 30 days
Established in 1969

126 HO CHING CHEONG INVESTMENT CO., LTD.

7/F Justen Centre
46-52 Wai Ching Street
Yaumatei, Kowloon
Hong Kong
(852) 770-2817 ; fax: (852) 3-770-0235;
telex: 34556 HCCIC HX

These friendly people will meet you more than half-way (they're eager for the business). They sell only a limited range of products, but if you want bamboo products such as toothpicks, chopsticks, ashtrays, skewers and small restaurant items, this is the place. They will also welcome customers' designs, which they can accommodate in one of their three factories in China. Free price lists are available on request, or fax them for a price-quote on any items. Payment is accepted with IMO or bank draft in U.S., Canadian or Hong Kong dollars.

✔ Mail orders accepted
✔ Phone orders accepted
✔ Good bargain-hunting
Minimum order: no minimum
Shipping method: airmail or surface mail
Shipping time: 4-6 weeks
Returns policy: all goods guaranteed

127 HOLLYWOOD MAGIC, INC.

6614 Hollywood Blvd.
Hollywood, CA
U S A 90028
(213) 464-5610

This place is just a few blocks from my sister's loft on Hollywood Blvd., and close to Mann's Chinese Theater (where all the star's footprints are in the cement out front). It's a truly dreadful neighbourhood, which is why, if you're in the market for magic supplies and sleight-of-hand gear, you'll be relieved to be able to shop by mail. The catalogue is $4, refundable on your first order. Payment is accepted with Visa, M/C, IMO or cheques in U.S. funds.

✔ Mail orders accepted
Minimum order: no minimum
Shipping method: UPS or mail
Shipping time: 2 weeks
Returns policy: all goods guaranteed

128 HOLST, INC.
1118 W. Lake, Box 370
Tawas City, MI
U S A 48764

This source sells weathervanes (crowing rooster, galloping horse) made with friction-free bearings to allow for free movement in the smallest breeze. Each comes with mounting materials. Just be careful you don't fall off the roof! Information pamphlet is free. Payment is accepted with IMO or cheque.

✔ Mail orders accepted
Minimum order: no minimum
Shipping method: mail
Shipping time: 2-4 weeks
Returns policy: 20-day money-back guarantee

129 HOLY JEWELRY
c/o Royal Hotel
Ratchadamnoen Ave.
Bangkok
Thailand
(662) 222-9111

A friend recommended this place to me for custom-crafted jewellery. They prefer to work from a photograph, so if you see a piece of jewellery in a magazine that you like, they can copy it, nearly exactly. They use real gemstones, or ones you supply. Remember that set gemstones, and the settings themselves, are dutiable coming into Canada. When you write, direct your inquiry to "Mrs. Lamai" and request a price-quote before ordering. No catalogue is available. Payment is accepted with VISA, M/C, or Amex only.

✔ Mail orders accepted
✔ Good bargain-hunting
Minimum order: one item
Shipping method: airmail, insured
Shipping time: 2-3 weeks
Returns policy: no returns on custom work unless faulty

130 HONEST PHOTO & AUDIO SUPPLIES

Shop A1, G/F, Bo Yip Bldg.
10 Peking Road, Tsim Sha Tsui
Kowloon
Hong Kong
(852) 369-1323; 368-9962; 366-0972

I have friends who swear by the deals they've had from this place on cameras, small electronics, and tape recorders, but I found the people a trifle sullen and unfriendly. Take that caution to heart, or consider dealing instead with 47th Street Photo in New York if you're a worrier. Otherwise, their prices are very good compared to domestic. Price lists are available, but you're better off to send them a note with the specifics of what you're after and see if they can supply. Don't forget to add in import duty and F.S.T. Payment is accepted with VISA, M/C, Amex and IMO.

✔ Mail orders accepted
Minimum order: no minimum
Shipping method: airmail, insured
Shipping time: 2-3 weeks
Returns policy: all goods guaranteed but returns are slow

131 HORCHOW CATALOGUE

Subscriptions Department
P.O. Box 620048
Dallas, TX
U S A 75262-0048
(214) 888-9700; U.S. toll-free: (800) 527-0303;
fax: (214) 888-9797

Roger Horchow is known as the King of Mail Order — and that's high-quality mail order. Each of the 10 to 12 catalogues produced annually features completely new and different items collected worldwide, including fine gifts, apparel, furniture, linens, placemats, decor accents, jewellery, luggage, rugs, china, boudoir accents, chatchkas (but only of the finest quality), silver, frames, quilts, trivets, gadgets, watches, men's items (including some wonderful ties), cookware (oh, those brass pots), hammocks and even nature tapes from the Audubon Society. Though a one-year subscription to those 10 to 12 catalogues normally costs $5 to U.S. addresses, and $10 to Canada, they will send our readers one copy free, if you mention this book. Some goods are discounted, too, in periodic sale catalogues. Their motto: "We're not satisfied until you are!" Payment is accepted via VISA, M/C, Amex, Diners Club, Discover card, IMO or cheque (U.S. funds).

- ✔ Special offer to readers
- ✔ Mail orders accepted
- ✔ Phone orders accepted

Minimum order: no minimum
Shipping method: mail
Shipping time: 2 weeks
Returns policy: returns: ship prepaid and include packing slip
Established in 1973

132 HUNTER'S OF HONG KONG

Ocean Terminal
Shop 122
Kowloon
Hong Kong
(852) 723-0155; (852) 368-6061

Hunter's of Hong Kong sells only the most prestigious china and crystal from names like Lladro, Herend, Wedgwood, Royal Doulton and Boehm at prices 20 to 40 percent less than local retail. Their sales sheets are updated with periodic price lists, which are all free. Payment is accepted with VISA, M/C, Amex or IMO.

- ✔ Mail orders accepted
- ✔ Phone orders accepted

Minimum order: no minimum
Shipping method: airmail or surface mail (insured)
Shipping time: 4-6 weeks surface mail
Returns policy: all goods guaranteed

133 ICEMART MAIL-ORDER DEPARTMENT

235 Keflavik Airport
Iceland
U.S. toll-free: (800) 431-9003

These beautiful Icelandic sweaters, jackets, capes, mitts, caps, laprobes and blankets cost about half what you'd pay at home. No catalogue is available, but a full-colour brochure showing all the styles is sent to you airmail for $2. Payment on orders is accepted with VISA, M/C, Amex or Diners Club.

- ✔ Mail orders accepted
- ✔ Phone orders accepted
- ✔ Good bargain-hunting

Minimum order: no minimum
Shipping method: airmail or surface mail

Shipping time: 2-6 weeks
Returns policy: all goods unconditionally guaranteed
Established in 1970

134 IKEA MAIL ORDER
West Edmonton Mall, Phase III
2556 - 8770 - 170th St.
Edmonton, Alberta
Canada T5T 4M2
(403) 444-2345; Can. toll-free: (800) 661-9807;
fax: (416) 226-6750

Not everybody knows that the Vancouver Ikea store is the prototype (and a very successful one, too) for all of its North American expansion plans. Ikea managed to stay profitable even in the bleakest recession days. How? By great customer service, good pricing and brilliant marketing plans. Even their catalogue has extra offers, including coupons that allow you to dine in their in-store cafeterias, get a chit equal to the cost of the meal, then apply that total amount to items in the store. Goods in the free annual catalogue may be mail-ordered if you don't live near a retail branch. Included in the available merchandise are innovative home furnishings, cookware, wall coverings, carpets, toys, knock-down furniture (for office, workshop or home), shelving, party supplies, decor accents, lamps, sofas, linens and bedding. Catalogues are mailed from Edmonton, and fax service is in Toronto, and of course, the whole chain originated in Sweden. Payment is accepted with VISA, M/C, IMO or cheques.

✔ Mail orders accepted
✔ Phone orders accepted
✔ Good bargain-hunting
Minimum order: no minimum
Shipping method: Canada Post or freight
Shipping time: 1-3 weeks (depends on goods)
Returns policy: all goods unconditionally guaranteed

135 IMPACT PUBLICATIONS
10655 Big Oak Circle
Manassas, VA
U S A 22111-3040
(703) 361-7300; fax: (703) 335-9486

This direct-from-the-publisher source sells hard-to-find career, job-search, travel and shopping books from their own list. Included are the best travel/shopping books ever, by Drs. Ron and Caryl Krannich, a husband-and-wife team who have lived and worked (and shopped) in the places they write about, including the South Pacific, the Caribbean, Southeast Asia, Australia and Papua New Guinea, and Indonesia. Their first book, *Shopping in Exotic Places*, is a treasure no traveller should be without. The catalogue is published annually and is free. Payment is accepted with VISA, M/C, IMO or cheques. Institutions may make billing arrangements.

✔ Mail orders accepted
✔ Phone orders accepted
Minimum order: no minimum
Shipping method: mail or UPS
Shipping time: 2 weeks
Returns policy: all goods guaranteed

136 IMPOSTER COPY JEWELS
651 Gateway Blvd., Suite 900
South San Francisco, CA
U S A 94080
(415) 358-9775 (store); (415) 588-1800 (corporate office)

Nancy Olsen can sell you an exact replica of Princess Di's wedding ring for $40 (U.S.). Well, not an exact replica: the stones are "faux." Duplicates of those fabulous David Webb animal bracelets are about the most expensive items she sells, and those are only $200. The trick with these fakes is that the settings are solid and expensive-looking, and the fake gemstones actually have more sparkle than real ones. Nancy claims that Jackie Onassis, Barbara Stanwyck and Princess Diana herself all wear fake jewellery, and you can, too. The annual catalogue and price list are free, and they will gladly price-quote any item you are seeking. Sometimes they will have something in stock that replicates your magazine tear-outs, so it's worth writing to inquire. Payment is accepted with VISA, M/C, Amex, IMO or cheques (U.S. funds only, please).

✔ Mail orders accepted
✔ Phone orders accepted
✔ Good bargain-hunting
Minimum order: no minimum
Shipping method: airmail or UPS
Shipping time: 2 weeks
Returns policy: all goods guaranteed
Established in 1984

137 INDUSTRIAL REVOLUTION
2306 Granville St.
Vancouver, B.C.
Canada V6H 3G3
(604) 734-4395; fax: (604) 736-2925

Industrial Revolution is a joy to shop in, and nearly as much fun by mail. They carry state-of-the-art lighting, closet organizers, space savers, patio furniture, giftware, fireplace mantels, office accessories, and imports from Italy, England, France and Germany, to name but a few. Catalogues for each product category (e.g., separate one for "home organizers") plus sales and discount flyers are free. Payment is accepted with VISA, M/C, IMO and cheques. They have a "mail order discount program," which means that purchases up to $100 get a 10% discount, up to $500 receive 20% and up to $2500 receive 25%. Purchases over $2500 get a special quotation.

✔ Mail orders accepted
✔ Phone orders accepted
✔ Good bargain-hunting
Minimum order: no minimum
Shipping method: Canada Post or shipping for large pieces
Shipping time: 2 days to 2 weeks
Returns policy: all goods guaranteed to satisfy (30 days)

138 INTERNATIONAL BANK OF ASIA
X'mas Mail Order Catalogue
Customer Service Department
G.P.O. Box 13198
Hong Kong
880-3669

This glossy catalogue (in Chinese and English) is published only at Christmas, by one of Asia's major banks. It includes high-end extravagances like watches, gold coins, jewellery, children's toy robots, electronics, sculpture, novelties and executive toys. Prices quoted are in HK dollars (divide by approximately seven to get Canadian dollars). Payment is accepted by VISA, M/C, and cheques payable to "Times Direct Marketing."

✔ Mail orders accepted
✔ Phone orders accepted
Minimum order: no minimum
Shipping method: airmail or surface mail
Shipping time: 2-3 weeks
Returns policy: 14 days free trial

139 IROQRAFTS LTD.

RR #2
Ohsweken, Ontario
Canada N0A 1M0
(416) 765-4206; fax: (416) 765-5633

Iroqrafts is one of North American's largest suppliers of native Indian art and crafts, and since they don't give dealers a discount, their prices are much less than you'd pay in a retail store. They carry items you won't find anywhere else, including: totems, carvings, posters, art, moccasins, beads, birch-bark canoes, bear rugs, papoose carriers, hobby supplies, headbands, beadwork, books, Inuit art and soapstone carvings, and many, many items from the Iroquois band. The catalogue is updated periodically and costs $2 (refundable with first order) and they prefer that you send them a 9 x 12 SASE for reply. They will do C.O.D. in Canada on phone orders. Otherwise, they prefer payment by Canadian Money Order or bank draft. No personal cheques. Ontario residents add P.S.T.

✔ Mail orders accepted
✔ Phone orders accepted
✔ Good bargain-hunting
✔ SASE required
Minimum order: minimum $25 order, or pay $2 surcharge
Shipping method: Canada Post or CanPar
Shipping time: "24 hours 95% of the time"
Returns policy: all goods guaranteed

140 J. CREW

One Ivy Crescent
Lynchburg, VA
U S A 24506
(804) 385-6700; (212) 886-2500; U.S. toll-free: (800) 562-0258

Arthur Cinader runs this mega-operation like a family business, though catalogue sales in excess of $150 million annually have become the norm in the half-dozen years since J. Crew began marketing its wares. Included in the catalogue offerings are upmarket, casual sportwear, exhibiting what Cinader calls "understated flair," plus Shaker cotton

sweaters, "weathered" T-shirts, men's tweed jackets and men's and women's business attire. They also sell active-wear and swimwear, and all garments are from their original J. Crew lines. They will send gifts to your friends, with a message on a price-free "invoice" included. Ten catalogues are published yearly, some including clearance items or sales flyers, and all are free, but can only be sent to U.S. addresses. Shipping cost is a fixed $3.95, again to U.S. addresses only. Payment is accepted with VISA, M/C, Amex, IMO or cheques.

✔ Mail orders accepted
✔ Phone orders accepted
Minimum order: no minimum
Shipping method: mail or UPS to U.S. address ONLY; Fed. Ex costs more
Shipping time: 1-2 days
Returns policy: all goods guaranteed satisfactory
Established in 1984

141 J. FLORIS LTD.
89 Jermyn Street
London SW1Y 6JH
England
(71) 930 2885

In 1730 Juan Famenias Floris sailed from his native island of Minorca to seek his fortune in England. It was daring of this young Mediterranean stranger to set up shop in the ritzy quarter of St. James, almost opposite the splendid new church that Christoper Wren had built, but Floris was a visionary in his time. And there they've been ever since, building a reputation known the world round. Nowadays, you can order directly from them from a great selection of toiletries, perfumes and shaving accessories for ladies and gentlemen. They are best known for a wonderful range of English flower perfumes. Their quality and service set them apart. Please note that no exchanges or refunds are given. A full-colour catalogue is produced every spring and is free, on request. Payment is accepted by VISA, M/C, Amex, IMO, Access, Diners Club and cheques.

✔ Mail orders accepted
✔ Phone orders accepted
Minimum order: no minimum
Shipping method: airmail or surface mail
Shipping time: 2 weeks
Returns policy: no returns or refunds
Established in 1730
By appointment to the Queen and Prince of Wales

142 THE J. PETERMAN COMPANY
257 Midland Ave.
Lexington, KY
U S A 40507
(606) 231-7064; U.S. toll-free: (800) 231-7341

My friend Michael has a long horseman's coat his brother sent him from Australia as a joke. Tastes have caught up to it, and now that that coat has become a fashion statement, Michael refers to it as his "J. Peterman coat," even though it didn't come from this catalogue. That's a testimony to the wisdom of John Peterman himself and to his success in marketing a very few, but carefully selected items, by mail. Peterman's idea is that people want quality in what they buy, but they also want romance. The classic horseman's duster is a perfect example. Peterman ran a little ad in the *New Yorker* and the *Wall Street Journal* and sold coats all over the world, including 2,000 in a single order to "a mysterious gentleman in Japan." As Peterman says, "Well, the coat is magnificent. Simple, functional, handsome, extremely well made, affordable and yes, romantic." His entire catalogue reflects that philosophy, from the counterfeit mailbag, to the coal miner's bag, to the Panama hat, 1920s bathing suit, Gatsby shirt, Mephisto shoes, simple-but-primo leather boots, Babe Ruth bat, Montblanc pen or the Gaugin hat. Catalogues are produced for spring and fall and are free to our readers. Payment is accepted with VISA, M/C or C.O.D.s (the latter to U.S. addresses only).

✔ Special offer to readers
✔ Mail orders accepted
✔ Phone orders accepted
✔ Good bargain-hunting
Minimum order: no minimum
Shipping method: mail
Shipping time: 48 hours
Returns policy: "Absolute satisfaction" or money back. "Period."

143 J.W. DEVITT
648 East Hastings St.
Vancouver, B.C.
Canada V6A 1R1
(604) 251-4744

Devitt's sells office furniture, stationery supplies, printing and calculators at good prices year-round, and at sale prices each winter. Their "Office Trends" flyers are free. Payment is accepted with VISA, M/C, cheque or purchase order where credit has been established.

✔ Mail orders accepted
✔ Phone orders accepted
Minimum order: no minimum
Shipping method: Canada Post or shipping firms
Shipping time: depends on item
Returns policy: all goods guaranteed
Established in 1978
Member: Canadian Independent Stationers

144 JAFFE BROS. INC.
P.O. Box 636
Valley Center, CA
U S A 92082
(619) 749-1133

Jaffe Bros. sell natural foods. They have organic dried fruits, dates, nuts, edible seeds, dehydrated veggies, nut butters, jellies, jams, honey, carob confections, juices, bee pollen, dried coconut, unrefined salad oils, tree-ripened olives, herb teas and even organic, low-salt, Kosher dill pickles. They sell unrefined natural sea salt and Mother Earth tortilla chips in both tamari and no-salt varieties. The catalogue is updated in November and is free. Payment is accepted via VISA, M/C, IMO or cheque.

✔ Mail orders accepted
✔ Phone orders accepted
✔ Good bargain-hunting
Minimum order: no minimum
Shipping method: mail or UPS
Shipping time: 1 - 2 days
Returns policy: defective goods must be reported within 10 days

145 JAKE'S FAMOUS PRODUCTS, INC.
4910 N. Basin Ave.
Portland, OR
U S A 97217
(503) 226-1420

This company has a reputation in the Pacific Northwest for high standards in its gourmet foods. Among the favourites are smoked salmon, smoked salmon paté, smoked trout paté, Jake's clam chowder, gift packs, chocolate truffle cakes, chocolate truffle sauce and Irish whiskey sauce. The brief but detailed (and full-colour) catalogue is renewed every August and is free. Payment is accepted by VISA, M/C, Amex, Discover card, or IMO, and C.O.D. orders can be sent to U.S. addresses.

✔ Mail orders accepted
✔ Phone orders accepted
Minimum order: no minimum
Shipping method: mail or UPS
Shipping time: 4 days
Returns policy: 100 percent guarantee on everything
Established in 1892

146 JAY NORRIS SELECT
P.O. Box 940
Montreal North, P.Q.
Canada H1H 5T6
(514) 325-0260

If you live in Canada and have never heard of Jay Norris, you must have been sleeping in the woods like old Mr. Van Winkle! This outfit is one of our more active mail order houses, sending national mailings out in bulk to all main centres. Just in case you don't know how to find them, here are the basics: A one-year "subscription" to their catalogues costs $1, but if you write as one of our readers, they'll put you on the list free. If you fail to purchase after a period of time, your name will be deleted. They sell novelties, clothing, chatchkas, gifts, trivets, linens, placemats, a few business supplies, cosmetics, jewellery, books, lingerie, exercise equipment and some furniture and accessories. They even had "The King of Clocks," a guitar-shaped creation with a picture of Elvis, highlighted with gold. Sales and clearance prices are very low. Payment is accepted by VISA, M/C or cheque. A shipping "credit" certificate is given with each order fulfilled, to be used against the next order's shipping costs. Quebec residents, add 9 percent P.S.T.

✔ Special offer to readers
✔ Mail orders accepted
✔ Phone orders accepted
✔ Good bargain-hunting
Minimum order: no minimum
Shipping method: Canada Post
Shipping time: 2 weeks
Returns policy: 90-day money-back guarantee
Established in 1975
Member: Canadian Direct Marketing Association

147 JESSICA'S BISCUIT
Box 301
Newtonville, MA
U S A 02160
(617) 965-0530

Bob Rome sells cookbooks by mail, many of them hard to find. His catalogue is changed as often as six times a year, depending on what's available. Shipping costs about $3.50 in the U.S. Catalogues (about six each year) cost $2. Payment is best by VISA, M/C or cheque.

✔ Mail orders accepted
✔ Phone orders accepted
Minimum order: no minimum
Shipping method: mail or UPS
Shipping time: depends on time of year
Returns policy: satisfaction guaranteed

148 JEWELAND
World Jewels Trade Center Ltd.
987 Silom Road
Bangkok 10500
Thailand
(662) 233-8388; 233-8389; 235-1254; 235-1255

This place is also known as the "Gem Supermarket." It is housed within the same building as the Institute of Gemology, so students and practising gemologists (such as Dale Mearns — see entry under "Rama Trade") can buy at a discount. A positively staggering assortment of diamonds, rubies, sapphires, garnets, amethysts, emeralds and everything else you can imagine is sold here. There are also necklaces, antique jewellery and artifacts. Everything is sold on a price-quote basis, which means you really must know what you're doing so you can specify the weight of the stone in carats, the colour, intensity, and so on. If you feel you can't do all this on your own, contact Dale Mearns to act on your behalf. Payment to Jeweland is accepted with VISA, M/C, Amex, IMO or cheques.

✔ Mail orders accepted
✔ Phone orders accepted
✔ Good bargain-hunting
Minimum order: no minimum
Shipping method: airmail, insured
Shipping time: 2-6 weeks
Returns policy: goods cannot be returned or exchanged

149 JIM THOMPSON SILK COMPANY
9 Suriwongse Road
Bangkok
Thailand
(662) 234-4900

Jim Thompson himself is the central figure in an unsolved mystery in Bangkok. He disappeared one evening after dining with friends, and has never been found. However, the silk trading company he established is among the finest in the world. In recent years, it has become a little touristy, but the wares are still good and the values are there in silk clothing, ties, yard goods, upholstery fabrics, jewellery boxes, pillow shams, scarves and the like. A catalogue is published periodically and updated with price lists as required. Both are available free. Payment is accepted with VISA, M/C, Amex or IMO.

✔ Mail orders accepted
Minimum order: no minimum
Shipping method: surface mail or airmail
Shipping time: 5-6 weeks surface mail
Returns policy: all goods guaranteed; yard goods can't be returned

150 JOHN DEERE
Moline, IL
U S A 61265
(309) 765-8000; U.S. toll-free: (800) 544-2122

John Deere has a reputation for quality goods and this varied catalogue emphasizes that point. Here you'll find lawn and garden furniture, playhouses, wagons, and fine household and garden supplies of every description. The seasonal catalogue is free, and you'll keep receiving them if you order something. Payment is accepted with Visa, M/C, IMO or cheque (U.S. funds only, please).

✔ Mail orders accepted
✔ Phone orders accepted
Minimum order: no minimum
Shipping method: UPS, Fed Ex or U.S. postal service
Shipping time: 3-4 weeks, depending on item
Returns policy: all goods guaranteed

151 JOHN LOBB LTD., BOOTMAKER
9 St. James Street
London SW1A 1EF
England
(71) 930-3664/5

John Lobb is the official bootmaker to HRH Queen Elizabeth; HRH Prince Philip, the Duke of Edinburgh; HRH Prince Charles, the Prince of Wales; and a host of kings and European royalty spanning more than a century. When you contact them, they will send you a complex measuring form from which they custom-make a last to match your foot. Alternatively, you can send them a pair of comfortable shoes and they will create a last to fit it exactly, replicating your actual feet as closely as possible. Their styles do not change from season to season, or even from year to year, as they are established classics. And for all this luxury, you will pay dearly, but you may find no finer footwear anywhere on the planet. Every shoe or boot they make is hand-crafted from the finest leather to individual measurements. Their catalogue is "permanent"; they also supply photos of styles, all free to readers of this book. Payment is accepted via VISA, M/C, Amex, IMO, Cheque, Access or Eurocard.

✔ Special offer to readers
✔ Mail orders accepted
✔ Phone orders accepted
Minimum order: no minimum
Shipping method: mail or airmail
Shipping time: approximately 6 months
Returns policy: returns only if dissatisfaction proven
Established in 1862
Member of everything; see text

152 KATHLEEN'S ARAN KNITS
Upper Main Street
Mountcharles
County Donegal
Ireland
73-35108

Kathleen's knitters create custom sweaters of the traditional "Aran" type knits, at very reasonable prices. All sweaters are hand-knit from 100-percent sheep's wool. They also sell blankets, throws, bedspreads, capes and tweeds. No catalogue is available, but you can request a free brochure and price list. These are all custom orders. Payment is accepted with VISA, M/C, Amex and IMOs in pounds sterling.

✔ Mail orders accepted
✔ Good bargain-hunting
Minimum order: no minimum
Shipping method: airmail or surface mail
Shipping time: 4-8 weeks (depends on goods)
Returns policy: all items guaranteed or full refund
Established in 1976

153 KENDAL PLAYING CARD SALES

3, Oakbank House, Skelsmergh
Kendal, Cumbria
LA8 9AJ
England
0539 722055

This specialty house is run by collectors Lorna and Maurice Collett for other collectors interested in contemporary and unusual old playing cards. They spent three weeks in Western Canada last year and found virtually no cards to add to their personal collection, which they suggest indicates a need for good sources elsewhere — and that's where they come in. Although not manufacturers, they acquire and resell interesting playing cards from around the world, via a free catalogue they reprint once or twice a year as the need arises. Included in the vast array of playing cards are decks with movie stars in the picture cards, some with birds, Japanese women, literary figures and even a deck featuring members of the living Royal family. There are some exotic tarot decks, as well, many at very reasonable prices. Did you know that German suits are leaves, acorns, hearts and bells; that Swiss suits are bells, flowers, shields and acorns; and that Italian suits are batons, cups, swords and money? Who says mail order isn't educational? The Colletts do not accept credit card payment, but do take Canadian currency in cheques drawn on Canadian banks. The catalogue is free by surface mail, and they'll send it airmail for $1, but please send cash (or a U.S. bill if you can't find a Canadian one), as their bank charges them $10 to cash your cheque. Payment by IMO is preferred (Canadian funds).

✔ Mail orders accepted
Minimum order: no minimum
Shipping method: surface or airmail; for airmail send $1 Cdn. (bill)
Shipping time: "next day dispatch"
Returns policy: all goods guaranteed or money refunded

154 KING SOUND

1312 New Road, Bangkrak
Bangkok
Thailand
(662) 233-1015

By my reckoning, this is one of the cheapest places anywhere to find good, brand-name cassette recorders and small electronics. I priced Sony professional recording-Walkman models that sell for 45 percent more here at home, and these units are not stripped of all their accessories the way they sometimes are in Hong Kong. It's certainly

worth writing them for a price-quote on an item you're contemplating buying. They do not have a price list or catalogue. Payment is accepted with VISA, M/C, Amex or IMO.

✔ Mail orders accepted
✔ Phone orders accepted
✔ Good bargain-hunting
Minimum order: no minimum
Shipping method: airmail, insured
Shipping time: 2 weeks
Returns policy: all goods guaranteed or money back

155 KINGS SLAP SHOP
8808 S. Sepulveda Blvd.
Los Angeles, CA
U S A 90045
(213) 215-1084

This is the home of official souvenirs and apparel from the L.A. Kings hockey team. Also available are mementoes and paraphernalia from the Dodgers, Lakers, Raiders and other teams. The catalogue is available free. Payment is accepted with Visa, M/C, Amex, Discover card, IMO or cheques in U.S. funds.

✔ Mail orders accepted
✔ Phone orders accepted
Minimum order: no minimum
Shipping method: UPS or mail
Shipping time: 10 days to 2 weeks
Returns policy: all goods guaranteed if returned unused

156 THE KNITWEAR ARCHITECTS
1926 West 4th Avenue
Vancouver, B.C.
Canada V6J 1M5
(604) 736-4383

Marg Meikle is a part-time CBC broadcaster in Vancouver, but her real passion is knitwear. She and partner Janice Tsuruda (who is the designer) produce a profusion of glorious designs for men's, women's and children's knitwear and supply entire kits (absolutely everything you need) to produce these unique creations. The permanent catalogue (updated periodically) is a work of art itself, and it will cost you $4 to see for yourself. Payment for kits is accepted by VISA, M/C, Amex, IMO or cheque. B.C. residents, pay P.S.T., too.

✔ Mail orders accepted
✔ Phone orders accepted
Minimum order: no minimum
Shipping method: mail, but mostly UPS
Shipping time: 2-3 weeks
Returns policy: all goods guaranteed; return for credit only
Established in 1987

157 KNOWLEDGE BOOKSTORE

Box 94000
Richmond, B.C.
Canada V6Y 2A2
(604) 660-2000

The Knowledge Network in B.C. runs this mail order branch, to sell VHS videos (shows like "Rockschool"; David Attenborough's natural history series; music, cooking, drama, personal development and teaching programs), plus records, prerecorded cassettes and posters. The catalogue is modest but detailed and free. Payment is accepted with VISA, M/C or cheques only.

✔ Mail orders accepted
✔ Phone orders accepted
Minimum order: no minimum
Shipping method: Canada Post
Shipping time: 2 weeks
Returns policy: all goods guaranteed

158 L.H. SELMAN LTD.

761 Chestnut St.
Santa Cruz, CA
U S A 95060
(408) 427-1177; U.S. toll-free: (800) 538-0766;
fax: (408) 427-0111

This source sells only one item: paperweights. They have classic styles, French and Scottish imports, Millefiori glass, and every imaginable kind for the collector. But you had better be serious, because the colour catalogue costs $15 (refunded on orders over $100). Otherwise, there's no minimum order. All prices include postage, and all paperweights are shipped insured. If you wish to have your purchase sent by Federal Express, that's extra. They accept fax orders, too. Tell them you are one of our readers when you write, and they'll send you a free package of information. Payment is accepted with VISA, M/C, IMO or cheques (U.S. funds only).

✔ Special offer to readers
✔ Mail orders accepted
✔ Phone orders accepted
Minimum order: no minimum
Shipping method: airmail or UPS (shipped insured)
Shipping time: 6-8 weeks, if not in stock
Returns policy: all goods guaranteed
Established in 1970

159 L.L. BEAN, INC.
Freeport, ME
U S A 04033
(207) 865-4761; toll-free: (800) 221-4221 (orders);
(800) 341-4341 (service)

When old L.L. started this firm almost 80 years ago, I doubt he ever imagined the company's mail order sales would top $520 million (U.S.) in a single year, but there it is. More than 6,000 items are featured in their frequent catalogues, including T-shirts, bikes, luggage, watches, cameras, electronics, binoculars, hammocks, gardening supplies, outdoor furniture, cookware, dog beds, drinking glasses, fishing gear, camping gear, hiking gear, sleeping bags, tents, bike helmets, outdoor goods, outdoor apparel, shoes, clothing, accessories, hats, rain gear, parkas, sweaters, moccasins, dresses, skirts, shorts, jeans, fishing, camping, hiking and hunting gear, sleeping bags, camp stoves, tents, kayaks, canoes, snorkels, paddles, hiking boots, and deck shoes. Catalogues are produced 22 times a year and mailed out free. Payment is accepted with VISA, M/C, Amex, IMO and cheques.

✔ Mail orders accepted
✔ Phone orders accepted
✔ Good bargain-hunting
Minimum order: no minimum
Shipping method: mail or UPS
Shipping time: 1-2 weeks
Returns policy: refund or exchange
Established in 1912

160 L.M. MEDIA MARKETING
9575 Côte de Liesse
Dorval, P.Q.
Canada H9P 1A3
(514) 631-9010

These are unique entries, as their goods are entirely free. They list hundreds upon hundred of free films and videos that you may borrow if you return them pre-paid (means: you pay return postage). The only hitch is you must write to them representing a group of some sort, even if it's one you "invented" to qualify for ordering. Most topics are meant to promote a group, country or activity, while some are purely educational. You are also asked to fill out an "audience report card" (for their on-going research) and return it with the materials you've borrowed. This address serves Quebec, Prince Edward Island, Nova Scotia, Newfoundland and New Brunswick.

✔ Mail orders accepted
✔ Phone orders accepted
✔ Good bargain-hunting
Minimum order: no minimum
Shipping method: Canada Post
Shipping time: 1 week
Returns policy: see text

161 L.M. MEDIA MARKETING
115 Torbay Road, Unit 9
Markham, Ontario
Canada L3R 2M9
(416) 475-3750

These are unique entries, as their goods are entirely free. They list hundreds upon hundred of free films and videos that you may borrow if you return them pre-paid (means: you pay return postage). The only hitch is you must write to them representing a group of some sort, even if that group is "Elm Street Parents" or "Concerned Singles Group" or another assemblage you've created for the purpose of ordering. This address serves all of Ontario and Manitoba and offers many films and videos not available to other L.M. Media Marketing areas. You are also asked to fill out an "audience report card" (for their on-going research) and return it with the materials you've borrowed.

✔ Mail orders accepted
✔ Phone orders accepted
✔ Good bargain-hunting
Minimum order: no minimum
Shipping method: Canada Post
Shipping time: 1 week
Returns policy: see text

162 L.M. MEDIA MARKETING
15161 Fraser Hwy.
Surrey, B.C.
Canada V3R 3P2
(604) 588-2214; fax: (604) 588-2214

These are unique entries, as their goods are entirely free. They list hundreds upon hundred of free films and videos that you may borrow if you return them pre-paid (means: you pay return postage). The only hitch is you must write to them representing a group of some sort, even if that group is "Elm Street Parents" or "Concerned Singles Group" or another assemblage you've created for the purpose of ordering. Most topics are meant to promote a group, country or activity (e.g., "The Trouble with Weeds" from B.C.'s Ministry of Forests promotes weed control). Some are purely educational, and teacher's aids are included. You are also asked to fill out an "audience report card" (for their ongoing research) and return it with the materials you've borrowed. This address serves B.C., Alberta, Saskatchewan, the Yukon and Northwest Territories.

✔ Mail orders accepted
✔ Phone orders accepted
✔ Good bargain-hunting
Minimum order: no minimum
Shipping method: Canada Post
Shipping time: 1 week
Returns policy: see text

163 LA PIÑATA
No. 2 Patio Market
Old Town N.W.
Albuquerque, NM
U S A 87104
(505) 242-2400

This source sells every kind of piñata you can imagine: Santa, Batman, bears, elephants, pigs, frogs, penguins, witches, etc. They usually come in small, medium or large. They also sell extravagant-looking (but inexpensive) paper flowers. A brochure and price list is available for $1 to cover postage. Payment is accepted with VISA, M/C, IMO or cheques in U.S. currency.

✔ Mail orders accepted
✔ Good bargain-hunting
Minimum order: no minimum
Shipping method: mail or airmail
Shipping time: 2-3 weeks
Returns policy: all goods guaranteed
Established in 1961

164 LANDS' END DIRECT MERCHANTS

1 Lands' End Lane
Dodgeville, WI
U S A 53595
(608) 935-9341; Can. toll-free: (800) 356-4444;
hearing impaired: (800) 541-3459

Lands' End is probably the most fun you can have catalogue shopping. Their catalogue covers have featured everything from comic strip 90-lb. weaklings transformed by a "super T-shirt" to Norman Rockwell-style illustrations circa 1950, to a bald guy with a cold head wanting a warm hat for the winter! Inside is more people-pleasing, with wholesome, hard-wearing clothing for the whole family, including shirts, ties, belts, sportwear, women's casual clothes, outfits for tykes to teens, jeans, luggage, shoes, boots, hats and even bathing suits. Catalogues are published monthly and are free. Once you get on their mailing list, it seems as though they send you catalogues forever! Payment is accepted by VISA, M/C, Amex, IMO, cheque or bank draft.

✔ Mail orders accepted
✔ Phone orders accepted
✔ Good bargain-hunting
Minimum order: no minimum
Shipping method: mail or Federal Express (the latter not to P.O.boxes)
Shipping time: filled within 24 hours
Returns policy: absolute unconditional guarantee

165 THE LANGUAGE LABORATORY

47 Richards Ave.
Norwalk, CT
U S A 06857
Canada toll-free: (800) 367-4534

The Language Laboratory sells educational cassettes and videos to help people learn foreign languages. Call for a free brochure, toll-free. Payment is accepted with Visa, M/C, Amex, Diner's Club, IMO or cheque.

✔ Mail orders accepted
✔ Phone orders accepted
Minimum order: no minimum
Shipping method: airmail or surface mail only to Canada; UPS to U.S. points
Shipping time: averages 2-4 weeks
Returns policy: everything returnable within 30 days
Established in 1969

166 LAO SONG HANDICRAFTS
69 Soi 19, Sukhumvit Road
Bangkok
Thailand
(662) 253-2948

This is the main outlet for 22 Hill tribe villages in Northern Thailand, producing original handicrafts, placemats, Christmas ornaments, baskets, unique stuffed animals, potholders and incredible weavings and artifacts. Their catalogue is produced annually and includes most of their offerings, with prices. They are amazingly cheap! Payment is accepted with VISA, M/C, Amex, and IMO.

✔ Mail orders accepted
✔ Good bargain-hunting
Minimum order: no minimum
Shipping method: surface or airmail
Shipping time: 2-6 weeks
Returns policy: no returns

167 LAUREL BURCH, INC.
410 Townsend St.
San Francisco, CA
U S A 94107
(415) 890-9061; U.S. toll-free: (800) 722-8724

This "Gallerie by Mail," as they call themselves, sells art prints, T-shirts, jewellery, tote bags, coffee mugs and other novelties. Many of the items are unique and unusual. The catalogue is published periodically and is free. Payment is accepted with Visa, M/C, Amex, IMO or cheque (U.S. funds).

✔ Mail orders accepted
✔ Phone orders accepted
Minimum order: no minimum
Shipping method: UPS or post
Shipping time: 2 weeks
Returns policy: all goods guaranteed

168 LE BARON OUTDOOR PRODUCTS LTD.
8601 St. Laurent Blvd.
Montreal, P.Q.
Canada H2P 2M9
(514) 381-4231; Toronto: (416) 225-3322;
Mississauga: (416) 629-2300

These retail outlets in Quebec and Ontario sell diverse lines of name-brand merchandise for the outdoors at discount prices, through a glossy, 350-page catalogue. Included is fishing equipment, hunting and camping gear, apparel, footwear and specialty items, such as hip-waders. The catalogue costs $1. Payment is accepted by VISA, M/C, IMO and cheque. Since goods are shipped from Montreal, Quebec residents pay P.S.T.

✔ Mail orders accepted
✔ Phone orders accepted
✔ Good bargain-hunting
Minimum order: no minimum
Shipping method: mail or UPS
Shipping time: 10 days
Returns policy: all goods guaranteed

169 LE TRICOTEUR
Pitronnerie Road Estate
Saint Peter Port, Guernsey
Channel Islands
Guersney 26214

This is the classic fisherman's sweater you'd pay twice the price for here in a woollens shop. Each garment is hand-knit with the traditional waterproof quality from the unprocessed wool, still full of all its natural lanolin. No catalogue is available. Instead, there's a free flyer, price list and yarn samples. Payment is accepted with VISA, M/C, Amex, Diners Club and Eurocard.

✔ Mail orders accepted
✔ Good bargain-hunting
Minimum order: no minimum
Shipping method: surface post or air
Shipping time: 4-6 weeks
Returns policy: money-back guarantee
Established in 1964

170 LEARNING AT HOME
Dept 9010
P.O. Box 270
Honaunau, Hawaii
U S A 96726
(808) 328-9669

This source offers learning resources for families and is particularly useful for youngsters growing up in rural Canadian communities without access to excellent educational materials. There are video and cassette tapes, books and parent guidebooks. The catalogue is free. Payment is accepted with Visa, M/C, IMO or cheque (U.S. funds, please).

- ✔ Mail orders accepted

  Minimum order: no minimum
  Shipping method: UPS or mail
  Shipping time: 2-4 weeks, depending on item
  Returns policy: all goods guaranteed

171 LILLIAN VERNON CORPORATION

510 South Fulton Avenue
Mount Vernon, NY
U S A 10550
(914) 633-6400

Here's another success story that started as a family business on the kitchen table. Nowadays, Lillian Vernon ships an average of 30,000 orders a day across the U.S. The hitch for Canadian customers is that they will not ship to Canada, so you'll have to find a friend or relative in the States who will receive goods for you. Among the items are giftware, chatchkas, hammocks, watches, jewellery, clothing, placemats, garden accessories, toys, miniatures, purses, kitchen accessories, closet organizers, bath accessories, stationery, decorative room accents, and fine leather goods. A total of 14 regular catalogues and three sale catalogues are produced yearly, averaging 104 pages each and featuring 700 different products. All are free and are mailed to Canadian addresses even though the goods ordered are not. Payment is accepted via VISA, M/C, Amex and Discover cards.

- ✔ Mail orders accepted
- ✔ Phone orders accepted
- ✔ Good bargain-hunting

  Minimum order: no minimum
  Shipping method: Canadian customers must ship to friends in USA
  Shipping time: 2 weeks
  Returns policy: all goods guaranteed
  Established in 1951

172 LIMERICKS LINENS LTD.

Limerick House
117 Victoria Avenue
Southend-on-Sea, Essex SS2 6EL
England
(0702) 353427; 343486

Manager Daniel Page told me that their experiences in selling to the U.S. have not been good, so that it is only cost-effective for them if they charge for their catalogue (in Canadian currency). That way, they can

send your catalogue out immediately, instead of waiting for enough orders to send a lot out in bulk. Their catalogue is worth it, with everything in the way of household linens featured at very attractive prices. There are two catalogues printed a year, one each for spring and autumn. Cost of each is $3 (Cdn.). There is also a made-to-measure service for your special needs. Payment is accepted with VISA, M/C, Amex, Access, Diners Club and cheques payable in pounds sterling.

✔ Mail orders accepted
✔ Phone orders accepted
Minimum order: no minimum
Shipping method: airmail or surface mail
Shipping time: 1 week
Returns policy: "free replacement if faulty and postage costs"

173 LITTLE SWITZERLAND
P.O. Box 887
St. Thomas, VI
U S A 00804
(809) 776-2010; U.S. toll-free only: (800) 524-2010

Little Switzerland is one of those off-shore specialty houses you hear about, but never seem to find. This one handles only the top-line, finest brand names and guarantees customer satisfaction. Although you'll be responsible for all import duties and taxes when your goods arrive at the local post office, you should save about 25 percent over comparable goods purchased at home, plus this firm will accept Canadian currency at par with U.S. dollars. Best savings are on jewellery and china. All prices are quoted by phone (or mail) and prices do not appear in their catalogue. The catalogue is published once yearly, in the fall, and is free if you mention this book. Payment by VISA, M/C, Amex, IMO or Diners Club.

✔ Special offer to readers
✔ Mail orders accepted
✔ Phone orders accepted
✔ Good bargain-hunting
Minimum order: no minimum
Shipping method: mail only
Shipping time: 3 days till shipping
Returns policy: 30-day money-back guarantee

174 LOCAL HOUSE CO. LTD.
Bangkrak
Bangkok
Thailand
(662) 234-8919

Here's a spot for Thai handicrafts, dolls, folk art, relics and Hill tribe weavings and fabrics. A price list only is available, but if you're after a particular item, write to inquire. Payment is accepted with VISA, M/C, Amex, but IMO, cheque or bank draft is preferred.

✔ Mail orders accepted
Minimum order: no minimum
Shipping method: surface mail
Shipping time: 6-8 weeks
Returns policy: no returns

175 LOUIS CHOCK
74 Orchard St.
New York, NY
U S A 10002
(212) 473-1929

This place has been down on Orchard Street almost forever and is filled with bustling clerks and brown stock boxes of name-brand goods, such as Hanes, Vassarette, BVD, Supp-Hose, Christian Dior, Burlington hosiery, Botany 500 cotton pyjamas, and men's items from Oscar de la Renta. They have some beautiful terry robes and 100 percent cotton boxers for men. A full size range of all Hanes pantyhose and stockings is carried. There's a small catalogue and it is free. Payment is accepted with VISA, M/C and cheques (U.S. funds only, please).

✔ Mail orders accepted
✔ Phone orders accepted
✔ Good bargain-hunting
Minimum order: no minimum
Shipping method: airmail or parcel post
Shipping time: 2 weeks
Returns policy: 30-day money-back guarantee
Established in 1921

176 M B I FLIGHT GEAR
47 Richards Ave.
Norwalk, CT
U S A 06857
Canada toll-free: (800) 367-4534

This mail order source sells luggage. There is no catalogue available, but they will send you a descriptive brochure free if you call — and the call is free Canada-wide, too. Payment is accepted with Visa, M/C, Amex, Diner's Club, IMO and cheque.

✔ Mail orders accepted
✔ Phone orders accepted
Minimum order: no minimum
Shipping method: airmail or surface mail only to Canada; UPS to U.S. points
Shipping time: averages 2-4 weeks
Returns policy: everything returnable within 30 days
Established in 1969

177 M.M. POONJIAJI & CO.

42-Anandilal Podar Marg.
Bombay - 400 002
India
312412 (B); 255475 (Res.)

This firm has been in business for more than 100 years, selling "Ship" brand chutneys, fruit and mango pickles, curry powder and curry paste worldwide. They have won many awards for their products. Each bottle is hand-wrapped in poly bags and carefully packaged to avoid breakage while shipping. Minimum order is 12 bottles or tins, at a minimum cost of $60 (U.S.) and the quality is guaranteed to satisfy: their motto is "Customer Is Always Right." A recipe booklet is shipped with catalogue requests, if you mention this book. Flyer and price list (which are free on request) are published in April and October. All payment must be in U.S. currency. They request a "demand draft" of $60 (U.S.) in advance with your order.

✔ Mail orders accepted
✔ Phone orders accepted
✔ Good bargain-hunting
Minimum order: 12 bottles or tins
Shipping method: by surface mail
Shipping time: 15 days
Returns policy: quality is guaranteed
Established in 1883

178 MAJESTIC COUNTERFEIT JEWELS

9496 Brighton Way
Beverly Hills, CA
U S A 90210
(213) 271-6663

If you've always wanted expensive jewellery, but felt you couldn't afford it, do what the divas of Hollywood do and buy counterfeits, copied in perfect detail from famous originals in 14K or 18K white or yellow gold, at a fraction of the price. This source specializes in custom creations and will copy any design, so your fantasy bracelet from the pages of a fashion magazine could be transformed into a very convincing duplicate. All stones come with a lifetime guarantee and Majestic's written "Hippocratic" oath of confidentiality, promising not to reveal their customers' names. They also sell a full line of designer replica watches, hand-knotted pearls and "knock-off" perfumes. The colour catalogue is free, and sometimes out of print, so it might be necessary to wait a month or more for a reply. Payment is accepted with Visa, M/C, Amex, Diner's Club, Discover card, or with IMO or cheques in U.S. currency.

✔ Mail orders accepted
✔ Phone orders accepted
✔ Good bargain-hunting
Minimum order: no minimum
Shipping method: UPS or insured mail
Shipping time: 2-3 weeks, depending on availability
Returns policy: all goods guaranteed

179 MARK'S WORK WEARHOUSE

#30 - 1035 64th Ave. S.E.
Calgary, Alta.
Canada T2H 2J7
(403) 255-9220; Can. toll-free: (800) 661-1266

While primarily operating retail outlets across Canada, Mark's Work Wearhouse frequently fills orders for people in remote areas of Canada, at logging camps, steel mills, and so on. Included in their stock is work clothing, sportwear, boots, rain gear, jeans (Levi red-tab jeans a specialty), shirts, shorts, T-shirts, sweats (or "comforts" as they prefer to call them), sports and duffle bags, steelworker safety boots, hiking boots, lunch boxes, sailing boots, joggers, and casual wear for men and women. Sales flyers and an extensive, full-colour "shopping guide" are published frequently throughout the year and are free. Payment is via VISA, M/C or cheque.

✔ Mail orders accepted
✔ Phone orders accepted
✔ Good bargain-hunting
Minimum order: no minimum
Shipping method: mail or UPS (where routes exist)
Shipping time: 1 week
Returns policy: all goods guaranteed

180 MARKS & SPENCER HAMPERS
3770 Nashua Drive
Mississauga, Ontario
Canada L4V 1M6
(416) 676-1910, ext. 471

Marks & Spencer offers a Christmas gift pack and hamper service to the U.K. mainland. These include an opulent selection of gourmet foods, traditional favourites or wines. A special 10-percent discount is offered to our readers for early orders. Deliveries in Great Britain take place about 10 days to a week before Christmas via TNT Express (included in cost of hampers). Payment is accepted via VISA, M/C, IMO or cheque, but not cash. Hmmph!

✔ Special offer to readers
✔ Mail orders accepted
✔ Phone orders accepted
Minimum order: no minimum
Shipping method: TNT Express
Shipping time: specific delivery period
Returns policy: food items non-returnable unless defective

181 MARSHALL'S FUDGE
308 East Central Avenue
P.O. Box 639
Mackinaw City, MI
U S A 49701
(616) 436-5379; (616) 796-9490; U.S. toll-free: (800) 343-8343

Another family-run operation, this one boasts roots in the U.S. going back over 100 years. Today the Marshalls have added to their line of hand-made fudge and candies with flavours like strawberry and piña colada, as well as the many variations of chocolate blends. Other items you can order include gift packs, nut brittles, almond bark, pecan logs, nuts, caramel corn, salt water taffy and bulk chocolate (some sugar-free). The old family recipes originated on Mackinac Island. If you are senior and shop there in person, you receive a discount. The prices are very reasonable, in any case. Catalogues are produced in May and December and are free. Payment is accepted by VISA, M/C, Amex, Carte Blanche, Diners Club, Discover card, IMO or personal cheques.

✔ Mail orders accepted
✔ Phone orders accepted
Minimum order: 1 pound minimum
Shipping method: mail or UPS
Shipping time: 1 day

Returns policy: return unused portion in original package for replacement
Established in 1926

182 MARY MAXIM
75 Scott Avenue
Paris, Ontario
Canada N3L 3G5
(519) 442-2266; fax: (519) 442-4520

Mary Maxim is yet another fixture in the mail order scene, and a welcome source of bargains for people interested in knitting, sewing, needlepoint and crafts. The catalogue includes patterns for sweaters, afghans, hooked rugs (and kits), stitchery, baby items, quilting accessories, batting, shoulder pads, plastic canvas kits and more. The catalogue is $2, but our readers may request a sample catalogue free. Payment is accepted with VISA, M/C, IMO or cheques. Ontario residents pay P.S.T.

✔ Special offer to readers
✔ Mail orders accepted
✔ Phone orders accepted
✔ Good bargain-hunting
Minimum order: no minimum, but bonus gifts with minimum $35 orders
Shipping method: Canada Post
Shipping time: 1-2 weeks
Returns policy: all goods guaranteed
Established in 1952

183 MAURY ISLAND FARMING COMPANY
Box L
Vashon, WA
U S A 98070
(206) 463-5617; U.S. toll-free: (800) 356-5880

This family-owned farm is genuinely concerned with customer satisfaction. I have friends on Vachon Island who have stickers saying "I'm stuck on Maury Island jam," so you know their reputation is good. There's more fruit than sugar in every jar of their jams, such as strawberry and boysenberry, or preserves, jellies and toppings. Their catalogues are printed three times a year, in spring, summer, and fall (in time for Christmas) and are free. They'll gladly fill gift orders and ship them to your friends with your enclosure. Payment may be made through VISA, M/C, Amex, IMO or personal cheque.

✔ Mail orders accepted
✔ Phone orders accepted
Minimum order: no minimum
Shipping method: mail or UPS
Shipping time: 24 hours from receipt of order
Returns policy: replacement or money back if not satisfied

184 MAXWELL'S ARTISTS MATERIALS LTD.
Waterfront Station, 601 West Cordova St.
Vancouver, B.C.
Canada V6B 1G1
(604) 683-8607

Maxwell's is a long-established Vancouver art supply retailer and modest mail order outlet. Included in their fine selection are Staedtler pens, Winsor & Newton inks and brushes, Bienfang fine art papers, and many art supplies and stationery needs. Catalogues are periodical and are free. Payment is accepted by VISA, M/C or cheques.

✔ Mail orders accepted
✔ Phone orders accepted
Minimum order: no minimum
Shipping method: Canada Post
Shipping time: 2 weeks
Returns policy: all goods guaranteed; you pay return postage

185 McMANUS & MORGAN
2506 West 7th Street
Los Angeles, CA
U S A
(213) 387-4433; (213) 387-2717

This is a source for artists' supplies, print-making materials and, above all else, fine art papers. They stock marbled sheets from Europe, parchment, rice paper from Asia, and every pattern, weight and composition you can imagine, including the sought-after British Cockerell papers (the kind with that coloured, feathery pattern often seen on the inside of well-made, hard-bound books). They also stock the best selection of decals you've ever seen. There are fairy-tale characters, Arthur Rackham-type illustrations, animals, birds, and flights of fancy. They mostly price-quote on specific items by phone, but will send a full (free) price list, on request. Payment is accepted only with IMO or cheques in U.S. currency.

✔ Mail orders accepted
✔ Phone orders accepted
Minimum order: no minimum
Shipping method: UPS (U.S. points) or U.S. Postal Service
Shipping time: 2-3 weeks
Returns policy: no returns unless defective

186 MELLINGER'S INC.
2310 W. South Range Rd.
North Lima, OH
U S A 44452-9731
(216) 549-9861; U.S. only: (800) 321-7444

Mellinger's is a family-run business selling every form of gardening supply and nursery stock you can imagine. This is as extensive a catalogue as you'll find in the gardening business anywhere — and prices are very competitive. All plants are guaranteed a full year and all supply merchandise is fully warranteed by the manufacturer. Although supplies are shipped quickly, plants are often delayed to arrive at the appropriate time for their planting — and this is calculated according to the part of North America in which you reside so you can put your tree or shrub into the ground the day it arrives. They offer no special discounts, but strive to keep their everyday prices down. The catalogue costs $1.50 if mailed outside of the U.S. and it is published every November and March (non-refundable) but our readers may request one free copy. Payment accepted by VISA, M/C, IMO or cheque.

✔ Special offer to readers
✔ Mail orders accepted
✔ Phone orders accepted
✔ Good bargain-hunting
Minimum order: $10 if ordering on VISA or MasterCard; no minimum for cheques
Shipping method: mail only
Shipping time: supplies 2-3 days; plants see text
Returns policy: all plants guaranteed 1 full year
Established in 1926

187 MERLO'S CUTLERY
Sherman Oaks Galleria
15301 Ventura Blvd.
Sherman Oaks, CA
U S A
(818) 990-6776

This family-run business specializes in knives for cooks, hunters, collectors and hobbyists. They also stock cutlery at very competitive prices, and often offer sale prices on special lines. They will send you their colour brochure and price list free, on request. Payment is accepted with Visa, M/C, Amex, Discover, IMO or cheques in U.S. funds.

✔ Mail orders accepted
✔ Phone orders accepted
Minimum order: no minimum
Shipping method: UPS or mail
Shipping time: "order filled promptly"
Returns policy: all goods guaranteed

188 METROPOLITAN MUSEUM OF ART
255 Gracie Station
New York, NY
U S A 10028
(212) 570-3694

These people seem reluctant to sell their goods — they're that difficult. Why bother to send their stupid dollar and wait endlessly for the catalogue? Because the catalogue is gorgeous full-colour and loaded with lavish illustrations, beautiful Christmas cards, faithful museum-quality reproductions, tapestries, jewellery and more. It's even frustrating to call, but worth the hassle. Their catalogue appears in the fall, in time for Christmas ordering and costs (as I whined) $1, which you might find easier to obtain and send in U.S. currency so they won't be confused by receiving a loony and wondering what the heck it is. Payment is accepted by VISA, M/C, Amex or cheques drawn in U.S. funds.

✔ Mail orders accepted
Minimum order: $15 for credit card orders; otherwise no minimum
Shipping method: mail
Shipping time: 30 days
Returns policy: difficult, but possible

189 MINERVA STREET CHOCOLATE
1052 Olivia
Ann Arbor, MI
U S A 48104
(313) 996-4090

Judy Weinblatt's truffles were dubbed among the best ten in the world by *Chocolatier* magazine, and it's no wonder. Among her offerings are praline, vanilla bean, cheesecake (wow!), brandy, rum, mocha, orange and the *pièce de résistance*, "hazelnut crunch caramel." There are many different assortments available. All truffles are hand-dipped, of course. Our readers may write for free information about the company and price lists, but remember, you can only order to a U.S. address, sorry. Payment is accepted via VISA, M/C or Amex.

✔ Mail orders accepted
✔ Phone orders accepted
Minimum order: no minimum
Shipping method: UPS to U.S. points only
Shipping time: 1 week
Returns policy: all goods guaranteed
Established in 1980

190 MINNETONKA BY MAIL
P.O. Box 444
Bronx, NY
U S A 10458
(212) 365-7033

These people sell a beautiful line of moccasins to fit men, women and even tiny infants. Some are beaded, tassled, sheepskin-lined, or accented with Southwest silver medallions. There are also boots, boating shoes and other casual footwear — all in all, more than 150 styles to choose from. Prices are about 20 percent under retail. Colour catalogues are produced in spring and fall and cost $1 (refundable on first order). Payment is accepted in U.S. funds via IMO only.

✔ Mail orders accepted
Minimum order: no minimum
Shipping method: mail or UPS
Shipping time: 21 days to 2 weeks
Returns policy: unworn goods (or imperfects) exchanged or refunded

191 MOON SHINE TRADING CO.
P.O. Box 896
Winters, CA
U S A 95694
(916) 753-0601

Another family-run business, this one began with "just 180 pounds of Yellow Star Thistle, northern California's most magnificent offering." Now they sell a full selection of gourmet honeys, each 85-90 percent varietally pure (means the bees stuck to the intended flower patch and didn't shop around). They also offer a range of wonderful nut butters and chocolate nut spreads "to die for." Discounts of 10 percent are given

on goods purchased by the case. The catalogues are reprinted for spring and fall and are free. Plus, they'll send our readers their history and an assortment of recipes in a free folder just for writing. Payment is accepted via VISA, M/C or IMO, but cheques must be payable in U.S. funds, drawn on a U.S. bank.

✔ Special offer to readers
✔ Mail orders accepted
✔ Phone orders accepted
✔ Good bargain-hunting
Minimum order: $15 (U.S.)
Shipping method: mail or UPS
Shipping time: 3-5 days
Returns policy: all goods guaranteed; write or call before returning
Established in 1979

192 MOORE BUSINESS SUPPLIES

Suite 450, Mississauga Executive Centre
Four Robert Speck Parkway
Mississauga, Ontario
Canada L4Z 1S1
Can. toll-free: (800) 387-7810; Ont. toll-free: (800) 387-7830;
Que. toll-free: (800) 387-7840

Every manner of computer supply is sold here, from diskettes to printer stands, to three-part NCR paper (hard to find at local suppliers), to power-surge bars to chairs and complete workstations. They also do custom-printing of letterhead, cards and labels, and offer free samples of each. The free full-colour catalogue is published for spring and fall. Fax orders may be sent to (416) 270-3130. Payment is accepted with VISA, M/C, Amex, IMO or cheque, or you can be billed for the shipment, but that delays the order.

✔ Mail orders accepted
✔ Phone orders accepted
✔ Good bargain-hunting
Minimum order: no minimum
Shipping method: parcel post or freight (freight charges extra)
Shipping time: depends on method of shipping
Returns policy: all goods money-back guaranteed

193 MORAVIAN SUGAR CRISP COOKIES

Rt. #2, Box 431, Friedberg Road
Clemmons, NC
U S A 27012
(919) 764-1402

Evva (Mrs. Travis F.) Hanes makes paper-thin "flavour-full" Moravian sugar crisp cookies from an old family recipe that has been handed down, quite literally, for generations. Each cookie is rolled, cut and packed by hand, and shipping is prompt, to ensure freshness. Each selection of cookies is wrapped in individual stacks in a tin container and mailed in an incredibly heavy-duty carton to minimize breakage. Considering the delicacy of the cookies themselves, it is amazing that they arrive so completely intact. These are a wonderfully good (and penny-conscious) Christmas present, particularly as all prices include postage within the States, so you can save time and money with gifts to American friends. To Canada, postage is charged according to weight (approximately $5 Cdn.) on the $13 selection of sugar crisps and ginger crisps, but can this be too steep for the "best cookies in the world"? They accept phone orders year-round, except at Christmas. Their modest (but illustrated) catalogue is published once yearly, in September, and is free. Payment is acceptable by cheque or IMO.

✔ Special offer to readers
✔ Mail orders accepted
✔ Phone orders accepted
✔ Good bargain-hunting
Minimum order: no minimum
Shipping method: by mail, airmail or UPS
Shipping time: overnight shipment
Returns policy: all goods guaranteed

194 MOTHERCARE BY MAIL
Cherry Tree Road
Watford, Herts
WD2 5SH England
Watford 33577; telex 264009

Mothercare is yet another example of ingenuity paying off. Eventually, every mother-to-be or new mother learns of this source from a friend, so here's the scoop: they sell maternity wear you're not likely to find elsewhere, they even stock stretch-mark creams and nipple creams to prevent problems. They have every imaginable convenience for the new baby, too, and clothing and active-wear for children up to age eight (they say age 10, but Canadian kids are a little bigger). They are very efficient in filling orders. Some items are dutiable coming into Canada. A special Canadian edition of their catalogue is published in February, so be sure to request that one. Ordering in any given season entitles you to the next one automatically, and they are always free. Payment is accepted with VISA, M/C, Amex, Access, Eurocard, IMO or cheque. All prices quoted are in Canadian dollars.

✔ Mail orders accepted
✔ Phone orders accepted
✔ Good bargain-hunting
Minimum order: no minimum
Shipping method: surface or airmail; extra fee for parcels by air
Shipping time: 4-6 weeks surface mail
Returns policy: all goods guaranteed or money back (2 weeks)

195 MOUNTAIN EQUIPMENT CO-OP

428 West 8th Ave.
Vancouver, B.C.
Canada V5Y 1N9
(604) 872-7858; Can. toll-free: (800) 663-2667;
fax: (604) 872-4088

Mountain Equipment Co-op started the B.C. trend toward manufacture and supply of truly superior outdoors equipment and apparel, rivalling the best available anywhere else in the world. The 72-page full-colour catalogue is available free each winter and could include outdoorsy photos you've taken if you submit them with your name, location of shot, your return address and releases for any identifiable people in the pictures. Your reward, if they are accepted, is actual cash money in payment. Though Mountain Equipment Co-op (a real co-op you join for life for $5) operates big stores in Toronto, Calgary and Vancouver, they pull in 10 percent of their $28-million annual sales from mail order alone, so they're very conscientious about keeping their mail order customers happy. Their goods include hiking, camping, climbing, fishing, hunting and outdoors gear, tents, sleeping bags, backpacks, ropes, harnesses, footwear, hiking boots, kayaks, marine wear, floatation vests and much more. Payment is accepted with VISA or M/C and a 2-percent discount is given for payments with cash (IMOs) or cheques.

✔ Mail orders accepted
✔ Phone orders accepted
✔ Good bargain-hunting
Minimum order: no minimum but you must join co-op for $5 (lifetime)
Shipping method: Canada Post or UPS
Shipping time: 2-3 weeks, depending on item
Returns policy: all goods guaranteed against defects
Established in 1971

196 MR. ROMANCE
Romance Center
422 East Sixth Street
Tucson, AZ
U S A 85705-8553
(602) 623-4133; U.S. toll-free: (800) 444-7662;
fax: (602) 623-4133

Langdon Hill, dubbed "Mr. Romance" by *People* magazine, didn't actually get married to his wife Em on Donahue, but a video-taped portion was shown there later. Langdon himself looks more like Beaver Cleaver than Gerry Mathers does, and he has a wholesome approach to the whole idea of romance, so it's no wonder that his catalogue is filled with sweet thoughts, inspired gifts for lovers, and nice, nice ideas to keep your relationship joyful. The catalogue itself is mailed out monthly and includes readers' letters, prizes and items like a romantic bubble bath kit, chocolate chip cookies, the "I'm nuts over you" boxed nuts, gourmet chocolates in a heart-shaped box, and so on. A sample catalogue is free to our readers. New to the line is Victorian lingerie, custom-made to your measurements. They've even been creating Victorian-era bridal gowns and accessories (at much less than you'd pay for a wedding gown in a traditional retail outlet). Payment is accepted with VISA, M/C, IMO or cheque (U.S. funds).

✔ Special offer to readers
✔ Mail orders accepted
✔ Phone orders accepted
Minimum order: no minimum
Shipping method: mail or UPS
Shipping time: 7 days for custom-order
Returns policy: all goods guaranteed 100 percent
Established in 1981

197 MR. SPICEMAN
615 Palmer Rd.
Yonkers, NY
U S A 10701
(914) 961-7776; (914) 576-1222

You will save about 40 percent of what you would pay for spices, condiments, housewares, gadgets, provisions, teas, bulk chocolate, gummi bears, Bortz gold foiled coins, and herb teas at retail outlets. Mr. Spiceman also sells brands you will recognize, such as Knorr sauces and soups and Maggi seasonings. Spices are sold in one-pound sizes to the consumer. The catalogue is published every October and costs $1 (refunded on first order). Payment is accepted with VISA, M/C, and personal cheques payable in U.S. funds.

✔ Mail orders accepted
✔ Phone orders accepted
✔ Good bargain-hunting
Minimum order: no minimum
Shipping method: mail or UPS
Shipping time: "a few days"
Returns policy: 10 days to return for refund or exchange
Established in 1965

198 MUSEUM OF FINE ARTS, BOSTON
P.O. Box 74
Boston, MA
U S A 02117-0074
(617) 267-9300; U.S. toll-free: (800) 225-5592

Like most prominent museums worldwide, this one offers superior gift items including museum reproductions, desk calendars, art, posters, jewellery, scarves, sculpture, silk ties, art books, decor accents, pens, children's books (and hard-to-find pop-ups), gift wrap, greeting cards, toys, musical instruments, board games and executive toys. Membership for individuals costs $35 annually and allows you a 10-percent saving on purchases, so if you plan to be a big spender, it might be wise to join. Catalogues are printed in July and November and a subscription to both costs $1. You can also get their poster catalogue free. Payment is accepted with VISA, M/C or Amex.

✔ Mail orders accepted
✔ Phone orders accepted
Minimum order: no minimum
Shipping method: mail or UPS
Shipping time: 10 working days; more at Christmas
Returns policy: full guarantee or money refunded

199 MUSEUM OF MODERN ART
Mail Order Department
11 West 53rd St.
New York, NY
U S A 10019-5401
(212) 708-9888; (212) 708-9746

The Museum of Modern Art offers several catalogues featuring posters, art reproductions, furniture, artifacts, objets d'art, greeting cards and limited edition prints. The Christmas catalogue is $3. Payment is accepted with VISA, M/C, Amex, IMO and cheques (U.S. funds only).

✔ Mail orders accepted
✔ Phone orders accepted
✔ Good bargain-hunting
Minimum order: no minimum
Shipping method: mail or UPS
Shipping time: 3 weeks
Returns policy: returns possible if dissatisfied

200 MUSIC FOR LITTLE PEOPLE
P.O. Box 1460
1144 Redway Dr.
Redway, CA
U S A 95560
(707) 923-3991

Music for Little People focuses, naturally on children, offering videos, tapes and records on ethnic and classical themes, as well as the popular (but less commercial) items kids beg for. There are also musical instruments, some very inexpensive. The catalogue is free. Payment is accepted with Visa, M/C, IMO or cheques (U.S. funds, please).

✔ Mail orders accepted
✔ Good bargain-hunting
Minimum order: no minimum
Shipping method: UPS or mail
Shipping time: 1-2 weeks
Returns policy: all goods guaranteed

201 MYRON MANUFACTURING CORP.
1361 Huntingwood Drive
Scarborough, Ontario
Canada M1S 4L3
(416) 291-9000

Mike and Elaine Adler run this large manufacturing plant like the family business it is, with much attention to customer service and satisfaction. They produce calendars, desk diaries, pocket memos, address books, pens, business planners, greeting cards and logo watches. The catalogue is produced every August and is free. This offer extends only to businesses. Payment is accepted via Amex, IMO, cheque or C.O.D. in Canada. Ontario residents add P.S.T.

✔ Special offer to readers
✔ Mail orders accepted
✔ Phone orders accepted
✔ Good bargain-hunting

Minimum order: some minimums, but it depends on what you are ordering
Shipping method: Canada Post, UPS, CanPar, Swiftsure
Shipping time: 4-6 weeks
Returns policy: unconditional 100-percent money-back guarantee
Established in 1949

202 NAT SCHWARTZ
549 Broadway
Bayonne, NJ
U S A 07002
(201) 437-4443; U.S. toll-free: (800) 526-1440;
fax: (201) 437-4903

Nat Schwartz runs such a family business that he's likely to answer his phone himself, or maybe you'll talk to his mother, Rose. Whoever it is, the discounts are fantastic, ranging from 20 to 70 percent off first-line (no seconds) name brands in china, silver, crystal, chatchkas and giftware. You'll recognize names like Waterford, Wallace, Lennox, Wedgwood, Royal Doulton and Spode, among many others. As a special gift to our readers, the free catalogue includes "how to care for china, crystal and sterling" and "how to design your tabletop," which is one of their specialties. They can also advise you about co-ordinating patterns from china to silver to linens, so you can lay a perfect table every time. Shipping of breakables includes insurance. Fax orders are welcome. Payment is accepted with VISA, M/C or cheques.

✔ Special offer to readers
✔ Mail orders accepted
✔ Phone orders accepted
✔ Good bargain-hunting
Minimum order: no minimum
Shipping method: mail or UPS; $4 to ship flatware; $5 for crystal or china
Shipping time: 48 hours shipping
Returns policy: all goods 100-percent guaranteed to please
Established in 1967

203 NATIONAL GEOGRAPHIC SOCIETY
P.O. Box 2118
Washington, D.C.
U S A 20013
(202) 857-7000

The National Geographic Society is a North American institution, but their mail order goods are neither stodgy nor lacklustre. In fact, they offer a small but splendid assortment of inexpensive gifts, including globes, maps, atlases, calendars, wonderful books and, naturally, subscriptions. A particularly good value is a subscription for *National Geo World*, perfect for children age 8 to 14, and a bargain if you're mailing to youngsters in the U.S. Gift cards, carrying your own personal message (and hand-written by one of Santa's elves, we presume), may be included with the announcement of your gift. In the States, a year's subscription costs $8.95; in Canada it's steeper at $12 (U.S.), or $15 (Cdn.). Other countries pay a still higher rate. The Christmas catalogue is free. Payment is preferred by IMO or cheque for subscriptions. Gift items can be billed to you later.

✔ Mail orders accepted
Minimum order: no minimum
Shipping method: mail
Shipping time: 2-6 weeks
Returns policy: a little difficult, but possible

204 NATIONAL PUBLIC RADIO
NPR Customer Service
P.O. Box 55417
Madison, WI
U S A 53705
(608) 263-4892; U.S. toll-free: (800) 235-TAPE

If you love NPR programming, this source will be a bonanza for you. Program cassettes are available for every topic under the sun, including education, social sciences, the humanities, science, media, the arts, and such personalities as Dick Cavett, Mickey Mantle, Roger Ebert, Mr. Rogers, Gahan Wilson (the bleak-humoured cartoonist), novelist Kurt Vonnegut, Phyllis Diller, Joan Rivers, Carl Reiner, and the list goes on and on. There's classic (and classical) music, plays, readings, interviews, commentary, foreign affairs, business, history and archival material. It's fascinating just reading the catalogue. That catalogue is published annually (costs $3) and is supplemented by the quarterly *Cassette Gazette*, which costs $2. Free flyers are mailed out periodically, too. By the way, pre-recorded tapes come into Canada duty-free. Payment is accepted with VISA, M/C, IMO or cheques. Recognized institutions (libraries, schools, etc.) may use purchase orders, but only for orders over $50.

✔ Mail orders accepted
✔ Phone orders accepted
Minimum order: no minimum unless using purchase order (orders over $50)
Shipping method: mail
Shipping time: 2-3 weeks
Returns policy: no returns
Established in 1970

205 NATIONAL WILDLIFE FEDERATION
1400 Sixteenth Street, N.W.
Washington, D.C.
U S A 20036-2266
(202) 797-6800

The National Wildlife Federation is a lobbying and umbrella group that has been working to protect U.S. wildlife for over half a century. They sell magazine subscriptions (like *Ranger Rick* and *National Wildlife*), fine nature books, and audiovisual teaching aids. Naturally, they promote memberships, too, but you need not join to buy their goods. They also distribute the highly collectable Wildlife Conservation stamps every year. Catalogues are produced periodically and are free. Payment is made after they invoice you for goods ordered.

✔ Mail orders accepted
Minimum order: no minimum
Shipping method: mail
Shipping time: 2 weeks
Returns policy: not applicable
Established in 1938

206 THE NATURE CO.
P.O. Box 2310
Berkeley, CA
U S A 94702
(415) 644-1337; U.S. toll-free: (800) 227-1114

The highlight here is Nature, and all items reflect the theme, from videos and books to clothing, jewellery, hiking supplies, art prints and even bird feeders. The catalogue is updated seasonally and is free. Payment is accepted with Visa, M/C, Amex, IMO and cheques in U.S. funds.

✔ Mail orders accepted
Minimum order: no minimum
Shipping method: UPS or mail
Shipping time: 2 weeks average
Returns policy: all goods guaranteed

207 NEBS BUSINESS FORMS LTD.
330 Cranston Crescent
Midland, Ontario
Canada L4R 4V9
Ont.: (800) 461-7531; Can. toll-free: (800) 461-7572

This brilliant idea for office supplies and forms is a secret every small business should learn. They custom-imprint small quantities of specialized forms for prices any fledgling operation can afford. They also ship free if you pre-pay and their service is toll-free and really fast. So if you need three-part invoices or inexpensive letterhead and cards for your company, this is the place to turn. They also sell labels, shipping aids and rubber stamps. If you wonder about the name, it's originally American, as in "New England Business Services," where the company has been established for ages. Catalogues are automatically mailed seasonally to regular customers and your first one is free, of course. Payment is via cheque or arranged credit (billing after shipment, but you pay shipping charges). No C.O.D.s.

✔ Mail orders accepted
✔ Phone orders accepted
✔ Good bargain-hunting
Minimum order: no minimum
Shipping method: Canada Post or UPS
Shipping time: 24 hour fulfillment
Returns policy: all goods guaranteed or replaced free

208 NEIMAN-MARCUS
1618 Main St.
Dallas, TX
U S A 75201
(214) 741-6911

Surely the grand-daddy of all mail order houses, this one started with a dedication to customer service and that's what keeps them so strong today. They are often consulted for TV stories about bizarre gift possibilities, like the "his and her gift camels," real camels, that is. Everything is in their catalogue, from men's and women's apparel, to sporting goods, executive toys, cookware and gifts of every description. Catalogues cost between $5 and $7, depending on which edition it is. Write to inquire. Payment is accepted via VISA, M/C, Amex, IMO or cheques.

✔ Mail orders accepted
✔ Phone orders accepted
Minimum order: no minimum
Shipping method: mail or UPS
Shipping time: 2 weeks
Returns policy: all goods unconditionally guaranteed
Established in 1907

209 NEW BIG MAN COMPANY
Room 607, Universal Commercial Bldg., 6/F
No. 69, Peking Road, Tsim Sha Tsui
Kowloon
Hong Kong
(852) 367-5357; 739-3087

David Chan runs this operation and offers custom tailoring for men and women by tailors trained in the Shanghai method (best tailors) of fitting and finishing. It's difficult to have this work done without fittings, but sometimes they can copy an article of your own clothing. They also occasionally can sell you copy watches of famous brands. No catalogue is available, but they will price-quote on individual requests. Payment is accepted with VISA, M/C, IMO or cheques.

✔ Mail orders accepted
✔ Good bargain-hunting
Minimum order: no minimum
Shipping method: air or surface mail
Shipping time: 3-4 weeks
Returns policy: no returns on custom goods unless alteration required

210 NEW ROOTS NUTRITION
2581 West Broadway
Vancouver, B.C.
Canada V6K 2E9
(604) 734-4536

These helpful people sell high-quality vitamins at a discount, and also mail order hypo-allergenic formulas, vapour-control cookware, juicers and ionizers and "cleansing programs." Their catalogue is available year-round and is free. Payment is accepted with Visa, M/C, IMO or cheque.

✔ Mail orders accepted
✔ Phone orders accepted
✔ Good bargain-hunting
Minimum order: no minimum
Shipping method: Canada Post
Shipping time: 1 week
Returns policy: all goods guaranteed; appliances under warranty

211 NEW UNIVERSAL
1144-46 New Road
Bangkok
Thailand
(662) 234-3514

Another source that treats customers fairly; however, you'll still have to enter into some correspondence to bargain for a low price. Be sure you know what you're doing before ordering! This place sells unset gemstones at savings up to 75 percent off Canadian prices. They will send you a flyer and price list free. Payment is via VISA, M/C, Amex or IMO.

✔ Mail orders accepted
✔ Good bargain-hunting
Minimum order: no minimum
Shipping method: airmail
Shipping time: 2-3 weeks
Returns policy: returns possible, but slow

212 NURHAN CEVAHIR
Istiklal Cad. Bekar sok.12/4
Beyoglu
Istanbul
Turkey
144 41 23; 144 35 10

Nurhan Cevahir sells one type of item only: genuine block meerschaum pipes. His price list is updated around New Year's every year and is free. Payment is accepted with VISA, Amex, Access, Choice, En Route, IMO or cheque (U.S. funds only).

✔ Mail orders accepted
Minimum order: no minimum
Shipping method: airmail to Canada
Shipping time: 2 weeks
Returns policy: replacement possible

213 ORIENTAL PACIFIC
Room 601-5 Sands Building
17, Hankow Rd.
Tsim Sha Tsui, Kowloon
Hong Kong
(852) 724 2633

This is one of the first places I head to when I visit Hong Kong and their mail order service is wonderful, even if they do insist on sending goods on a slow boat from China. They manufacture machine-made and hand-knit sweaters for stores and specialty designers worldwide, and the items offered in their catalogue are overruns, samples or their own lines (copied exactly from the originals, which they make anyway). The only thing missing sometimes is the designer label. I bought my daughter a hand-knit 100-percent wool sweater there with an Abercrombie and Fitch label in it, for $40 Canadian, which I considered on the expensive side until I saw the same sweaters in A & F for $380! Expect discounts of 30-90 percent off North American retail. Their nominal catalogue and price lists are updated sporadically and are free. At this writing, they have temporarily suspended their mail order service due to a shortage of staff, but they fervently promised me they will start it up again if the demand is great enough, so write! Payment is accepted with Visa, M/C or Amex.

✔ Mail orders accepted
✔ Good bargain-hunting
Minimum order: no minimum
Shipping method: surface mail
Shipping time: 5-6 weeks
Returns policy: all goods guaranteed, but returns are slow
Member: Hong Kong Trade Association

214 P.G.N. SALES

5813 Beresford St.
Burnaby, B.C.
Canada V5J 1K1
(604) 435-8495; fax: (604) 435-8495

This wholesaler of educational art supplies will sell directly to you by mail. Discounts increase according to the size of the order (to a maximum of 25 percent), but the real plus here is the high quality of the products: Berol of England paints are highlighted, as well as inks, lettering supplies, pens and nibs, watercolours, excellent fabric dyes, glue, marking pens, artist's paints, books and daycare supplies. The catalogue is reprinted every year, usually in July or August, and is free to our readers. Payment is accepted by IMO or cheques, and with steady customers or established institutions they ship the stock first and invoice later.

✔ Special offer to readers
✔ Mail orders accepted
✔ Phone orders accepted
✔ Good bargain-hunting
Minimum order: no minimum
Shipping method: Canada Post or courier (costs more)
Shipping time: 2 days
Returns policy: all returns accepted and credited or refunded

215 PAPRIKAS WEISS IMPORTER

1546 Second Avenue
New York, NY
U S A 10028
(212) 288-6117

Edward Weiss runs the family business in the same tradition as his father before him. They began importing Hungarian paprika and added on to the line until, today, they are one of the top importers of gourmet foodstuffs and cookware. Here's a sampling of the fine goods they stock: herbs, spices, coffee, teas, salamis, Hershey's golden almond bars,

Guittard chocolate and white chocolate (in bulk), fancy vinegars, chestnuts, crème de marrons, foie gras and patés from Louis Henry (Strasbourg) like smoked goose paté, liver paté and Baudoin truffles. There's also Dobosh torte, Viennese Ildefonso chocolates, chocolate sugar plums, pfeffernusse (a traditional German Christmas confection), jams, jellies, preserves, cheeses, dried mushrooms, cod roe paté, gold foil coins, Van Houten cocoa, honey, butters, hams, strudel dough, syrups, fruitcakes, pasta, Sabatier cooks' knives, aprons, cookbooks, cookware, Hungarian records and gift packs. Whew! Catalogues are published in each of the four seasons and are free. Payment is accepted by VISA, M/C and Amex only.

✔ Mail orders accepted
✔ Phone orders accepted
Minimum order: $10 (U.S.)
Shipping method: goods can only be shipped to U.S. pick-up point
Shipping time: 1 week
Returns policy: all goods guaranteed
Established in 1889

216 PARADISE PRODUCTS, INC.
P.O. Box 568
El Cerrito, CA
U S A 94530
(415) 524-8300

Here's the place for party supplies: theme parties, Oktoberfest, Hallowe'en, casino night, dress black-and-white, you name it. The catalogue is a delight of ideas and inspiration for party people. You'll save as much as 50 percent on all orders. The catalogue costs $2. Payment is accepted with VISA, M/C, IMO or cheques in U.S. funds.

✔ Mail orders accepted
✔ Phone orders accepted
✔ Good bargain-hunting
Minimum order: $30 (U.S.)
Shipping method: mail or airmail
Shipping time: 2-3 weeks
Returns policy: all goods guaranteed
Established in 1953

217 PARFUMERIE CATHERINE
6, Rue de Castiglione
75001 Paris
France
426 13 155; or fax: 426 13 227

You'll save up to 40 percent on French perfumes and cosmetics by ordering directly from Catherine. They carry an extensive list of brand lines, such as Chanel, Dior, Lancome, Stendhal and Orlane, with perfumes, colognes, body lotions and other cosmetics represented. They will charge you $9 (U.S.) to ship a two-pound parcel. They are also very reliable about sending gifts directly to your friends, with hand-written cards carrying your personalized greetings if you carefully print the instructions and write or fax them clearly. Their price-list-style catalogue is published once a year, usually in April or May, and is free. They accept payment via VISA, M/C, Amex, IMO, Access, Eurocard, JCB card or cheques.

✔ Mail orders accepted
✔ Phone orders accepted
Minimum order: no minimum
Shipping method: airmail or surface mail
Shipping time: 2 weeks
Returns policy: they replace or reimburse for all defective goods
Established in 1955

218 PARIS INTERNATIONAL INC. ("THE LITTLE OLD BREAD MAN")
500 Independence Ave. S.E.
Washington, DC
U S A 20003
(202) 544-6858

Clyde Brooks and his wife lived in Paris until after the war and acquired a taste for baguettes. Brooks himself had done some baking during their Paris stint, during the bread shortage, and when they returned Stateside, he discovered he couldn't find pans that would produce the right-shaped loaves. So, like any good entrepreneurial American, he devised a way to make his own. Now he sells them by mail at prices about 40 percent below retail market value. Even though you pay higher postage fees to have them sent to Canada, you probably couldn't even buy them in this country. He also sells pans for San Francisco sour dough loaves, and "whole oven" baking sheets (measure your oven to ensure they will fit). The loaf pans come with free, detailed bread-making recipes and instructions. They do not accept phone orders. An order sheet and product description will answer your written inquiry. All payment must be in U.S. funds via cheque or IMO.

✔ Mail orders accepted
✔ Good bargain-hunting
Minimum order: no minimum

Shipping method: mail or UPS
Shipping time: shipped within 5 days of order
Returns policy: return for refund if not satisfied

219 PARON CHOCOLATIER
1038 Lexington Ave.
New York City, NY
U S A 10021
(212) 744-2888

Harriot Sessa is the chocolatier responsible for imagining popcorn coated in rich, dark chocolate, and for dreaming up her delectable Cookie Chip Chocolates, which are small chunks of cookie dipped in semi-sweet chocolate, then stuck together in hunks of wonder! Sessa's goods are found at Bonwit Teller, Stern's and Neiman-Marcus, but you can order direct from her in New York. Catalogues are published every June and January and are free. Payment is accepted via VISA, M/C, Amex, or in some form of U.S. currency.

✔ Special offer to readers
✔ Mail orders accepted
✔ Phone orders accepted
Minimum order: no minimum
Shipping method: ship to Canada via UPS only
Shipping time: 1 week
Returns policy: all goods guaranteed

220 PECAN ST. SWEETS
4839 Don Drive
Dallas, TX
U S A 75247
(214) 634-2825; U.S. toll-free only: (800) 882-NUTS

This place sells gourmet nuts of all kinds, including peanut brittle, pralines, divinity, pecan chewies, peanut logs, and their specialty, jars of frosted pecans (which I've tasted, and they're delicious). Sylvia Cohen and her family have been cooking up these Dallas specialties for more than 30 years, and boy, is she eager to please! She told me, "Get me the business, and we'll add an 800 number in Canada!" Their policy is they will do "whatever necessary to satisfy a customer's need." Naturally, they'll send your gift to American or Canadian friends with a gift card from you. Catalogues are published for Valentine's Day, Mother's Day and Christmas and are free to our readers. Payment is accepted by C.O.D. (U.S. only, of course), VISA, M/C, Amex, IMO, Diners Club or Discover card.

✔ Special offer to readers
✔ Mail orders accepted
✔ Phone orders accepted
Minimum order: no minimum
Shipping method: mail, UPS, courier
Shipping time: 3 days to process order
Returns policy: goods guaranteed 100 percent

221 PETER JONES
Sloane Square
London SW1W 8EL
England
(71) 73-3434

Peter Jones is not quite so posh as the Knightsbridge stores we all know about in London, but their stock is much the same and their prices better. Household items you might find include linens, fine china, silver and crystal, yard goods and upholstery fabrics, and gifts. Catalogues are published seasonally and are free. Payment is accepted only by IMO, bank draft or cheques, in pounds sterling.

✔ Mail orders accepted
✔ Good bargain-hunting
Minimum order: no minimum
Shipping method: mail or airmail
Shipping time: 2-4 weeks
Returns policy: all goods guaranteed
Established in 1877

222 PIED PIPER CATALOG
2922 N. 35th Ave., Suite 4
Drawer 11408
Phoenix, AZ
U S A 85061-1408
(602) 272-1853

These people produce a catalogue for "gifted children," featuring games, toys, learning materials, sports equipment and science projects. Their catalogue is free. Payment is accepted with Visa, M/C, Amex, IMO or cheques in U.S. currency.

✔ Mail orders accepted
Minimum order: no minimum
Shipping method: UPS or post
Shipping time: 2-3 weeks
Returns policy: all goods guaranteed

223 PIERRE DEUX
428 N. Rodeo Drive
Beverly Hills, CA
U S A
(213) 550-7265

When I was quilting in the late '70s, I used to travel to Paris and stay with a girlfriend in the trendy (and very upscale) 7ième arrondissement, just around the corner from Pierre Deux's showroom. Having been shooed away when I went in during daylight hours to enquire about "coupons" (remnants), I prowled the streets on garbage night, but always came up empty-handed. These days, I pay the full price, but reluctantly. In addition to wonderful French provincial floral print fabrics, they sell Laura Ashley-style dresses, separates, totes, pillows, curtains and upholstery, for very high prices, but the dumpster-diving doesn't work in L.A. either, so what's a seamstress to do? The catalogue is $4. Payment is accepted with Visa, M/C or Amex only.

✔ Mail orders accepted
Minimum order: no minimum
Shipping method: UPS or U.S. Mail
Shipping time: 2-6 weeks, depending on season
Returns policy: no returns on cut yard-goods

224 PLAYERS CHESS & GAME SHOWROOM
1710 Silverlake Blvd.
Los Angeles, CA
U S A
(213) 665-5729

These people are the publishers of *Chess News*. Naturally, they carry chess paraphernalia and supplies, backgammon sets, bridge computers, books on chess, and even Monopoly in foreign languages. A flyer and price list are available on request, free. Payment is accepted with Visa, M/C, Amex, Diner's Club, IMO or cheque.

✔ Mail orders accepted
✔ Phone orders accepted
Minimum order: no minimum
Shipping method: UPS or mail
Shipping time: 2-4 weeks, depending on stock
Returns policy: all goods guaranteed

225 POINTER JEWELLERY CO. LTD.
Room 605, Prosperity House
10, Granville Road, Tsim Sha Tsui
Kowloon, Hong Kong
(852) 739-1892; 739-1900 ; fax: (852) 3-311-0060

This family-run business sells jewellery and unset gems at near-wholesale prices, but, as with all overseas gemstone purchases, be sure you are specific in your description of what you want and have an independent appraisal done to ascertain the "real" value of your purchases, particularly for the purposes of domestic insurance coverage. Remember that unset stones enter Canada duty-free, but you will have to pay F.S.T. based on the amount you have paid, so be sure they send you a receipt—otherwise Canada Customs assesses the stones at Canadian values and you'll pay more. Price lists or price quotes (by phone or fax) are available on request. Payment is accepted with IMO or bank draft in a variety of currencies.

✔ Mail orders accepted
✔ Phone orders accepted
✔ Good bargain-hunting
Minimum order: no minimum
Shipping method: surface or airmail; request insurance and registration
Shipping time: 2-6 weeks, depending on method
Returns policy: all goods guaranteed to be as represented

226 THE POPCORN FACTORY
P.O. Box 4530
Lake Bluff, IL
U S A 60044
(312) 295-9633; (312) 362-6670;
U.S. toll-free: (800)858-1000

The Popcorn Factory is just that: the mail order arm of the famous stores near Chicago. They sell every manner of plain and coated popcorn and in fancy tins like Coca-Cola, Sandra Boynton, Mickey Mouse, personalized party tins, and reproduction antique Coke tins. They also feature the wonderful Rachel's brownies, popping supplies, mints and seasonal specialties, such as "gummy bunnies" for Easter. Their catalogues change seasonally and are free. Order to Canada, add 40 percent (!) to their prices, so you might consider ordering to a U.S. drop point. A handy way to send Christmas gifts, of course. Payment is accepted by VISA, M/C, Amex, and Discover card, or by IMO or cheque (U.S. funds).

✔ Mail orders accepted
✔ Phone orders accepted
✔ Good bargain-hunting
Minimum order: no minimum

Shipping method: mail or UPS
Shipping time: 3 - 4 weeks
Returns policy: all goods guaranteed

227 PT & P (THAILAND) CO. LTD.

285 Bangkok Bazaar, Rajadamri Rd.
Bangkok
Thailand
(662) 253-8800; fax: (662) 294-4122

Here is a source for PVC (leather-look) wallets, briefcases, journals, address books, plastic files and wedding registers. Their stock is quite extensive, and they update their catalogue and colour flyer frequently with periodic price lists, all free. Payment is accepted with VISA, M/C, Amex, IMO or cheque, though they prefer bank drafts above all.

✔ Mail orders accepted
✔ Phone orders accepted
✔ Good bargain-hunting
Minimum order: no minimum
Shipping method: airmail or surface mail
Shipping time: 2-6 weeks (depends on method)
Returns policy: "your complete satisfaction guaranteed"

228 PUBLIC BROADCASTING SERVICE

Signals Catalogue
P.O. Box 70870
St. Paul, MN
U S A 55170-0252
U.S. toll-free only: (800) 669-9696 ;
U.S. customer service: (800) 669-5225

Signals is the PBS catalogue and includes promotional items bearing the familiar PBS logo on sweatshirts, mugs and tote bags. There are also video tapes available from popular programs like "Bill Moyer's Journal", "Fawlty Towers" (remember that one where Basil was beating his car with half a tree?) and the Sherlock Holmes series. Catalogues are published six times a year, for spring, late spring, summer, fall, winter and holiday, and are free. Payment is accepted with VISA, M/C, Amex, Discover card, IMO or cheques.

✔ Mail orders accepted
Minimum order: no minimum
Shipping method: mail or UPS
Shipping time: 2 weeks
Returns policy: all goods guaranteed
Established in 1981

229 PUR ET SIMPLE INC.

431 Corey Road
Ayer's Cliff, P.Q.
Canada J0B 1C0
(819) 838-4203; (819) 838-5705 ; Can. toll-free number available soon; call 800 Information to check

Pierre LaCombe and Hannah Obermeir create or personally screen all the products available through this environment-friendly company. All goods are "ecologically and ethically sound," from self-fastening cotton diapers to beeswax crayons, and from household cleaners to cosmetics. They also assure themselves that manufacturers from whom they buy do not pollute or use animals in testing. Their catalogue is $3, but as a special offer to our readers, they will send you a sample catalogue free (please quote the name of this book when you write). Payment is accepted with Visa or M/C (but you'll have to order $30 worth); or with IMO or cheque. C.O.D.s are possible within Canada, but there's a small surcharge. Shipping costs about 10 percent of your order.

✔ Special offer to readers
✔ Mail orders accepted
✔ Phone orders accepted
✔ Good bargain-hunting

Minimum order: no minimum if paid by cheque; $30 if charged to credit card
Shipping method: UPS, C.O.D. or regular Canada Post mail
Shipping time: 4-6 weeks
Returns policy: goods guaranteed, but you pay shipping and return
Established in 1988
Member: Canadian Association for Environmental Products and Service

230 RADIO SHACK

Box 34,000
Barrie, Ontario
Canada L4M 4W5
nearest retail store

Radio Shack primarily operates retail outlets in North America, but if you live in a remote area, they will mail order goods to you, if you pay postage. You can write to get on their mailing list. All catalogues are fully illustrated, contain current pricing and are free. Mail order payment with Radio Shack must be by credit card: VISA, M/C, Amex or Radio Shack card.

✔ Mail orders accepted
✔ Phone orders accepted
✔ Good bargain-hunting

Minimum order: no minimum
Shipping method: Canada Post
Shipping time: 2-3 weeks
Returns policy: all goods guaranteed; you pay postage on returns

231 RAMA TRADE
844 Greenchain
False Creek
Vancouver, B.C.
Canada V5Z 3Z6
fax only: (604) 874-4535; or fax directly to Bangkok: (011) 662-235-1744

Though Dale Mearns is from an old establishment family in British Columbia, she somehow acquired a knack for wheeling and dealing, which led her into the business of importing goods, clothing and valuable artifacts and relics from Southwest Asia many years ago. She's a great bargain sleuth and haggler, so she buys items for a fraction of their value here. Years ago, she became friends with magazine publisher Richard Murray, and now they have a happy association in Rama Trade. Dale is in Vancouver during the summer months, and Richard stays in Bangkok year-round. They will find, and buy for you, anything that can legally be acquired in Southwest Asia: silks, quilted pillow cases, antique Hill tribe textiles, diamonds and other gems, artifacts, relics, even custom-made eyeglasses. Naturally, their prices are very good. They will not take phone orders, but you can write to the Vancouver address, or fax directly either to Vancouver or Bangkok with your requirements, and they will reply via fax about the item's availability, cost and how long it will take to find it and ship it to you. Payment is accepted with IMO, cheque, bank draft or traveller's cheques, all in Canadian currency.

✔ Mail orders accepted
Minimum order: no minimum
Shipping method: airmail; large items crated and shipped
Shipping time: 5-6 weeks
Returns policy: returns only if goods faulty
Established in 1972

232 RAMMAGERDIN H.F.
P.O. Box 751
121 Reykjavik
Iceland
354-1-1122

If you've been looking for a source for fabulous (surprisingly inexpensive) sweaters, this is it! The styles are high fashion, appealling and practical (warm). There are mainly sizes for men and women, but a few kids' items, too. For the knitter, there are wonderful wools (they'll send cards of samples) and sweater kits. There are souvenir T-shirts and sweats, too. There's no minimum order from the huge, colour catalogues (usually printed in April or May), but there is a minimum of eight skeins for wool (price is only $3.50 per skein by surface mail). All prices include postage to Canada. Catalogues cost $2 (U.S.) refundable on your first order. Payment is accepted by VISA, M/C, Amex, Diners Club, IMO or cheque.

✔ Special offer to readers
✔ Mail orders accepted
✔ Phone orders accepted
✔ Good bargain-hunting
Minimum order: no minimum
Shipping method: airmail or surface mail
Shipping time: about 4 weeks
Returns policy: all goods can be returned for exchange or refund

233 THE READER'S CATALOG
250 West 57th St.
New York, NY
U S A 10107
(212) 333-7900; U.S. toll-free: (800) 882-8770;
fax: (212) 307-1973

This huge compendium, reference catalogue is published to help you find hard-to-locate books, particularly if you live in areas with bookstores that have trouble special-ordering books for you. More than 40,000 of "the best books in print" are listed in 15 main categories and 208 subcategories. This is a research-junkie's paradise. The catalogue itself may be ordered and sent as a gift anywhere in North America. Each entry is briefly annotated, so you know roughly what the subject matter of the book is. The catalogue is updated each year. Goods are shipped into Canada airmail for an 8 percent surcharge (or send them to a U.S. address, being mindful of the fact that UPS will not deliver to a postal box). For yet another $8 (U.S.), the order can be shipped by Federal Express. Extra bulletins of forthcoming books may be sent to you free if you send in your name and address with a short list of the subjects in which you are interested. Payment is accepted with VISA, M/C, Amex and cheque, and fax orders are welcome, too.

✔ Mail orders accepted
✔ Phone orders accepted
Minimum order: $15 (U.S.)
Shipping method: UPS; airmail to Canada (add 8 percent to order)

Shipping time: 2 weeks
Returns policy: call first before returning merchandise, prepaid

234 REGAL GIFTS & GREETINGS
939 Eglinton Ave. East
Toronto, Ontario
Canada M4G 2L6
(416) 425-3130

Barbara Canning-Brown, who is director of marketing for this long-established Canadian catalogue sales firm, is also the chairman of the Canadian Catalogue Council. Regal Gifts is a bit of a dark horse among mail order houses, because their sales are carried out by individuals who acquire the catalogue and sell to their friends and co-workers. There are many incentives for doing this, including nice discounts on your own purchases. Anyone can participate, and you don't have to worry about being shipped cartons of greeting cards — your letter will merely bring you a free copy of their current catalogue. Inside, are tempting photos of novelties, coffee mugs, stuffed toys, decor accents, cookware and kitchen utensils, luggage, and of course, cards. Payment is accepted with VISA, M/C or cheque and C.O.D.s within Canada.

✔ Mail orders accepted
Minimum order: no minimum, but you must "join"
Shipping method: Canada Post or UPS
Shipping time: 2-4 weeks
Returns policy: all goods unconditionally guaranteed
Established in 1928
Member: Canadian Direct Marketing Association

235 RIC CLARK HEARING AIDS
9530 Langdon Ave.
Sepulveda, CA
U S A 91343
(818) 892-6636

Ric Clark claims to sell hearing aids otherwise sold nationally by dealers under another brand name — only his prices are about half. Payment is required by cheques payable in U.S. dollars or by U.S. dollar money orders. A $10 (U.S.) deposit is required for trial orders. Phone orders are not taken. Hearing aids are not dutiable and Ric marks the package "Hearing Aids, No duty, Medical device" and has no problem. Ric says that about a quarter of his business is repeat, another quarter comes from referrals from satisfied customers and the rest is word of mouth and advertising. His guess is the saving on buying directly from him is

about $300 "but this depends on how greedy [your local] dealer is, and they are a greedy lot." All of Ric's merchandise is covered by a one-year guarantee against defects in materials or workmanship, but not against breakage or damage caused by dropping. Any defective aid is repaired or replaced at their cost, no charge of any kind to you. Note that some types of deafness are not helped by a hearing aid. Check with your physician to determine your needs. Catalogue is reprinted as they add new goods or "as the mood strikes us" and is free. Payment is preferred in IMO payable in U.S. dollars. Cheques are also accepted but you'll have to wait for them to clear, which delays your shipment a little.

✔ Mail orders accepted
✔ Good bargain-hunting
Minimum order: no minimum
Shipping method: prices include 1st class postage
Shipping time: same day shipping
Returns policy: 30 day money-back trial
Established in 1968

236 ROBINSON'S MAPLE PRODUCTS
RR #2
Auburn, Ontario
Canada N0M 1E0
(519) 529-7857

This family operation produces an assortment of sizes and forms of Ontario maple syrup, from the syrups themselves, to maple candy and specialty treats. A flyer and price list is available free, on request. Payment is accepted with IMO or cheque, and large corporate gift orders are possible, too.

✔ Mail orders accepted
Minimum order: no minimum
Shipping method: Canada Post or UPS
Shipping time: 1-2 weeks, depending on supply
Returns policy: all goods guaranteed

237 ROCKWOOD GARDENS LTD.
501 Harris St.
Rockwood, Ontario
Canada N0B 2K0
(519) 856-9539

I hesitated about including this entry because the tactics they use to hustle business are, well, such a hustle, but they do have good products, at what I've found to be very fair prices, so here they are. These folks sell seeds, bulbs, tree stock and plants, plus combo packages that work out to a very low unit price. The catalogue and seasonal flyers are free, in fact, you'll be hard-pressed to get off their mailing list once you're on. You'll also get a large number of mailings telling you that you've "qualified" to win this or that, but generally, you'll "win" a package of seeds and nothing more, so don't be conned. Payment is via IMO or cheques.

✔ Mail orders accepted
Minimum order: no minimum
Shipping method: Canada Post
Shipping time: 2 weeks
Returns policy: all goods guaranteed

238 ROGER'S CHOCOLATES
913 Government Street
Victoria, B.C.
Canada V8W 1X5
(604) 384-7021

These bonbons are famous worldwide. They've even been served in Buckingham Palace and the White House, so I'm not alone in claiming they're the best chocolate confections on the planet! The eccentric C.W. Roger first opened his shop in Victoria's heyday, when even Sarah Bernhardt stopped in town to perform. Today, the candies are made fresh daily from C.W.'s original, secret recipes. They can be shipped anywhere in the world boxed in their distinctive checkerboard or foil wrappers, or in seasonal packaging or keepsake tins. There are plain creams in peach (my passion), pineapple, rum and more, and nut-filled versions, such as "Cherry Nut Delight" with walnuts and brazils. There are also toffees, chews, mint wafers and hard candies. A descriptive, colour brochure, order form and price list are available free. Payment is accepted with Visa, M/C, Amex and cheques.

✔ Mail orders accepted
✔ Phone orders accepted
Minimum order: no minimum
Shipping method: UPS or Canada Post
Shipping time: shipped within 48 hours
Returns policy: all goods guaranteed
Established in 1885

239 ROMSHOPS, TREASURES OF THE ROM
Shop By Mail
100 Queen's Park
Toronto, Ontario
Canada M5S 9Z9
(416) 586-5842; fax: (416) 586-5863

Another museum source, this one is Toronto's Royal Ontario Museum, and though the offerings are modest, there's so much less hassle with customs. Some of the items are quite wonderful, including fine sculpture, reproductions, art, posters, books and greeting cards. There are dinosaur Christmas ornaments (and earrings!), Beatrix Potter board games, fossil kits, a copy of the priceless Mallorytown glass pitcher, unique (and inexpensive) jewellery, coffee mugs, and a baby sleeping bag I particularly fancy. The catalogue is free. Payment is accepted with VISA, M/C and cheques.

✔ Mail orders accepted
Minimum order: no minimum
Shipping method: Canada Post
Shipping time: 2 weeks
Returns policy: all goods guaranteed

240 ROSS-SIMONS JEWELERS
9 Ross-Simons Dr.
Cranston, RI
U S A 02920-9848
(401) 463-3131; U.S. toll-free: (800) 556-7376;
fax: (401) 463-8599

Ross-Simons is a large outfit, offering major brands at discount prices. Among the luxury items they stock are Lennox china, Wedgwood, Royal Doulton, Spode, Waterford crystal, Wallace sterling and other flatware, plus fine jewellery (such as watches, diamonds and pearls). There is also a broad selection of faux jewellery, framed in 14K or 18K white or yellow gold. Overstock is cleared out by periodic sales, right in the catalogue itself. Catalogues are published as required and are free to our readers. Payment is accepted by VISA, M/C, Amex, Access, Carte Blanche, Diner's Club, Discover, En Route and IMO. Fax orders are also accepted.

✔ Mail orders accepted
✔ Phone orders accepted
✔ Good bargain-hunting
Minimum order: no minimum
Shipping method: mail or UPS
Shipping time: 2-3 weeks
Returns policy: all items guaranteed
Established in 1952

241 ROWENA'S AND CAPTAIN JAAP'S JAM & JELLY FACTORY
758 West 22nd Street
Norfolk, VA
U S A 23517
(804) 627-8699; U.S. only: (800) 627-8699

Rowena and Captain Jaap make their own line of wonderful jams, jellies, sauces and a delectable almond pound cake. Their distinction comes from the unusual and delicious flavours of their products, created with home-made attention. Shipping charges are listed on their order form. Discounts are available on corporate gifts. Deadline for Christmas giving is December 20 for shipping to your American friends. Catalogues are published for spring, summer and fall and are free. Payment is accepted by C.O.D. (U.S. only), VISA, M/C and Choice card.

✔ Mail orders accepted
✔ Phone orders accepted
Minimum order: no minimum
Shipping method: UPS
Shipping time: 2 - 4 days
Returns policy: "complete satisfaction guaranteed"

242 S.E. RYKOFF & CO.
P.O. Box 21467
Market St. Station
Los Angeles, CA
U S A 90021
(213) 624-6094; (213) 622-4131; (800) 421-9873

S.E. Rykoff is a supplier of gourmet restaurant fare that makes their line available to the public by mail order. They sell high quality foods and "cookware of distinction." Discounts (of about 10 percent) apply to volume orders of products they regularly stock. Catalogues are published four times a year, in January, April, July and October and one is free only if you mention this book. They accept VISA, M/C and Amex.

✔ Special offer to readers
✔ Mail orders accepted
✔ Phone orders accepted
Minimum order: no minimum
Shipping method: they will ship only to U.S. destinations
Shipping time: 2 weeks
Returns policy: goods are guaranteed for 30 days

243 SAN FRANCISCO HERB CO.
250 14th Street, Dept APB
San Francisco, CA
U S A 94103
(415) 861-7174 ; toll-free in U.S.: (800) 227-4530;
in Calif.:(800) 622-0768

Here's a wholesaler that really understands mail order. Not only are their prices exceptional on a host of kinds of pot-pourri, spices, curry, health foods, edible nuts and seeds, sprouting seeds, teas, fragrance oils, herbs and botanicals, dehydrated veggies and much more, but you actually check off your order on their clever catalogue, refold the whole works (they've pre-printed their return address on it) and send it back to them to order. Readers of this book are offered a free catalogue, of course, plus 30 free recipes, just for writing. Generally speaking, on large orders you'll save 10 to 15 percent. Please note that minimum order is $30 (U.S.). The catalogue is refreshed twice a year, for February and August and is free. C.O.D. orders are filled only for the continental U.S. and those over $300 must be prepaid or via IMO. Cheques are accepted only in U.S. funds. Otherwise, payment is best by VISA or M/C.

✔ Special offer to readers
✔ Mail orders accepted
✔ Phone orders accepted
✔ Good bargain-hunting
Minimum order: $30.00 (U.S. funds) minimum
Shipping method: mail or UPS
Shipping time: 48 hours
Returns policy: all goods guaranteed; return within 15 days

244 SAXKJAERS
53 Koomagergade
1150 Copenhagen K
Denmark
(45) 1-110777; fax: (011-45) 1-3272107

Scandinavia offers a large number of giftware merchants, and this is one of the oldest. They sell collectors' plates, giftware, china, crystal, figurines, jewellery, hand-painted porcelain, brassware, dolls and other unusual items, all at lower prices than you'd pay at home. The catalogue is glossy and well-illustrated with colour photos and costs $2 (refundable on first order). Payment is accepted with VISA, M/C, Amex, Eurocard or IMO.

✔ Mail orders accepted
Minimum order: no minimum
Shipping method: surface mail (includes insurance)

Shipping time: 3 weeks
Returns policy: all goods guaranteed
Established in 1904

245 SEARS CANADA INC.
108 Mutual Street
Toronto, Ontario
Canada M5B 2C9
(416) 362-1711

Sears Christmas catalogue is its largest, naturally, often running to 400 pages or more. At that time of year, they emphasize gifts which can be sent anywhere in Canada, postage-paid. These gifts will include a card from you. The Christmas "Wish Book" often includes a supplement of discounted or unique gift items, too. Catalogues are published 12 times a year, with two of those being the "major" books, and three seasonal books for Christmas, mid-winter and summer, as well as numerous sales supplements and flyers. Catalogues now cost $4, but that is refunded on your first purchase, if it's over $25. If you continue to buy $25 worth of goods between editions, catalogues will come to you free.

✔ Mail orders accepted
✔ Phone orders accepted
✔ Good bargain-hunting
Minimum order: $25 to get free catalogue; otherwise, no minimum
Shipping method: mail or delivery to nearest catalogue sales office
Shipping time: 3-4 days
Returns policy: all goods guaranteed
Established in 1953

246 SEARS CANADA INC. ATLANTIC
7101 Chebucto Rd.
Halifax, N.S.
Canada B3L 1N3
(902) 454-5111

Sears is Canada's premier mail order house, fulfilling orders at counters in 1,600 catalogue sales offices from coast to coast. As one company official quipped: "If a place has two people and a dog, we've got a catalogue sales office there." Goods include dolls, toys and children's clothing, housewares, cookware, bedding and linens, electronics, men's and women's apparel, shoes, boots, hiking, fishing, hunting and camping gear, furniture, jewellery, sportswear, household goods, and gift packs, including some very fine fruitcakes. There's much more, of course. See other Sears listings for more details.

- ✔ Mail orders accepted
- ✔ Phone orders accepted
- ✔ Good bargain-hunting

Minimum order: $25 to get free catalogue; otherwise, no minimum
Shipping method: mail or delivery to nearest catalogue sales office
Shipping time: 3-4 days
Returns policy: all goods guaranteed
Established in 1953

247 SEARS CANADA INC. QUEBEC

3075 Thimens Blvd.
St. Laurent, P.Q.
Canada H4R 2V5
(514) 335-5000

Sears operates mail order offices across Canada and carries on business in Quebec in both official languages. The catalogues are available in all Sears retail stores nationwide, of course, but surprisingly, they're also found at Coles bookstores and W.H. Smith. In areas not served directly by Sears, this is one of the addresses to which you may write for a catalogue. Please read other Sears entries also, for the complete picture.

- ✔ Mail orders accepted
- ✔ Phone orders accepted
- ✔ Good bargain-hunting

Minimum order: $25 to get free catalogue; otherwise, no minimum
Shipping method: mail or delivery to nearest catalogue sales office
Shipping time: 3-4 days
Returns policy: all goods guaranteed
Established in 1953

248 SEARS CANADA INC. WEST

1050 Broad Street
Regina, Sask.
Canada S4R 5E1
(306) 569-1711

Most Canadians are familiar with the Sears name. They've operated under the Simpsons-Sears banner since 1953, and before that, Simpson's history in Canada stretches back to the late 1920s. Hardly a Canadian in any small town would not remember the local Simpson's or Sears outlet from the main street. Even today, mail order makes up a huge (and

profitable) chunk of their business, so they are ever-eager to please. Payment, however, is accepted only by cheque, money order or Sear's card, but they will do C.O.D. orders, which is a great convenience if you want to check out the goods at the counter before paying for them.

✔ Mail orders accepted
✔ Phone orders accepted
✔ Good bargain-hunting
Minimum order: $25 to get free catalogue; otherwise, no minimum
Shipping method: mail or delivery to nearest catalogue sales office
Shipping time: 3-4 days
Returns policy: all goods guaranteed
Established in 1953

249 SELECT ORIGINS INC.
Box N
Southampton, NY
U S A 11968
(516) 288-1382; toll-free in U.S.: (800) 822-2092

Tom and Kristi Siplon's assortment of herbs and spices has been selected by the Book of Bests recommended in the *New York Times* Gourmet Shopper. Their stock includes sun-dried tomatoes from California, imported chili, olives, cooking oils, vinegars, pepper, peppercorns, mushrooms, Sable and Rosenfeld antipasto, Vermont maple syrup, flavoured sugars, teas, Turbinado vanilla sugar, Lindt chocolate (in bulk), Grand Finale dessert sauces and gift packs of every size and description.They will send you their catalogue (printed four times a year, seasonally), free. Payment is accepted by VISA, M/C, Amex, and IMO.

✔ Mail orders accepted
✔ Phone orders accepted
Minimum order: no minimum
Shipping method: air or UPS
Shipping time: 2-3 days
Returns policy: refund if not completely satisfied

250 SEVA FOUNDATION, C/O SEVA SERVICE SOCIETY
Suite 204-1965 West 4th Avenue
Vancouver, B.C.
Canada V6J 1M8
(604) 733-4284; fax: (604)732-6433

This international service organization provides medical assistance to third-world countries. One of the ways they raise money is by marketing craft and specialty items through their catalogue. The catalogue features wind-chimes, jewellery, Nepali silk purses, Navaho rugs, baby hats and paper products. Payment is accepted by VISA, M/C, IMO or cheques.

✔ Mail orders accepted
Minimum order: no minimum
Shipping method: Canada Post or UPS
Shipping time: 2 weeks
Returns policy: all goods guaranteed

251 SEVENTH GENERATION

Colchester, VT
U S A 05446-1672
(802) 655-4500 ; U.S. toll-free: (800) 456-1198

Here you'll find "Products for a Healthy Planet," and lots of them. These folks have turned ecology and recyling into a big business, but they haven't lost sight of you, the customer, or of the basic tenets of their philosophy. They sell recycling materials, games, books, and natural household and garden products, many hard-to-find elsewhere. Their catalogue is free. Payment is accepted via Visa, M/C, Amex, IMO or cheque (U.S. funds, please).

✔ Mail orders accepted
✔ Phone orders accepted
Minimum order: no minimum
Shipping method: UPS or post
Shipping time: 2 weeks
Returns policy: all goods guaranteed

252 SHAKER WORKSHOPS

P.O. Box 1028
Concord, MA
U S A 01742
(617) 646-8985

This source offers quality reproductions of Shaker furniture at reasonable prices. Included in their colourful catalogue are tiny baskets, miniature Shaker animals, Shaker tables, tape-back rockers and occasional chairs, soft dolls, oval wooden boxes, books, samplers, cross-stitch kits and kits for making furniture. There are also pieces of furniture shipped assembled and finished. Most of the wood used is rock maple. A sample catalogue is free to our readers. Catalogues are published twice yearly: spring/summer and fall/winter, with items featured reflecting the seasonal nature of the publication. Payment is accepted with C.O.D. (U.S. only), VISA, M/C, Amex, Access and Discover cards.

✔ Mail orders accepted
✔ Phone orders accepted
Minimum order: no minimum
Shipping method: mail or UPS
Shipping time: 10 working days after receipt
Returns policy: credit or refund if returned in 30 days

253 SHANGHAI ARTS & CRAFTS
190-208 Nanjing Road (W)
Shanghai
China
276530; fax: (21) 272908

This is a factory wholesale outlet that makes wooden crafts, Christmas ornaments, wooden rocking horses, toy sleighs, wooden cars, and best of all, wonderfully detailed dollhouse miniatures you won't find anywhere else in the world. There's even a tiny, perfectly detailed, hand-painted wooden Chinese folding-screen. The colour catalogue, with separate price list, is free. Payment is via IMO or bank draft. Inquire about payment and shipping details before ordering. Most items can come through Customs (especially if they are gifts) duty-free.

✔ Mail orders accepted
Minimum order: no minimum
Shipping method: airmail or surface mail
Shipping time: 4-6 weeks
Returns policy: all goods guaranteed

254 SHANGHAI SILK-KNIT CARPET FACTORY
342 Lingling Road
Shanghai
China
311-823; cable: 6242

This factory routinely wins the "Golden Cup" in the national competitions for quality in silk-carpet weaving in China. This is the place to have custom carpets woven at a fraction of their domestic cost. Some patterns are standard and can be ordered in a number of available sizes, but custom work takes longer, costs more and requires careful correspondence or telexing back and forth before you begin. A full-colour flyer illustrates on-hand styles and is free. Payment is accepted with IMO or bank draft, but please negotiate method of payment and shipping details before you order.

✔ Mail orders accepted
✔ Good bargain-hunting
Minimum order: inquire about minimum sizes
Shipping method: surface mail (ship)
Shipping time: 3-4 months if not in stock
Returns policy: all work guaranteed, but returns difficult

255 THE SHARPER IMAGE
650 Davis Street
San Francisco, CA
U S A 94111
(415) 445-6100; U.S. toll-free: (800) 344-4444;
U.S. customer service: (800) 344-5555

Included in their glossy, full-colour and very inviting catalogues are executive toys, electronics, gadgets, novelties, luggage, jewellery, watches, binoculars, posters, games, sports gear, moccasins, exercise equipment, and brand names such as Sony, Panasonic, Casio, and the famous Vuarnet Skilynx sunglasses, to name but a few. More than 20 million people read their monthly catalogues! They have stores in 66 U.S. locations, and a location in Zurich, Switzerland (Lowenstrasse 32 CH8001, if you're visiting there). Catalogues to U.S. addresses are free, but to send them to Canada, there's an annual subscription fee of $24 (U.S.). Often, if you call your nearest U.S. location, a friendly salesperson will sidestep the rules and send you a sample, gratis. They will mail goods to Canada, but you might find a U.S. drop-off spot faster and easier. Payment is accepted via VISA, M/C, Amex, Carte Blanche, Diners Club, Discover card, IMO or cheque.

✔ Mail orders accepted
✔ Phone orders accepted
Minimum order: no minimum
Shipping method: mail, UPS or Federal Express
Shipping time: orders filled within 48 hours
Returns policy: all goods guaranteed; return within 30 days

256 SHINAWATRA
Soi 23, 136 Sukhumvit Road; 94 Soi 23 Sukhumvit
Bangkok
Thailand
(662) 258-0515; (662) 258-3570

Please note in this listing there are two addresses, and two phone numbers. The stores are directly across the street from each other and you can write to either one. One building mainly sells cotton clothing, while the other has Thai crafts, silk yard goods, heavy fabrics for upholstery and clothing. Price lists are available for all goods, free. Payment is accepted with VISA, M/C, Amex or IMO.

- ✔ Mail orders accepted
- ✔ Good bargain-hunting

Minimum order: no minimum
Shipping method: airmail or surface mail
Shipping time: 5-6 weeks
Returns policy: cut fabrics may not be returned

257 SIMPSON AND VAIL
P.O. Box 309 - 38 Clinton St.
Pleasantville, NY
U S A 10570-0309
(914) 747-1336

This is perhaps the source for the largest variety of coffee and tea available by mail and they have more than six decades of experience, to boot. Their roster also includes specialty foods, tea pots, tea cozies and accessories, mustards, Mayacamas gourmet soups (all natural; no MSG), Donvier clean water maker, Krups coffee mills, nut mixes, Cartwright and Butler biscuits (from England), gift cannisters, Van Houten's cocoa, curry powder, chutneys, spices, sun-dried tomatoes and Jamaican hot sauces. Our readers are offered a 10-percent discount on their first order, so please mention this book. Catalogues are modest (but detailed in their information) and printed six to eight times a year. Payment is accepted with VISA, M/C, IMO or cheques.

- ✔ Special offer to readers
- ✔ Mail orders accepted
- ✔ Phone orders accepted

Minimum order: no minimum
Shipping method: mail or UPS
Shipping time: 2 days
Returns policy: all goods guaranteed to satisfy
Established in 1929

258 SMITHSONIAN INSTITUTION
Department 0006
P.O. Box 2456
Washington, DC
U S A 20073-0006
(703) 455-1700 (orders); customer service: (202) 357-1826

This is America's repository and, as such, offers a dignified selection of museum-related gifts, reproductions, art, posters, books, sculpture and toys. Catalogues are published six times a year, in January, February, March, July, September and October, and are free. If you become a member of the museum, all catalogue purchases are discounted 10 percent, and you will receive either "Air and Space" or the *Smithsonian Magazine*. Each catalogue has an expiration date on prices, so you'll

want to order from a current one. The museum will send our readers a free catalogue. Payment for goods is accepted by VISA, M/C, Amex or IMO (U.S. funds, please).

✔ Special offer to readers
✔ Mail orders accepted
✔ Phone orders accepted
✔ Good bargain-hunting
Minimum order: no minimum
Shipping method: mail
Shipping time: 2-3 days
Returns policy: 90 days guarantee, but each request individual

259 SOCKS GALORE & MORE

220 Second Avenue South
Franklin, TN
U S A 37064
(615) 790-7625; U.S. toll-free: (800) 626-SOCK

This national sock retailer operates sales outlets in many U.S. discount malls and sells internationally by mail or phone order. There is a vast array of socks, stockings and hosiery (as well as gift items such as tams and gloves) available in sizes to fit all family members. Discounts range from 20 to 80 percent off retail. Shipping to points in continental U.S.A. costs $2.75 (slightly higher to mail into Canada) and they will gladly send your gift to a friend anywhere in North America with a personalized enclosure card. Their catalogue is published twice yearly and updated with seasonal specials. Their motto: "You'll love our socks...we guarantee it!" Personally, I go for intaglio patterns woven into the socks I crave (of which there are precious few in this assortment) but there are a significant number of colours in each style and many interesting argyles and textures. A sample catalogue is free to our readers. Payment via VISA, M/C, IMO or cheque.

✔ Special offer to readers
✔ Mail orders accepted
✔ Phone orders accepted
✔ Good bargain-hunting
Minimum order: no minimum
Shipping method: UPS, mail, airmail, courier
Shipping time: goods shipped within 24 hours
Returns policy: all goods may be returned for refund or exchange

260 SONG SMAI CHAROENKRUNG COLLECTION
1197/1 Charoen-Krung Road
Bangkok
Thailand
(662) 233-8690

Very eager to do mail order business, this prospering clothing shop specializes in custom-made apparel, but also sells ready-made. You can send them your measurements (be accurate!) and a picture from a magazine and they can duplicate it reasonably well, and at very competitive prices. Their catalogue is updated periodically, but mostly they price-quote on individual orders. Payment is accepted with VISA, M/C, Amex, IMO or cheque.

✔ Mail orders accepted
✔ Phone orders accepted
✔ Good bargain-hunting
Minimum order: no minimum
Shipping method: airmail or surface mail
Shipping time: 2-3 weeks, including custom work
Returns policy: "guaranteed satisfaction"

261 SPECIALTY FOOD SHOP
200 Elizabeth Street
Toronto, Ontario
Canada M5G 2C4
(416) 977-4360

This mail order service is unique in Canada. They supply more than 400 food and medical items for people on restricted diets. The foods run the gamut from puddings and juices to gluten-free mixes, low-calorie jams and jellies, low-sodium soups, to foodstuffs with special dietary additives for nutrition. There is also a range of medical supplies, breast-feeding supplies, diet scales, feeding tubes and so on. The price lists (four per year) are free and fairly descriptive, but the annual catalogue actually lists every ingredient in each product and complete calorie values, sodium counts and the like for products reduced in those nutrients. The catalogue is $2. They are very efficient about mail orders, but will not ship perishables, such as fresh-baked or frozen foods. C.O.D. orders are possible in Canada only (Ontario residents add $2; other Canadians, add $3.50). Handling charges are an extra $4 (flat rate) and shipping charges are added to the final bill. Payment on non-C.O.D.orders is accepted with VISA or M/C only.

✔ Mail orders accepted
✔ Phone orders accepted
Minimum order: no minimum

Shipping method: Canada Post
Shipping time: 1 week
Returns policy: all items guaranteed; perishables not shipped
Branch of Carecor Health/Toronto General Hospital

262 SPEILZEUG-RASCH
Gerhart Hauptmann Platz 1
2000 Hamburg 1
Germany
(40) 337922

This long-established German toy supplier sells many brand name playthings at less than half what you'd pay at home. Included in their product lines are Steiff stuffed animals, Baufix construction sets, and model trains, dolls and teddy bears galore. Their large (250-page) glossy catalogue costs $4 (send two $2 bills). Payment is accepted with VISA, M/C, Amex, or IMO or bank draft in Deutschemarks.

✔ Mail orders accepted
✔ Good bargain-hunting
Minimum order: DM 50 (about $30 Cdn)
Shipping method: surface or airmail
Shipping time: 3-6 weeks
Returns policy: no refunds, just credit
Established in 1896

263 SPHINX DATE RANCH
4041 E. Thomas Road
Phoenix, AZ
U S A 85018
(602) 224-0195; U.S. toll-free: (800) 482-3283

This is the largest producer of Medjool dates in the U.S.A. so it stands to reason you can buy direct and save. The dates themselves are huge and virtually fibreless and very tender-skinned. Boxes start from the one-pound size, and discounts of 10 percent are offered on orders of $300 or more. Fancy gift boxes are available, too, and specialties, such as exquisite chocolate-covered dates.

✔ Mail orders accepted
✔ Phone orders accepted
✔ Good bargain-hunting
Minimum order: no minimum
Shipping method: mail or UPS
Shipping time: 48 hours
Returns policy: replacement or refund; they pay return postage

264 SPIEGEL
1515 West 22nd St.
Oak Brook, Illinois
U S A
(708) 986-8800 ; U.S. toll-free: (800) 345-4500

Spiegel is another of those names that is synonymous with mail order. Their goods tend to be a little more expensive than most, but then, they're dealing with higher calibre merchandise. Offerings include apparel, unique gifts, executive toys, home furnishings and accessories, cookware, and designs from DKNY, Liz Claiborne, Adrienne Vittadini, Christian Dior, Mario Buatta, Mikasa, in short, anything you can imagine. Catalogues are huge (up to 600 pages), lavish and cost $3 each, refundable against your first order. Ordering over a minimum amount brings you the next catalogue free. Payment is accepted with Visa, M/C, Amex, IMO or cheque.

✔ Mail orders accepted
✔ Phone orders accepted
Minimum order: no minimum
Shipping method: mail or UPS
Shipping time: 2 weeks
Returns policy: all goods guaranteed

265 STAMFORD HYGIENIC COLLECTION
P.O. Box 1160
Long Island City, NY
U S A 11101
(718) 389-6433; U.S. only: (800) 356-6325

Louis Schneider runs a fairly straightforward business, considering he's selling plain and fancy condoms, sexual devices and erotica by mail. When remitting in Canadian funds, you are expected to add 20 percent to catalogue prices to cover U.S. exchange, and the minimum order is $15. They prefer U.S. funds. I won't specify all the goods available, except to say that you wouldn't want this catalogue in the hands of your eight-year-old. On many of their shipments to Canada, printed matter has been confiscated by Customs under "the provisions of tariff item 99201-1" (you can guess what that is), so Stamford will no longer ship printed matter, books, films, games or playing cards in this country. The 40-page colour catalogue costs $3 and includes a 10-percent discount coupon you may use on your first order. Payment is preferred via VISA and M/C, though cheques in U.S. funds are acceptable.

✔ Mail orders accepted
✔ Phone orders accepted
Minimum order: $15 when paying in Cdn. funds or charging on credit cards

Shipping method: mail
Shipping time: 2 weeks
Returns policy: all goods guaranteed

266 STANLEY MARKET
G/F, 53-55 Chatham Rd.
Tsim Sha Tsui, Kowloon
G.P.O. Box 8757
Hong Kong
(852) 724-0180

Stanley Market takes the name of the touristy fishing village, but their bargains are strictly Hong Kong style, which means some goods are a wonderful deal; others are not, so select carefully. I like their linens and embroidered items the best, but there are also sweaters, Chinese jackets and Chinese arts and crafts, all available for mail order. Price lists are available free, on request, or you can ask for details on a specific item. Once you order from them and they know you mean to buy, they will send you more and more detailed information on available items, and the prices seem to decline as you bring back repeat business. Payment is accepted with IMO, but bank drafts are more efficient.

✔ Mail orders accepted
✔ Phone orders accepted
✔ Good bargain-hunting
Minimum order: no minimum
Shipping method: surface or airmail; specify "insured" if required
Shipping time: 4-6 weeks
Returns policy: difficult, but possible

267 STECHER'S LIMITED
27 Frederick Street
Port of Spain
Trinidad
West Indies
(623) 2586; (623) 5912

Run as a typical duty-free shop, this one also ships worldwide and will send your goods in $50 (U.S.) "unsolicited" gift parcels (non-dutiable) via parcel post, insured. They have more than 40 years' experience in this trade and will go out of their way to make it easy for you to buy from them. Included in their stock are many brand names, like Rosenthal crystal and Patek Philippe watches, and goods by Gucci, Cartier, Pierre Cardin and every perfume you can imagine. They import directly from the manufacturers (and import these goods tax free) so that their prices are generally a third to a half of U.S. prices. Shipping charges are extra. Their brochure is free to our readers. They will accept payment in Canadian or U.S. currency, but you may pay only by cheque or international money order except for in-person transactions in their shops.

✔ Mail orders accepted
✔ Phone orders accepted
✔ Good bargain-hunting
Minimum order: no minimum
Shipping method: airmail or surface mail
Shipping time: 1 week
Returns policy: all goods guaranteed
Established in 1949

268 STOCKHOLMS LEKSAKSMUSEUM (TOY MUSEUM)
Mariatorget 1C
116 48 Stockholm
Sweden
(08) 41 61 00; 40 44 92

This is an incredible experience for anyone who loves antique toys, and the tiny gift shop in the museum is not really geared to mail orders, but if you are diplomatic and persistent, you may be able to buy directly from them. They sell reproduction toys, novelties, and goods for collectors. There is no price list available, but they can sometimes quote on a particular item you are seeking — or a type of toy you collect. The actual museum is a wonder, three floors full of tin toys, tin figures, dolls, cars, games, ships, planes, tops, folk art and steam engines. My favourites are the children's books, but unfortunately, they are not for sale. A colour brochure about the museum itself is free for the writing. Payment, when they will sell you something, is via VISA, M/C, Amex, IMO or cheque.

✔ Mail orders accepted
Minimum order: no minimum
Shipping method: airmail or surface mail
Shipping time: 5-6 weeks
Returns policy: see text
Established in 1980

269 STOKES SEEDS
Box 10
St. Catharines, Ontario
Canada L2R 6R6
(416) 685-4255

I actually own a Stokes Seeds T-shirt, that's how big a fan I am. This seed house has been a point of reference on the Canadian landscape for more than seven decades, and needless to say, they've learned their trade well. The free catalogue is huge, detailed and well-organized and generously illustrated with both line drawings and photographs. There's a wealth of planting advice, too. I don't mind saying (as a garden hobbyist) this is my favourite national seed supplier. They are efficient and honest and supply good product. They have all kinds of useful garden equipment and supplies, as well. Shipping costs are prepaid, except for addresses far away, in which case you add 10 cents per pound for every 1,000 miles extra you are from St. Catharines, so Vancouverites would add 20 cents per pound. Let me point out, however, that seeds are fairly light, and it's unusual for home gardeners to be ordering even one pound of seeds at a time. Payment is accepted with IMO or cheques. C.O.D.s are possible, but can be costly, so Stokes discourages them.

✔ Mail orders accepted
Minimum order: no minimum
Shipping method: Canada Post; 10 cents/lb. for more than 1000 miles
Shipping time: 2 weeks; more in busy season
Returns policy: all goods satisfactory or money refunded
Established in 1919

270 SULTAN'S DELIGHT INC.

P.O. Box 140253
Staten Island, NY
U S A 10314-0014
(718) 720-1557; (718) 447-5098

Charles Farkouh operates a unique mail order house. He sells foodstuffs from the Middle East of every description, from baklava to olives, to halvah, to mango chutney, jams, syrups, turkish delight, turkish coffees (and coffee cups), filo pastry, candies, spices, nuts and seeds (edible), and much more. He also stocks a fez or two, Arab head-dresses, belly dancer supplies, musical instruments, henna, and belly dancing music by Eddie (the Sheik) Kochak and Hakki Obadia, whose expertise in this area I'm sure you know. Goods shipped in the continental U.S. go by UPS. Canadian orders are shipped by mail. Charles offers our readers a 10-percent discount on first orders, so be sure to mention this book when you write. Catalogues are renewed three times a year, September, March and June and are free. Payment is accepted by C.O.D. in the U.S., or by VISA, M/C, Amex and IMO.

- ✔ Special offer to readers
- ✔ Mail orders accepted
- ✔ Phone orders accepted
- ✔ Good bargain-hunting

Minimum order: $15 minimum
Shipping method: mail or UPS
Shipping time: 48 hours
Returns policy: full refund, including shipping if not satisfied

271 SUN & MOON JEWELLERY MANUFACTURING CO., LTD.

6/F, Flat D, Anson House
13-19, Lock Road
Kowloon
Hong Kong
(852) 721-1561; 723-0083

Another member of the respected Deepak Gems family, Deepak Mirpuri operates this factory in Hong Kong and exports cut but unmounted gems of every description worldwide. He showed me an amethyst when I was there in 1989 that I didn't buy, but it turned out to be valued at more than ten times his selling price in Canada. He offers my readers an additional 10 percent off any orders they place if they mention this book, and will match the best offer on a similar weight and colour stone you can get anywhere else (get it in writing and send him a copy). Price lists are available on request. Know what you're doing before ordering gems by mail! Payment is accepted with VISA, M/C, IMO or bank draft.

- ✔ Special offer to readers
- ✔ Mail orders accepted
- ✔ Phone orders accepted
- ✔ Good bargain-hunting

Minimum order: no minimum
Shipping method: airmail, insured
Shipping time: 2 weeks
Returns policy: all gems guaranteed or money refunded
Member: Hong Kong Tourist Association

272 SWEATER MARKET

15 Frederiksberggade
15-DK-1459 Copenhagen
Denmark
(1) 15 27 73

Their modest colour flyer illustrates 10 men's and women's styles in hand-knit, 100-percent wool sweaters, at about half the cost of those you would see in North America. There are also wool hats and vests. The flyer is free and is updated only as required. A new, comprehensive catalogue is being prepared. Payment is accepted in almost any currency, via IMO, cheque or travellers' cheques, or by VISA, M/C, Amex, Diners Club, JCB, Access card or Eurocard.

✔ Mail orders accepted
Minimum order: no minimum
Shipping method: airmail
Shipping time: 8-10 days by air; 6-8 weeks by ship
Returns policy: all goods guaranteed
Established in 1964

273 TAIGA WORKS
1675 West 2nd Ave.
Vancouver, B.C.
Canada V6J 1H3
(604) 736-0422

Taiga is another of Vancouver's great sources for sturdy outdoor gear and equipment. They also supply camping, hunting, fishing and hiking gear, as well as wetsuits and other marine accessories, a great line of sleeping bags and tents and some of the most practical backpacks around. The glossy 48-page annual catalogue is free. If you can contribute an outdoorsy photograph to their next catalogue, they'll even pay you in merchandise. Mark photos with location, your name and your return address. Payment is accepted with VISA, M/C or cheque, and they'll discount your order by 2 percent if you pay with cash or cheque.

✔ Mail orders accepted
✔ Phone orders accepted
✔ Good bargain-hunting
Minimum order: no minimum
Shipping method: Canada Post or UPS
Shipping time: 2 weeks
Returns policy: all goods guaranteed for lifetime of garment
Established in 1973

274 TALHEIM CRAFTWORKS, C/O JOSEPH E. WACK, PROP.
General Delivery
Center Point, WV
U S A 26339
(304) 782-2501

You used to have to drive up to West Virginia yourself to buy good hand-carved kitchen implements, but now this local woodcarver is selling his one-of-a-kind woodenware by mail. Included are ladles, scoops, bowls and other kitchenware, handcarved from native West Virginia hardwoods and finished with non-toxic oils for food use. The illustrated brochure is free, but send a long, self-addressed, stamped envelope (U.S. postage, please) for yours. Payment is preferred in U.S. funds via cheque or IMO.

✔ Mail orders accepted
✔ Phone orders accepted
✔ SASE required
Minimum order: no minimum
Shipping method: mail
Shipping time: 2 weeks
Returns policy: all work guaranteed

275 TERE HAGAN FLATWARE MATCHING SERVICE
P.O. Box 25487
Tempe, Arizona
U S A 85285
(602) 966-8838; U.S. toll-free: (800) 528-7425;
fax: (602) 966-8915

If you've discovered one of your good silver spoons went out with the garbage (and who hasn't?), this is the place to buy a replacement. They carry a vast array of discontinued patterns in sterling and silverplate flatware, and many current patterns, all at discounts of about 50 percent off retail. If you don't know the name of the pattern, send a photocopy (front and back so they can see both markings and hallmarks) or fax your order, and they'll let you know if they have it in stock. Our readers may request a free brochure showing some of the styles they stock. They will also send a free price list for any patterns you are collecting or replenishing. Payment is accepted via VISA, M/C, Amex, Discover card or cheques.

✔ Mail orders accepted
✔ Phone orders accepted
✔ Good bargain-hunting
Minimum order: no minimum
Shipping method: mail or UPS
Shipping time: 2 days
Returns policy: all guaranteed
Established in 1970

276 TERRITORIAL SEEDS (CANADA) LTD.

P.O. Box 46225, Station "G"
Vancouver, B.C.
Canada V6R 4G5
(604) 224-1010

I first met Mary Ballon when she had just started "Earthrise," a funky Harrowsmith-looking gardening shop on Vancouver's west side. Now she's moved on to running the Canadian arm of Steve Solomon's Territorial Seeds, a company that originated in nearby Eugene, Oregon, to harvest and market seeds expressly for the "maritime climate" of the West Coast. All are fresh seed, gathered from the year's harvest and designed to produce optimum fruits and vegetables in those special climate areas. They also sell gardening how-to books and "season extenders," cloth row-covers that make the growing season longer. An annual 64-page, large-format catalogue is published in early January and is free. Payment is accepted with VISA, M/C or cheques.

✔ Mail orders accepted
✔ Phone orders accepted
Minimum order: no minimum
Shipping method: commercial 4th class unless requested otherwise
Shipping time: within the same week
Returns policy: seeds are guaranteed, refund or replacement
Established in 1979

277 THAI LAPIDARY

277/122 Rama I Road
Bangkok
Thailand
(662) 214-2641

You might save as much as 75 or 80 percent on gems bought abroad, and Bangkok is one of the key sources, but you must know what you're doing, and what you are ordering, in the first place. This shop has a good reputation for reliability. They sell unset gems. A periodic flyer and price list are available free. Payment is accepted with VISA, M/C, Amex or IMO.

✔ Mail orders accepted
✔ Good bargain-hunting
Minimum order: no minimum
Shipping method: airmail
Shipping time: 2-3 weeks
Returns policy: all goods guaranteed

278 THE BARN
Market Street
Lehman, PA
U S A 18627
(717) 675-4232

Dorothy and Gary Baker run The Barn in Lehman, Pennsylvania, with the weaving done in the same dairy barn owned by the Major family for almost 200 years. This is the home of Heirloom Rag Rugs, their family business. They also operate Back Mountain Wood Stoves there. All rugs, from hall and stairway runners to room-sized rugs, are custom-made to your specifications, and at very reasonable costs. They also sell hand-stencilled rugs, a children's book (which won an American Book Award) by local author Beverly Major, hand-made teddy bears, hand-thrown pottery, a great-looking cast-iron teakettle, placemats, pillows, tote bags and clutch purses. Their colour catalogue is reprinted as needed and is free. Payment for goods is accepted via VISA, M/C, IMO or cheque.

- ✔ Mail orders accepted
- ✔ Phone orders accepted
- Minimum order: no minimum
- Shipping method: mail or UPS
- Shipping time: 4 to 8 weeks
- Returns policy: no returns; rugs are custom-made to your order
- Established for 200 years

279 THE GARDEN
Loblaws Mail Order Dept.
22 St. Clair Ave. East, Suite 601
Toronto, Ontario
Canada M4T 2S5
(416) 967-5623; Can. toll-free: (8... ...3-8880

NO LONGER IN BUSINESS

What a surprise (and what a good i... ...oblaws operates a mail order service for some of its ritziest goo... ...Fortnum and Mason gift packs, bronze sundials, garden acce... ...and tools, Museum of Modern art watering cans, pruning sa... ...geous gardening books, hammocks, garden furniture, beauti... ...arts, practical hats, wildflower seeds, rustic craft baskets, co... ...s, needlework kits, bird feeders, smoker-cookers, hickory c... ...anters, fancy dessert sauces and gourmet foods. The full... ...(handsome) catalogue is published for spring/summer... ...ree. Payment is accepted with VISA, M/C, Amex, IMO or cheq...

- ... orders accepted
- ...ione orders accepted
- Minimum order: no minimum

Shipping method: courier, free for orders over $30; $3 if less than $30
Shipping time: 3 weeks
Returns policy: all goods guaranteed satisfactory or full refund

280 THE PARAGON
89 Tom Harvey Road
Westerly, RI
U S A 02891
(401) 596-0134

Here's a source recommended to me by a friend, who swears by their prices for general household goods and family clothing. Their catalogue is free. Payment is accepted with Visa, M/C, IMO or cheque (U.S. funds only, please).

✔ Mail orders accepted
✔ Good bargain-hunting
Minimum order: no minimum
Shipping method: U.S. postal service
Shipping time: 2 weeks
Returns policy: all goods guaranteed

281 THE POSTILION
220 Old Pioneer Rd.
Fond du Lac, WI
U S A 54935
(414) 922-4170

The outspoken and eccentric Madame Liane Kuony is possibly Wisconsin's greatest cooking instructor. Certainly, her tiny restaurant is booked solid, and her culinary instruction classes — "not a look-see, have a recipe" as she says — are not for the timid, and neither are they meant for the casual cook. Caterers and chefs alike pay thousands to attend her school. It goes without saying that the few items Madame does put up for Christmas sale are extraordinary (but they are surprisingly inexpensive). Her tiny illustrated catalogue is available free for Christmas, and includes mocha-rum-filled yule logs, plum pudding and cognac hard sauce, gift boxes, fruit compotes, vinaigrettes, chocolates, chocolate sauces, and fibreless Imperial all-mango chutney. Inquiries are also welcome for her Postilion School of Culinary Art. She's quite a character and a delightful raconteur (we've had a number of conversations). Payment is accepted by IMO or cheques only (U.S. funds preferred).

✔ Mail orders accepted
✔ Phone orders accepted
Minimum order: no minimum
Shipping method: mail or UPS; yule log is shipped frozen in dry ice
Shipping time: 2 weeks
Returns policy: all goods guaranteed
Established in 1951

282 THE SWEETERY
P.O. Box 243
Anderson, SC
U S A 29622
(803) 224-8394

The Sweetery is known as South Carolina's finest dessert place. In the U.S., their prices include postage, and they will ship to all your friends or corporate colleagues in plenty of time for Christmas. Goods include their luscious Carolina cheesecake, praline cheesecake, chocolate Amaretto cheesecake, southern butter pecan chews, wonderful chocolate chip cookies, "uggly" cake (if it's "uggly," it has to taste great), Italian creme cake, a two-layer carrot cake, southern fruit cake, Swedish pecans (in season), and a moist brownie cake delivered in a three-pound pan and coated with thick white cream called Brownies'n'creme. Boy, I'm hungry! They use the freshest ingedients and make up recipes in small batches, so quality is high. Their free, illustrated flyer is updated every summer. Payment is accepted via VISA, M/C or IMO.

✔ Mail orders accepted
✔ Phone orders accepted
Minimum order: no minimum
Shipping method: mail or UPS
Shipping time: 10 days
Returns policy: all goods guaranteed; call collect with problems

283 THIMBLE COLLECTORS CLUB
47 Richards Ave.
Norwalk, CT
U S A 06857
Canada toll-free: (800) 367-4534

A big item in the collectables field is thimbles, and this is an example of where the name says it all. They will send you a full-colour, descriptive brochure for your toll-free call from anywhere in Canada. Payment is accepted with Visa, M/C, Amex, Diner's Club, IMO or cheque.

✔ Mail orders accepted
✔ Phone orders accepted
Minimum order: no minimum
Shipping method: airmail or surface mail only to Canada; UPS to U.S. points
Shipping time: averages 2-4 weeks
Returns policy: everything returnable within 30 days
Established in 1969

284 THOMPSON & MORGAN LTD.
London Road
Ipswich IP2 0BA
England
214226; telex 132483

Thompson & Morgan, Seedsmen, are the largest sellers of flower and vegetable seeds in the world, and a great many varieties are unique to them and unavailable elsewhere. I know of no other place to obtain their patented "Melon Squash" seed, which grows like a crook-necked squash, keeps like a winter melon, and smells and tastes like ripe canteloupe (raw or cooked!). They also sell "Asparagus pea," which is wonderful sautéed in butter and which can be planted in the most overgrown corner of the garden and still flourish and beat the weeds. For a time, they sold from a depot (with very limited stock) in Winnipeg (the depot is no longer operational and they soon hope to replace it), so it's best to write to the British head office, or the U.S. address, next in these listings. The seed catalogue is free. Payment is accepted with VISA, M/C, IMO or cheque (with order).

✔ Mail orders accepted
Minimum order: no minimum
Shipping method: airmail or surface mail
Shipping time: 3-4 weeks
Returns policy: refund or credit voucher
Established in 1855

285 THOMPSON & MORGAN, U.S.
P.O. Box 1308
Jackson, NJ
U S A 08527
(201) 363-2225; U.S. toll-free: (800) 274-7333;
fax: (201) 363-9356

This is Thompson & Morgan's U.S. affiliate, which carries virtually their entire line of seeds. I've had better luck ordering directly from England, but if you have a U.S. drop-off address, you might prefer the speed of UPS, compared to ordering from abroad. They currently send orders by UPS directly to Canadian addresses, but they are phasing this out, in the hope that they will replace their defunct Canadian mail house to better serve us in our own country. Please refer to the previous listing for description. Either way, most varieties clear Customs without hassle (call for Customs for advice BEFORE ordering, if in doubt) and enter Canada duty-free. Payment is accepted with VISA, M/C, IMO or cheque with your order.

✔ Mail orders accepted
✔ Phone orders accepted
Minimum order: no minimum
Shipping method: UPS to Canada (but phasing out; see text)
Shipping time: 7-10 days
Returns policy: credit voucher or refund
Established in 1978

286 TIBETAN REFUGEE SELF-HELP CENTRE
Havelock Villa
65, Gandhi Road, Darjeeling
(West Bengal)
India
2346 or 2552

These goods are produced according to age-old Tibetan traditions, using dyes and wool imported to India from Nepal. Carpet-making is their specialty, though they also feature other items in the full-colour, permanent catalogue, such as tapestries, hooked chair cushions, hand-woven belts, handknit sweaters, embroidered woven coats, caps, mufflers, gloves, socks, beautiful leather boots (plus traditional Tibetan styles), religious artifacts, authentic Tibetan dolls and greeting cards. Custom carpets can be made to any size, design or colour, and take about six months. All carpets, even custom ones, are very inexpensive by North American standards. Payment must be made in advance by cheque or bank draft payable to: "Tibetan Refugee Self-Help Centre, Darjeeling." Their account is with Grindlays Bank P.L.C. Darjeeling.

✔ Mail orders accepted
✔ Good bargain-hunting
Minimum order: no minimum
Shipping method: airmail or sea mail; maximum parcel weight 10 kg
Shipping time: 1 month; custom orders 5-6 months
Returns policy: no returns
Established in 1959

287 TILLEY ENDURABLES ADVENTURE CLOTHING
900 Don Mills Road
Don Mills, Ontario
Canada M3C 1V8
(416) 441-6141; Van.: (604) 732-4287;
Can. toll-free: (800) 387-0110

This is the home of the Tilley Endurable hat and a great selection of travel and adventure gear and apparel. You'll also find the famous Tilley hat, which comes in three styles (one of these in a brown, as compared to the classic beige that Tilley is known for) and 16 sizes. Hats cost $42-$55 and come with a lifetime guarantee. If you're buying a gift for a man, it's a good idea to sneak away one of his hats and take it to the store to check the size on their machine (you can mail it in, too, if your friend won't notice it's gone). Washing and drying the hats makes the hatband shrink a little for a tighter fit in cold weather, and the man simply has to stretch the hat over his knee to loosen it up for warm days. The catalogue is published every October. Payment is accepted by VISA, M/C, IMO and cheque. Since goods are shipped from Ontario, those residents pay P.S.T.

✔ Mail orders accepted
✔ Phone orders accepted
Minimum order: no minimum
Shipping method: mail or UPS
Shipping time: 2-3 weeks
Returns policy: lifetime guarantee
Established in 1981

288 TOUCH OF GEMS
1424 New Road
Bangkrak, Bangkok
Thailand
(662) 233-3043

This source sells Thai silk, garments and reproduction jewellery. They do not have a regular catalogue, but sell from colour flyers and price lists. Payment is accepted with VISA, M/C, or Amex.

✔ Mail orders accepted
✔ Good bargain-hunting
Minimum order: no minimum
Shipping method: airmail
Shipping time: 4-6 weeks
Returns policy: all goods guaranteed
Member: Tourism Authority of Thailand

289 TOWEL EXPRESS LIMITED
Rm 301, 3/F, Century Centre
44-46 Hung To Road
Kwun Tong, Kowloon
Hong Kong
(852) 342-5109; 344-1972; Cable: "HENHINHONG";
telex: 45732 HSANG HX

Towel Express is a wholesaler and manufacturer of towels, terry robes, slippers and gift packs, and they will not sell in small quantities by mail. Many of their clients are international department stores, and numbers of their very high-quality towels are monogrammed for sports clubs, department store private labels and so on. They will not do business with you if you are a "trifler" but are very friendly and eager to serve if you intend to buy reasonable quantities of their wares — and they will sell them to you at wholesale, which is about 70 to 80 percent off domestic retail. Catalogues are available free to serious customers. All prices quoted are in Hong Kong dollars. Payment is accepted with VISA, M/C, Amex, IMO or bank draft.

✔ Mail orders accepted
✔ Phone orders accepted
✔ Good bargain-hunting
Minimum order: $25 (Cdn.)
Shipping method: airmail or surface mail
Shipping time: 2-8 weeks
Returns policy: no returns except on defective goods

290 TOYS TO GROW ON
P.O. Box 17
Long Beach, CA
U S A 90801
(213) 603-8890; U.S. toll-free: (800) 542-8338

Here's a highly recommended source for toys, games and learning materials, some at great savings. The catalogue is published periodically and is free. Payment is accepted with Visa, M/C, IMO or cheques in U.S. currency.

✔ Mail orders accepted
Minimum order: no minimum
Shipping method: UPS or mail
Shipping time: 2-3 weeks
Returns policy: all goods guaranteed

291 TWEEDS INC.
1 Avery Row
Roanoke, VA
U S A 24012-8528
(201) 684-8185; U.S. toll-free: (800) 999-7997;
U.S. customer service: (800) 444-9449

Renegades from the J. Crew stable, the entrepreneurs who started this operation a scant three years ago are giving their former employers a run for their money. Their catalogue is aimed at a slightly more youthful market, and their goods are oriented towards continental, European-inspired fabrics and styles. They include their own line of sportswear, trendy, urbane tweeds, and classics-moved-uptown, for both men and women. Their operation, perhaps appropriately, is based in a 100-year-old, renovated brick mill in a rather tweedy part of New Jersey. They offer sales in their regular catalogues, as well as in periodic flyers. Their catalogue is produced five to seven times a year, with focus on the spring/summer and fall/winter editions, which are free, to U.S. addresses. They are working on Canadian distribution and expect to have that in place in 1991. Shipping to U.S. points by UPS costs a fixed $4.90. Federal Express costs more. Payment is accepted with VISA, M/C, Amex, IMO or cheques.

✔ Mail orders accepted
✔ Phone orders accepted
Minimum order: no minimum
Shipping method: UPS or Federal Express to U.S. addresses only
Shipping time: 48 hours, maximum
Returns policy: 100-percent guarantee
Established in 1987

292 U.S. AIR GIFT CATALOG
3825 West Green Tree Road
P.O. Box 17001
Milwaukee, WI
U S A 53217
(414) 352-0425; U.S. toll-free: (800) 558-8990

U.S. Air publishes a great gift catalogue spotlighting the usual executive toys, electronics, luggage, language tapes, novelties, and gifts, but the surprise is they have some hard-to-find gadgets, like very reasonable ski-bags, sporting gear, and an item I wish I'd seen in their catalogue before I paid too much for it at home: "The Gold Solution," a gold-plating liquid to refresh tired jewellery. There's even a laptop at a good price.

- ✔ Mail orders accepted
- ✔ Phone orders accepted

Minimum order: no minimum
Shipping method: UPS or mail to U.S. addresses only
Shipping time: 10 days to 2 weeks
Returns policy: all goods guaranteed

293 UNICEF CANADA
443 Mount Pleasant Road
Toronto, Ontario
Canada M4S 2L8
(416) 482-4444; Can. toll-free: (800) 268-3770, operator 738

Don't moan and say, "Everyone knows Unicef" because there are some surprises here. First of all, if you live outside of Ontario, you'll save P.S.T. by ordering directly. Secondly, they stock all kinds of wonderful items you never thought of, including art prints, custom stationery, games, jigsaw puzzles, cookbooks, coffee mugs, pop-up books and collectors' plates. Of course there are Christmas and greeting cards. The catalogue is published seasonally (Christmas) and is free. Payment is accepted with VISA, M/C, Amex, IMO or cheques. Ontario residents pay P.S.T.

- ✔ Mail orders accepted
- ✔ Phone orders accepted
- ✔ Good bargain-hunting

Minimum order: no minimum
Shipping method: Canada Post or UPS
Shipping time: 24-hour service by phone
Returns policy: "100-percent satisfaction guaranteed"
Established in 1946
Member: Canadian Direct Marketing Association

294 UNIVERSAL MANUFACTURING COMPANY
G.P.O. Box # 10700
Hong Kong
(852) 465-3323; 462-6601; fax: (852) 3-413-0016;
telex: 72686 LEYEN HX

With a factory located in the New Territories (almost a suburb of Hong Kong and Kowloon), these people can manufacture hair ornaments and costume jewellery at a tiny fraction of costs in North America, so there are bargains here, to be sure. They "assure that our articles are of satisfying quality and workmanship, of popular designs, attractively priced and punctually delivered." They can also create items to your supplied design and budget requirements. They do not offer a catalogue, but will send "samples and/or illustrations" on request. Payment can be arranged by Visa, M/C, IMO, cheque or bank draft, although the latter is preferable.

✔ Mail orders accepted
✔ Phone orders accepted
✔ Good bargain-hunting
Minimum order: no minimum
Shipping method: airmail or surface mail
Shipping time: 4-6 weeks
Returns policy: all goods guaranteed

295 UTHAI GEMS
23, 7 Soi Ruam Rudee
Bangkok
Thailand
(662) 252-4365

This store sells unset gems at about 70 percent below what you would pay in Canada. Unset gemstones are duty-free, but be sure they are shipped to you insured post. A price list is available, free. Please be certain you know what you want and can describe it accurately, to avoid disappointment, as returns are tedious and slow. Payment is accepted with VISA, M/C, Amex or IMO.

✔ Mail orders accepted
✔ Good bargain-hunting
Minimum order: no minimum
Shipping method: airmail
Shipping time: 2-3 weeks
Returns policy: returns accepted if not satisfied

296 VALLEY VIEW FARM
RR #2, Box 860
Stowe, VT
U S A 05672

Valley View Farm is a direct source for Vermont maple syrup, sold in sizes up to 1/2 gallon, if you're feeding pancakes to an army. These syrups make great gifts. Price list is free. Payment is accepted with IMO or cheques (U.S. funds, please).

✔ Mail orders accepted
Minimum order: package of four half-pints, $17
Shipping method: UPS (add $3 for shipping)
Shipping time: 1 week
Returns policy: all goods guaranteed

297 VERMONT'S CLEARVIEW FARMS
RR#1, Box 5070
Enosburg Falls, VT
U S A 05450
(802) 933-2537; toll-free in U.S. only: (800) 933-2537

Caroline Longe loves to feed people, and her reputation for fine gourmet goodies has spread far beyond her native state of Vermont. Included in her folksy catalogue are maple sugared almonds, maple syrup, mustards, relishes, chutneys, muffin mixes, sparerib maple basting sauce, sampler packs, gift packs, corporate gifts and preserves such as "Behind the Bush," a combination of blueberries, peaches and apples accented with 100-percent pure almond flavouring and almond slices. Though the goods are not bargain-priced, if you order early before Christmas, there's a modest discount of 5 percent. Any goods damaged in shipping are cheerfully replaced or refunded. They've recently added a crafts line to the available list. Their catalogue is published once or twice a year (usually spring and fall) and is free to our readers. Payment accepted with VISA or M/C.

✔ Special offer to readers
✔ Mail orders accepted
✔ Phone orders accepted
Minimum order: no minimum
Shipping method: mail, UPS, courier
Shipping time: 1 to 2 weeks
Returns policy: quick refund or replacement upon written complaint

298 VICTORIA & ALBERT MUSEUM
Cromwell Road
London SW7 2RL
England
(01) 938-8438; (01) 938-8433

Here you'll find many examples of cards, posters, art, artifacts, reproductions, dolls and other museum gifts from the Victoria and Albert period. Many items are truly unique. Postage is included in all costs. Gifts can be mailed to your friends anywhere, with a gift insert included with your best wishes. The free catalogue is printed once a year in time for Christmas and appears by late August. Orders may be charged to VISA, M/C, Amex, Access or purchased via IMO.

✔ Mail orders accepted
✔ Phone orders accepted
Minimum order: no minimum
Shipping method: airmail or surface mail

Shipping time: 10 days
Returns policy: goods refunded if returned in good condition

299 VICTORIA INTERNATIONAL KNIVES LTD.
1306 Government Street
Victoria, B.C.
Canada V8W 1Y8
(604) 383-2422

Here's a source of interest to the collector or the homemaker. There is everything from Swiss army knives to English darts, plus scissors, kitchen gadgets, cleavers, gold pocket watches, elegant cutlery, razors and sharpening stones. There are hand-made knives and commemorative pieces and even a Silva Swedish compass. A colour brochure and price quote are available, free. Payment is accepted with Visa, M/C, Amex, IMO or cheque.

✔ Mail orders accepted
✔ Phone Orders Accepted
Minimum order: no minimum
Shipping method: UPS or Canada Post
Shipping time: 2-4 weeks
Returns policy: all goods guaranteed
Established in 1976

300 VICTORIA'S SECRET
P.O. Box 182103
Columbus, OH
U S A 43272-4497
(212) 276-3131 ; U.S. toll-free: (800) 821-0001;
or (800) HER-GIFT

A very uptown lingerie manufacturer with boutiques in Paris and New York was thrilled when his line was accepted into Victoria's Secret catalogues. The goods run the gamut from the skimpy to the luxurious, including the same kinds of silkwear that Cybill Shepherd used to flounce around in on *Moonlighting*. Lingerie and stockings run about 30 percent off list, and there are periodic sales for regular customers, too. They also sell sweaters, dresses, leathers, suedes and denims. Catalogues are published seven times a year. A one-year subscription is $5; two years: $8. Payment is accepted with Visa, M/C, Amex or IMO in U.S. funds.

✔ Mail orders accepted
✔ Phone orders accepted
✔ Good bargain-hunting

Minimum order: no minimum, but you'll keep getting catalogues if you order
Shipping method: airmail or surface mail, or UPS
Shipping time: 2-4 weeks
Returns policy: money back on all goods returned in mint condition
Established in 1980

301 VILLAGE BOOKS
1210 11th Street
Bellingham, WA
U S A 98225
(206) 671-2626; U.S. toll-free: (800) 392-BOOK;
fax: (206) 734-2573

Charles and Dee Robinson (or "Chuck and Di" as their staff now call them) started this family operation a decade ago, and their expansion is obviously due to their love of books and their hand-picked (and really accommodating) personnel. Their mail order service is promoted by quarterly newsletters (free) and periodic sale supplements. They have a regular "bargain book section," too. Payment is accepted by VISA, M/C, Amex, Discover card or cheque. They'll accept fax orders, as well.

✔ Mail orders accepted
✔ Phone orders accepted
✔ Good bargain-hunting
Minimum order: no minimum
Shipping method: mail to Canada
Shipping time: 2 days
Returns policy: all goods guaranteed if returned in mint condition
Established in 1980
Member: American Booksellers' Association

302 THE VITAMIN EXPERTS
1818 West 4th Ave.
Vancouver, B.C.
Canada V6T 1M3
(604) 738-4114

This discount health food and vitamin supplement source claims to beat any price (for the same brand and item) anywhere in Canada. All vitamins are "natural source," and they also sell minerals, protein supplements, enzymes, amino acids and the like. Their catalogue is sometimes available, sometimes out of print, but they do maintain an active list of customers, so if your name is added, you'll receive up-to-date sale information periodically, all free. Payment is accepted only with plastic: Visa, M/C or Amex.

✔ Mail orders accepted
✔ Phone orders accepted
✔ Good bargain-hunting
Minimum order: no minimum
Shipping method: UPS or Canada Post
Shipping time: same day, if in stock
Returns policy: all items guaranteed; return unused portion
Member: Nutritional Research Clinic

303 W.O. LARSEN
Amagertorv 9,
1160 Copenhagen K
Denmark
(011) 45 33 12 20 50

Ole W.O. Larsen is a fourth-generation pipe maker, and his pipes are generally considered the finest in the world. Each is hand-made from Corsican briar by artisans who work in their own homes, according to an age-old Danish tradition of "freehand" carving. Each pipe produced is one of a kind and thus hard to show in a catalogue, but Ole does have a full-colour information sheet that pictures different sizes and shapes, so you'll know approximately what you are ordering. As he says: "Just in short I make maybe the finest pipe today, they are all truly handmade...as all are different and not mass-produced we do not make many pipes per year — but our name is known from Japan to America." They don't like to mail-order to places they have retailers, but they will sell to our readers individually, so be sure to mention this book to get the wholesale price. Payment is accepted by VISA, M/C, Amex, Diners Club, Eurocard and IMO.

✔ Mail orders accepted
✔ Phone orders accepted
✔ Good bargain-hunting
Minimum order: no minimum
Shipping method: airmail
Shipping time: at once, unless special-order
Returns policy: goods guaranteed
Established in 1864
Purveyors to the Royal Danish Court

304 W.S. ROBERTSON (OUTFITTERS) LTD.
40/41 Bank Street
Galashiels
Scotland
0896 2152

Scottish knitwear for men and women is available here. You'll find the luxurious Pringle of Scotland line, Lyle & Scott sweaters, Ballantyne knits and cashmere, lamb's-wool and Shetland knits by Braemar. You don't pay the V.A.T., so you'll save about 25 percent over comparable knits in Canada. Shipping costs are extra. Their full-colour catalogue is published twice yearly; spring and autumn. You will be added to their mailing list for $5 (Cdn.) and their price list is free. Payment is accepted with VISA, M/C, IMO, Access, Eurocard or cheque.

✔ Mail orders accepted
✔ Phone orders accepted
Minimum order: no minimum
Shipping method: airmail or surface mail
Shipping time: by return post
Returns policy: full refund or credit if dissatisfied
Established in 1815

305 WAYMARC
3179 Thunderbird Cres.
Burnaby, B.C.
Canada V5A 3G1
(604) 420-3633; phone collect to order

This outfit is a true wholesaler of office, industrial, store and manufacturing equipment, especially storage systems and shelving. They also sell filing items, closet organizers, electronics, folding tables, chairs, shipping supplies and handy step-stools. I actually bought a heavy-duty dolly from these folks years ago and have never found either a sturdier one, or one at a better price than I paid — and my friends and I continue to get a great deal of use from it (more than I'd ever have imagined). Their catalogue is fully illustrated and detailed and is free. Payment is accepted with VISA, M/C, IMO or with established credit (previous customers).

✔ Mail orders accepted
✔ Phone orders accepted
✔ Good bargain-hunting
Minimum order: no minimum
Shipping method: Loomis or truck-freight (F.O.B. Vancouver)
Shipping time: 24 hour-fulfillment
Returns policy: all goods guaranteed

306 WEALL & CULLEN GARDENERS SUPPLY INC.
400 Alden Road
Markham, Ontario
Canada L3R 4C1
(416) 479-9111; Can. toll-free: (800) 387-9777;
fax: (416) 479-1421

Mark Cullen, of the CBC's "Anything Grows," runs this supply house for avid gardeners, and he has assembled a number of unique and practical items for the home garden, including lawn decorations, wildflower seeds, gardening pants, Sheffield Pride handtools, faucets, sprinklers, Tilley Endurable hats, sundials, English Barbour clothing, "Lifetime" garden hoses (just what they claim to be), watering cans, cedar furniture and planter boxes, greenhouses and something called "solid water," a granular polymer that you mix with your soil mixture to slow-release water to your decorative plants — ideal if you're away on holiday. The catalogue is published seasonally and is free. Payment is accepted with VISA, M/C, Amex, IMO or cheques. Ontario residents add P.S.T. Fax orders are accepted, also.

✔ Mail orders accepted
✔ Phone orders accepted
Minimum order: no minimum
Shipping method: Canada Post
Shipping time: 2 weeks
Returns policy: all goods guaranteed (refund, credit, replacement)

307 WELLS INTERIORS
7171 Amador Plaza Road
Dublin, CA
U S A 94568
(415) 829-2610 ext.13 "Mail Order";
U.S. toll-free: (800) 547-8982; fax: (415) 829-1374

Wells offers discounts on pleated shades, woven blinds, wood blinds and vertical blinds, through a catalogue that is reprinted as prices fluctuate. The catalogue is free to our readers. Payment is accepted with VISA or M/C only. Add 10 percent to catalogue prices for orders to Canada. Fax orders are accepted.

✔ Special offer to readers
✔ Mail orders accepted
✔ Phone orders accepted
✔ Good bargain-hunting
Minimum order: no minimum
Shipping method: mail or UPS

Shipping time: 3-4 weeks
Returns policy: all goods guaranteed
Established in 1979

308 WESTAWAY AND WESTAWAY

62-65 Great Russell Street
London WC1A 2SL
England
(71) 405-4479

Here's an inexpensive source for Harris tweeds, cashmere and Shetland sweaters, kilts and tartans, wonderful Viyella shirts, and other British woollens. They publish their catalogue only sporadically, so you may have to be content with a flyer and price list. Payment is accepted with VISA, M/C, IMO (pounds sterling) or bank draft.

✔ Mail orders accepted
✔ Good bargain-hunting
Minimum order: no minimum
Shipping method: surface or airmail
Shipping time: 4-6 weeks
Returns policy: all goods guaranteed

309 WESTERN CANADA WILDERNESS COMMITTEE

20 Water Street
Vancouver, B.C.
Canada V6B 1A4
(604) 683-8220

This group sells posters, postcards, incredibly beautiful calendars, videos, and "Carmanah, Artistic Visions of an Ancient Rainforest," all to raise consciousness and money to preserve large forested areas from logging and other intrusions on the ecology of British Columbia. Needless to say, their promotional material is printed only as necessary and on recycled paper, at that. Price lists and flyers are free. The Christmas catalogue is $1. Members save 20 percent on purchases. Membership is $25 annually, but an inquiry will get you some free material without joining. Payment is via cheque. B.C. residents, add 6 percent P.S.T. to any purchase price.

✔ Mail orders accepted
Minimum order: no minimum
Shipping method: Canada Post; include $1 or 10 percent of order for postage
Shipping time: 1 week
Returns policy: all goods guaranteed

310 THE WHITEHEART COMPANY
9482 Dayton Way
Beverly Hills, CA
U S A
(213) 274-6671

This family business offers Caswell & Massey soaps, and a huge range of pot-pourri, even though formulated to please the males in your life. They also carry fine German cosmetics and scents, all at very reasonable prices. The catalogue is free. Payment is accepted with Visa, M/C, IMO or cheques in U.S. funds.

✔ Mail orders accepted
✔ Phone orders accepted
✔ Good bargain-hunting
Minimum order: no minimum
Shipping method: UPS or U.S. Postal Service
Shipping time: 2 weeks, or less
Returns policy: all goods guaranteed

311 WHOLE LIFE
RR #2
Powassan, Ontario
Canada P0H 1Z0
(705) 724-3000

Here you can find books, music and videos for health-conscious parents and professionals, including material on pregnancy, midwifery, childbirth, holistic health care and parenting. The catalogue is periodic and costs $2. Payment is accepted with IMO or cheques. Ontario residents add P.S.T.

✔ Mail orders accepted
✔ Phone orders accepted
Minimum order: no minimum
Shipping method: Canada Post
Shipping time: 2 weeks
Returns policy: all goods guaranteed

312 WIDE WORLD BOOKS & MAPS
401 N.E. 45th Street
Seattle, WA
U S A 98105
(206) 634-3453

This is the first travel book store established in the U.S., and if personal service means anything, it's a good indication of why they've been so successful. Joan Marsden prints a newsletter periodically, which she will send to you if you write. If no current newsletter is available, she will reply to you personally and let you know what is in stock. Now, that's customer service! Their slogan is "For travellers who love to read and readers who love to travel." They also sell maps and travel accessories, as well as their vast stock of travel books. Payment is accepted with VISA, M/C and Discover cards, or they will send C.O.D. to U.S. destinations.

✔ Special offer to readers
✔ Mail orders accepted
✔ Phone orders accepted
✔ Good bargain-hunting
Minimum order: no minimum
Shipping method: mail only
Shipping time: same day if in stock; or 2-6 weeks
Returns policy: store credit only on returns
Established in 1976

313 WILLIAMS-SONOMA
P.O. Box 7456
San Francisco, CA
U S A 94120-7456
(415) 421-4242

Here's the place for cooks: everything you could think of, from pots and pans, to utensils, cookbooks, gourmet equipment, aprons, kitchen machines and more. It's also a great source for gifts for the culinary whizzes among your friends. The catalogue is free. Payment is accepted with Visa, M/C, Amex, IMO or cheque.

✔ Mail orders accepted
✔ Phone orders accepted
Minimum order: no minimum
Shipping method: UPS
Shipping time: 1-2 weeks
Returns policy: all goods guaranteed

314 WING SUNG PEN FACTORY
27 Luo Fu Road
Shanghai
China
558014; cable: Shanghai 1845

This factory produces one thing only, and does a wonderful job of it. They make fancy cloisonné pens for export, and they are fairly sophisticated about dealing with Westerners, as is often the case with Shanghaiese Chinese (who are considered the "merchant-traders" in their own country). They prefer to deal in large quantities at true wholesale prices (which are about one-tenth of what you'd pay at home), but will sell to individuals, too. Be sure you sort out payment and shipping arrangements before ordering. Payment is accepted with IMO or bank draft.

- ✔ Mail orders accepted
- ✔ Good bargain-hunting

  Minimum order: prefers large orders (20 or more)
  Shipping method: airmail or surface mail
  Shipping time: 5-6 weeks, surface mail
  Returns policy: all goods guaranteed, but awkward to return

315 WING WAH TOYS CO.

156, Queen's Rd. East, G/F
Wan Chai
Hong Kong
(852) 528-1090

All kinds of toys are wholesaled from here at a discount. The good news is that the prices are very cheap; the bad news is that the "best" toys are made only for export and not carried here. They will price-quote on specific types of toys. Payment is accepted only with IMO or cheques.

- ✔ Mail orders accepted
- ✔ Good bargain-hunting

  Minimum order: no minimum
  Shipping method: surface mail
  Shipping time: 6 weeks
  Returns policy: no returns

316 WINNER TRADING CO.

P.O. Box 91355
Tsim Sha Tsui, Kowloon
Hong Kong
(852) 385-9665; 771-7414 ; fax: (852) 385-2179

Winner maintains a large showroom in Tsim Sha Tsui (the big tourist area in Kowloon) and rents out space to other wholesalers needing a local base. They sell fresh-water pearl necklaces from about $1 Cdn. and up, and also stock faux gemstones, costume jewellery, jewellery findings and jewellers' tools, as well as display stands, ring boxes, zip-top plastic bags of every size and promotional materials of every description. They frequently clear out outdated stock. Recent examples were mini disposable camera (110 film) for $2 Cdn each, a mini tool set for 60 cents, bags, purses, ball pens and more. They carry cloisonné vases, bracelets and brooches from China, stone carvings, musical instruments and artifacts. They will send a descriptive letter as a reply to your inquiry, followed by colour photos of anything you'd like details on, free. Payments may be negotiated by way of Visa, M/C or IMO, but they by far prefer bank drafts, payable in U.S. dollars. Most of their prices are quoted in U.S. currency.

✔ Mail orders accepted
✔ Phone orders accepted
✔ Good bargain-hunting
Minimum order: no minimum
Shipping method: insured parcel rate or air mail
Shipping time: 2-6 weeks, depending on method
Returns policy: all goods guaranteed

317 WINSOURCE CAMERA & VIDEO CO.
1/F, Shop 78, Admiralty Centre, Tower 1
18 Harcourt Road
Hong Kong
(852) 861-0631; 528-3702

Here's another Hong Kong favourite. I know a number of foreign journalists there who find their prices very good. I priced a couple of Sony Walkmans, and their prices were about 40 percent lower than Canada, but then, if you pay duty and F.S.T., you're no further ahead. They will price-quote (by mail or phone) on any brand-name item you wish to compare, including Panasonic, Sony, Toshiba, Nikon, Pentax, Canon, etc. Be sure to know the name and model number of each item and compare at home, first. Also remember that video equipment operates on an entirely different system than ours and is incompatible with it. Payment is accepted with VISA, M/C, Amex or IMO.

✔ Mail orders accepted
✔ Phone orders accepted
✔ Good bargain-hunting
Minimum order: no minimum
Shipping method: airmail, insured
Shipping time: 2 weeks
Returns policy: all goods guaranteed

318 THE WISCONSIN CHEESEMAN
P. O Box 1
Madison, Wisconsin
U S A 53701
(608) 258-3000; (608) 837-4100

This mail order gift house seems set up ideally for Christmas (or other seasonal) gift-giving. Obviously companies simply give them their entire mailing list to have favoured clients sent cheese packs, hams, smoked turkeys, jellies, jams, candy, and much more in every imaginable novelty package, basket, crate or container, and for every level of budget. Shipping within the continental U.S. costs $2.95 for each address up to nine and after that, shipping is free. Each address is allowed one name, one greeting and one arrival date. For Canadian deliveries, it costs $6.95 per address, and you may not send plants, fresh fruit, meats or salmon. Otherwise, there are more than 100 full-colour pages of gifts to choose from and, perhaps best of all, this huge catalogue is free. Payment can be made in U.S. funds by cheque or IMO, or deferred till February (if bought for Christmas) on your VISA, M/C, Amex or Diners Club cards.

✔ Mail orders accepted
✔ Phone orders accepted
✔ Good bargain-hunting
Minimum order: no minimum
Shipping method: mail or UPS
Shipping time: 2 weeks
Returns policy: all goods guaranteed
Established in 1946

319 WORLDWIDE CURIO HOUSE
Box 17095A
Minneapolis, MN
U S A 55417

If you've been looking for voodoo artifacts, tarot cards, books on mysticism, astrology, the paranormal, the occult and witchcraft, this is the place. They specialize in "mystic arts" goods and paraphernalia. Three distinct catalogues are published, and each is $1 (surface mail) or $2 (airmail). Payment is accepted with VISA, M/C, IMO or cheques (U.S. funds).

✔ Mail orders accepted
Minimum order: no minimum
Shipping method: mail or UPS
Shipping time: 2-3 weeks
Returns policy: all goods guaranteed

320 YOOLIM GEMS CO., LTD.
1180-2 New Road
Bangkok 10501
Thailand
(662) 235-1866; 234-0422; 234-8789; 233-3509 or 234-9940; or fax: (662) 236-3294

This is a true wholesale outlet, and consequently, they will only sell in large quantities (usually 10 each of any given style or item). They sell unset gemstones, gold or silver jewellery and an assortment of contemporary and antique-looking rings, earrings and a truly convincing line of Victorian to Art Deco style brooches and pins. They will supply customs invoices and certificates of origin to reduce or eliminate Canada Customs duty for unset stones. They also sell quantities of cut (facetted) garnet and high-quality cubic zirconia. Although catalogues are not available per se, they do have colour product sheets and price lists. Payment is via VISA, M/C, Amex or IMO.

✔ Mail orders accepted
✔ Good bargain-hunting
Minimum order: minimum orders in each product category; write to inquire
Shipping method: airmail, insured
Shipping time: 2-3 weeks
Returns policy: all goods guaranteed to be as specified

BIBLIOGRAPHY

There are number of fine books worth collecting that either pertain to mail ordering, or offer solid consumer advice about which particular goods and services you should choose. Some of these books will be available only through public libraries or remainder houses (if they are out of print). Others are as near as your local bookstore.

The Joy of Shopping
Elizabeth Hanson
Turnbull & Willoughby (1986)
This is obviously a light-hearted look at shopaholism, bargaining, wheedling and cajoling, coping with salespeople, and some surprisingly practical advice about "winning" in the marketplace.

Fine Flowers by Phone
Barbera Brooks
Atlantic Monthly Press (1989)
A thorough guide (including a smattering of Canadian sources) for ordering gift bouquets anywhere. Especially convenient if you want to send flowers to a friend in another part of North America.

Buying Jewelry
Anne Bingham
McGraw-Hill Paperbacks (1989)
Everything you need to know about buying gemstones, jewellery and precious metals.

How to Avoid Getting Ripped Off
(Essential but hard-to-find consumer facts for women)
Carol L. Clark, Ph.D.
Shadow Mountain, Deseret Book Company (1985)
Geared to American women, but very useful for its lists of contacts, information numbers and shopping strategies.

Antique Fakes and Their Detection
Raymond F. Yates
Award Books (paper) by arrangement with Harper & Row (1950)
A really insightful guide to tricks of the trade. Helpful for both the serious collector and the amateur, "recreational shopper."

The Complete Collector's Guide to Fakes and Forgeries
Colin Haynes
Wallace-Homestead Book Company (1988)

Subject-by-subject guidance to choosing between valued collectables and replications, particularly useful for the person shopping from mail order sources abroad.

The Toy Report
Canadian Toy Testing Council
updated annually
This comprehensive guide to children's playthings lists hundreds of toys by brand name and evaluates them according to play-value, money's worth and more. Each of the toys has been tested in Canadian homes with children of an appropriate age. Both good and bad reviews are included.

Complete Buyer's Guide
Reader's Digest
Reader's Digest Association (Canada) Ltd. (1982)
This is one of those massive books that gives you guidance on everything you could possibly even consider buying, and how to get the most for your money. Though almost a decade old, 95 percent of the content is still pertinent and worth knowing, and written for the Canadian consumer.

Consumer Reports
(yearly) Buying Guide
Consumers Union
Produced annually by this not-for-profit group, this is another exhaustive guide to actual "road-tests" of dozens of categories of appliances, electronics, health products, cosmetics, cars and what-have-you. Again, brand names are given and reviews are both critical and laudatory.

The Ultimate Shopper
Steve Winter
Living Skill Books (1987)
This home-spun, lifestyle book is designed to help you change your mode of dealing with consumer purchasing — and it does a pretty good job of it.

The Savvy Shopper
Judy Young Ocko and Larry Goodman
Ballantine (1982)
This insiders' guide to how retailers and merchandisers work behind the scenes is fascinating, if you can get beyond the embarrassing (and inaccurate) cursory sweep the authors have taken through Canadian retailing. In fact, all reference to Canada appears to have been added as

an afterthought after a phone conversation with a manager from "The Robert Simpson Company." Otherwise, it is an insightful and practical way to "wise up" to retailing practices.

Shoe Time
Aimee Liu and Meg Rottman
Arbour House (1986)
More than any human needs to know about the history, selection, wearing of and trivia pertaining to shoes.

Ski Tech's Guide to Equipment, Skiwear, and Accessories
Bill Tanler
John Muir Publications (1989)
A detailed guide to everything about the selection and maintenance of skiwear, including a large "what's new" section to bring you up to state-of-the-art.

The Art of Complaining
Phil Edmonston
Musson/General Publishing (1984)
This should really be entitled "The Art of Getting What You Want" because Edmonston's practical techniques for winning in the consumer jungle still work.

Consumer Beware!
Ellen Roseman
new press (1974)
The shocking thing about this book is how current it remains after more than 15 years in print. I find it sad to think how little advancement there has been in Canadian consumer legislation over these years, but that's fodder for another book, isn't it?

Who's Minding the Store?
Anthony J. Stokan
Stoddart (1989)
Ah, that's more like it. A book written from the Canadian perspective to guide retailers into the 21st century. Again, a great way to peek behind the scenes and learn how they pull those strings to make us buy. Forewarned is forearmed.

ALPHA INDEX

Note: all numbers in this index refer to entry codes, *not* page numbers.

NOTES